I0796905

AMERICA'S
TEST KITCHEN

Also by America's Test Kitchen

Umma

When Southern Women Cook

Food Gifts

America's Test Kitchen 25th Anniversary Cookbook

A Very Chinese Cookbook

Boards

Gatherings

The Skillet

Cook It in Your Dutch Oven

Cook It in Cast Iron

Ultimate Air Fryer Perfection

Kitchen Gear

Baking for Two

Everyday Bread

The Cook's Illustrated Baking Book

The Perfect Cookie

The Perfect Pie

The Perfect Cake

The Science of Good Cooking

Cook's Science

The New Cooking School Cookbook: Fundamentals

The New Cooking School Cookbook: Advanced Fundamentals

Mostly Meatless

Vegan for Everybody

Vegan Cooking for Two

Vegetables Illustrated

How Can It Be Gluten Free Cookbook Collection

The Complete Plant-Based Cookbook

The Complete Beans and Grains Cookbook

The Complete Mediterranean Cookbook

The Complete Cooking for Two Cookbook, 10th Anniversary Edition

The Complete Diabetes Cookbook

The Complete Vegetarian Cookbook

The Complete One Pot

The Complete Autumn and Winter Cookbook

The Complete Summer Cookbook

The Complete Modern Pantry

The Complete Salad Cookbook

The Complete America's Test Kitchen TV Show Cookbook

The Complete Cook's Country TV Show Cookbook

For a full listing of all our books:

CooksIllustrated.com

AmericasTestKitchen.com

Praise for America's Test Kitchen Titles

"The book is a treasure for its endless kitchen wisdom, heart-filled recipes, and deep-rooted respect for all generations that came before. It showcases home cooking at its best, ranging from sauces, banchan (side dishes), and a slew of kimchi, to gurgling stews, tantalizing meats, and not-too-sweet fare."

Epicurious on *Umma: A Korean Mom's Kitchen Wisdom & 100 Family Recipes*

A Best Cookbook of 2024

Los Angeles Times* on *When Southern Women Cook

"This 'very' Chinese cookbook from a father-son duo is a keeper. The book—ATK's first devoted to Chinese cooking—proves that you can teach and entertain in the same volume . . . All in all, it's one of the most charming works I've seen in years, and I already want to get a second copy."

Washington Post* on *A Very Chinese Cookbook

"An exhaustive but approachable primer for those looking for a 'flexible' diet. Chock-full of tips, you can dive into the science of plant-based cooking or just sit back and enjoy the 500 recipes."

Minneapolis Star Tribune* on *The Complete Plant-Based Cookbook

"This comprehensive guide is packed with delicious recipes and fun menu ideas but its unique draw is the personal narrative and knowledge-sharing of each ATK chef, which will make this a hit."

Booklist* on *Gatherings

"True to its name, this smart and endlessly enlightening cookbook is about as definitive as it's possible to get in the modern vegetarian realm."

Men's Journal* on *The Complete Vegetarian Cookbook

"A mood board for one's food board is served up in this excellent guide . . . This has instant classic written all over it."

Publishers Weekly* (starred review) on *Boards: Stylish Spreads for Casual Gatherings

"Reassuringly hefty and comprehensive, ***The Complete Autumn and Winter Cookbook*** by America's Test Kitchen has you covered with a seemingly endless array of seasonal fare . . . This overstuffed compendium is guaranteed to warm you from the inside out."

NPR on *The Complete Autumn and Winter Cookbook*

"If you're one of the 30 million Americans with diabetes, ***The Complete Diabetes Cookbook*** by America's Test Kitchen belongs on your kitchen shelf."

Parade.com on *The Complete Diabetes Cookbook*

"Another flawless entry in the America's Test Kitchen canon, *Bowls* guides readers of all culinary skill levels in composing one-bowl meals from a variety of cuisines."

BuzzFeed Books on *Bowls*

"***The Perfect Cookie*** . . . is, in a word, perfect. This is an important and substantial cookbook . . . If you love cookies, but have been a tad shy to bake on your own, all your fears will be dissipated. This is one book you can use for years with magnificently happy results."

HuffPost on *The Perfect Cookie*

"The book offers an impressive education for curious cake makers, new and experienced alike. A summation of 25 years of cake making at ATK, there are cakes for every taste."

Wall Street Journal* on *The Perfect Cake

"The go-to gift book for newlyweds, small families, or empty nesters."

Orlando Sentinel* on *The Complete Cooking for Two Cookbook

THE sheet pan

150+ Easy, Creative Meals from Your Most Versatile Pan

AMERICA'S TEST KITCHEN

Library of Congress Cataloging-in-Publication Data has been applied for.

ISBN 978-1-954210-52-3

America's Test Kitchen

21 Drydock Avenue, Boston, MA 02210

Printed in Canada

10 9 8 7 6 5 4 3 2

Distributed by Penguin Random House Publisher Services

Tel: 800.733.3000

Pictured on front cover: Lime-Glazed Salmon and Crispy Rice Salad (page 166)

Pictured on back cover: One Big Pancake (page 262), Zucchini, Leek, and Pea Soup with Crispy Prosciutto (page 111), Coffee and Fennel-Rubbed Boneless Short Ribs with Celery Root Salad (page 129)

Featured photography: Daniel J. van Ackere

Editorial Director, Books: Adam Kowit

Executive Food Editor: Dan Zuccarello

Deputy Food Editor: Stephanie Pixley

Executive Managing Editor: Debra Hudak

Project Editor: Elizabeth Carduff

Senior Editors: Camila Chaparro, Joe Gitter, Sacha Madadian, and Sara Mayer

Associate Editor: Claudia Catalano

Senior Photo Test Cook: José Maldonado

Test Cooks: Malcolm Jackson, Hannah Smokelin, and Stephanie Winter

Kitchen Intern: Janna Claassen

Additional Recipe Development: Garth Clingingsmith, Rebeccah Marsters, and Sandra Wu

Assistant Editor: Julia Arwine

Design Director: Lindsey Timko Chandler

Associate Art Director and Designer: Molly Gillespie

Photography Director: Julie Bozzo Cote

Senior Photography Producer: Meredith Mulcahy

Senior Staff Photographers: Steve Klise and Daniel J. van Ackere

Staff Photographer: Kritsada Panichgul

Additional Photography: Joseph Keller, Carl Tremblay, and Kevin White

Food Styling: Joy Howard, Sheila Jarnes, Catrine Kelty, Chantal Lambeth, Ashley Moore, Marie Piraino, Elle Simone Scott, Kendra Smith, Sally Staub, and Christine Tobin

Project Manager, Books: Kelly Gauthier

Senior Print Production Specialist: Lauren Robbins

Production and Imaging Coordinator: Amanda Yong

Production and Imaging Specialist: Tricia Neumyer

Production and Imaging Assistant: Chloe Petraske

Copy Editor: Cheryl Redmond

Proofreader: Ann-Marie Imbornoni

Indexer: Elizabeth Parson

Chief Executive Officer: Dan Suratt

Chief Content Officer: Dan Souza

Senior Content Adviser: Jack Bishop

Executive Editorial Directors: Julia Collin Davison and Bridget Lancaster

Senior Director, Book Sales: Emily Logan

contents

AMERICA'S
TEST KITCHEN

AMERICA'S
TEST KITCHEN

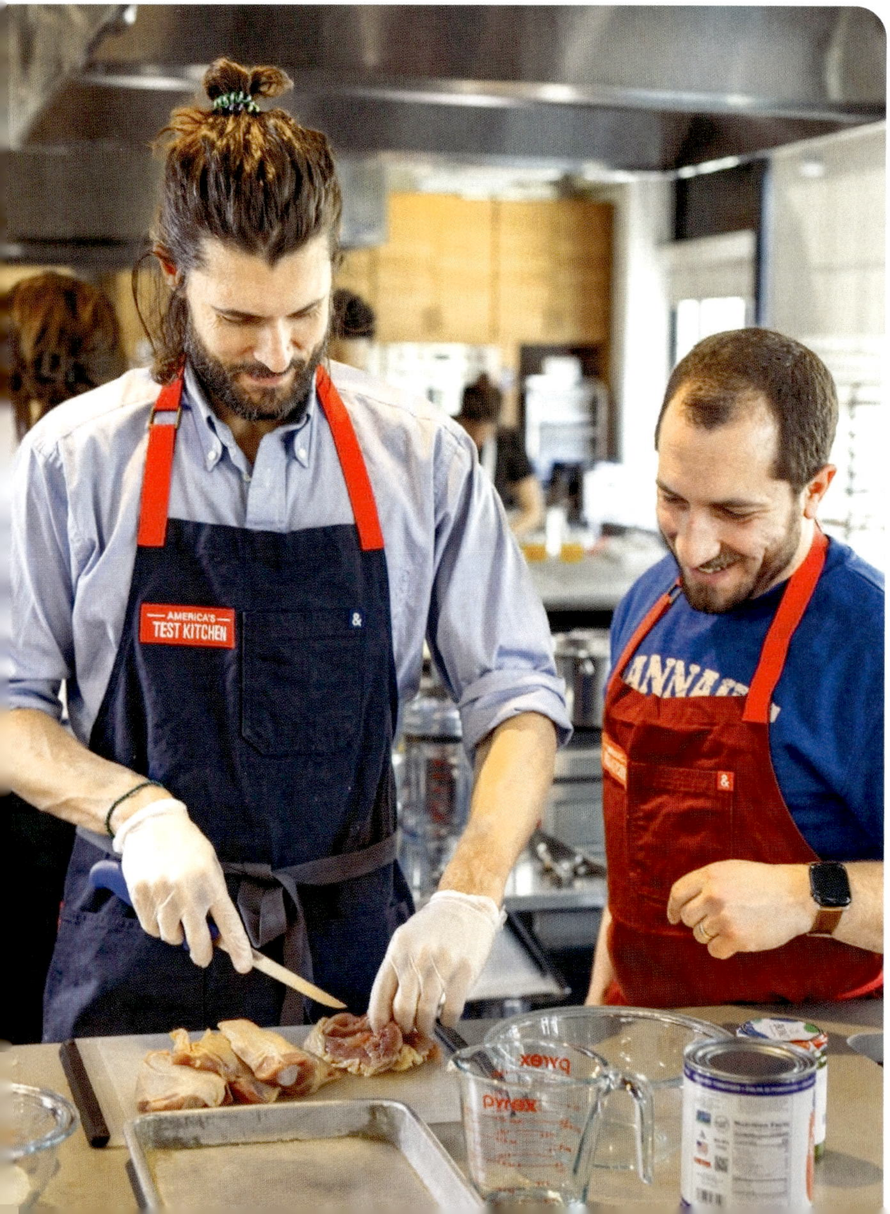

AMERICA'S
TEST KITCHEN

Welcome to America's Test Kitchen

This book has been tested, written, and edited by the folks at America's Test Kitchen, where curious cooks become confident cooks. Located in Boston's Seaport District in the historic Innovation and Design Building, it features 15,000 square feet of kitchen space including multiple photography and video studios. It is the home of *Cook's Illustrated* magazine and *Cook's Country* magazine and is the workday destination for more than 60 test cooks, editors, and cookware specialists. Our mission is to empower and inspire confidence, community, and creativity in the kitchen.

We start the process of testing a recipe with a complete lack of preconceptions, which means that we accept no claim, no technique, and no recipe at face value. We simply assemble as many variations as possible, test a half-dozen of the most promising, and taste the results blind. We then construct our own recipe and continue to test it, varying ingredients, techniques, and cooking times until we reach a consensus. As we like to say in the test kitchen, "We make the mistakes so you don't have to." The result, we hope, is the best version of a particular recipe, but we realize that only you can be the final judge of our success (or failure). We use the same rigorous approach when we test equipment and taste ingredients.

All of this would not be possible without a belief that good cooking, much like good music, is based on a foundation of objective technique. Some people like spicy foods and others don't, but there is a right way to sauté, there is a best way to cook a pot roast, and there are measurable scientific principles involved in producing perfectly beaten, stable egg whites. Our ultimate goal is to investigate the fundamental principles of cooking to give you the techniques, tools, and ingredients you need to become a better cook. It is as simple as that.

To get inspiration and expert instruction, download the America's Test Kitchen app or check out our social media channels for kitchen snapshots, exclusive content, video tips, and much more. You can watch us work (in our actual test kitchen) by tuning in to *America's Test Kitchen* or *Cook's Country* on public television or on our websites. Listen to *Proof* (AmericasTestKitchen.com/podcasts) to hear engaging, complex stories about people and food. Want to hone your cooking skills or finally learn how to bake—with an America's Test Kitchen test cook? Enroll in one of our online cooking classes.

However you choose to visit us, we welcome you into our kitchen, where you can stand by our side as we test our way to the best recipes in America.

facebook.com/AmericasTestKitchen

instagram.com/TestKitchen
youtube.com/AmericasTestKitchen

tiktok.com/@TestKitchen
x.com/TestKitchen

pinterest.com/TestKitchen

AmericasTestKitchen.com
CooksIllustrated.com
CooksCountry.com
OnlineCookingSchool.com

Join Our Community of Recipe Testers

Our recipe testers provide valuable feedback on recipes under development by ensuring that they are foolproof in home kitchens. Help the America's Test Kitchen book team investigate the how and why behind successful recipes from your home kitchen.

The Sheet-Pan Advantage

Introduction

What, you might ask, makes it necessary to devote a whole book to cooking meals with just a sheet pan? There is nothing sexy about these pans, unlike, say, an expensive skillet, a copper pan, or a gorgeous Dutch oven. But the sheet pan is actually the silent and unsung hero of our kitchens. In fact, we advise you to own several (two at the very least).

Sheet pans won't replace the other pans in your arsenal, nor should they, but they give you a whole new way to turn out boldly flavored meals with ease. And these sheet-pan recipes don't require the mastery of all sorts of cooking techniques. Don't get us wrong, cooking skills come into play when making them, but even if you are a novice, we've got your back.

There is both an art and a science to combining ingredients on a sheet pan so everything is perfectly cooked and seasoned once you arrive at the end. We show you how with more than 150 recipes in the pages that follow. Exciting pairings and bold flavors dominate in dishes such as **Miso Salmon with Kabocha and Cabbage** and **Coriander-Cumin Leg of Lamb with Radicchio Salad and Herb Relish**. We roasted, browned, charred, broiled, and steamed our way to success so you don't have to guess how things will turn out. Vinaigrettes and glazes are used in many ways, creative and easy spice rubs add instant flavor, while finishing touches like spiced oils and a wide array of sauces and toppings add big flavor and eye appeal. In fact these meals look so extraordinary on the pan, why not bring the pan to the table? Want to try your hand at creating your own sheet pan meals? See Sheet-Pan Improv (page 16), your guide to DIY meals.

We think you will be surprised by the recipes we reengineered to work on a sheet pan, like **Singapore Noodles with Chicken and Shrimp**; **Crispy, Creamy Macaroni and Cheese** (with frico topping); and **Eggplant Parmesan with Burrata and Basil**. You will find an abundance of weeknight meals such as **Baharat-Rubbed Steak Tips with Lemony Spinach and Pear Salad**, where combining sweet and savory flavors puts a fabulous steak dinner on your table in 30 minutes.

Once you realize all the ways you can press a sheet pan into service, it won't ever languish in your kitchen. The pans we use at home bear the scars of lots of use, always a sign of someone who loves to cook. On the pages that follow, we aim to make you a sheet pan devotee too. So put your sheet pans within reach—we guarantee you'll be using them constantly.

The Art of Arranging Ingredients

In developing the recipes in this book, we discovered a host of practical techniques for achieving great results in sheet-pan dinners (and breakfasts). But the linchpin of them all is how (and when) to arrange your ingredients on the pan. Here are some discrete examples of how strategic placement helps you to harness the power of the sheet and the oven to get the best results.

Use the Perimeter Strategically

The oven's steady heat makes the sheet pan's perimeter hotter than the middle, so we arrange hardy ingredients there while keeping those at risk of overcooking protected in the center. For **Roasted Gnocchi with Blistered Cherry Tomato Sauce** we place the starchy gnocchi around the perimeter and the tomatoes in the center. The tomatoes blister in the heat and slowly release their juices, which form a fragrant sauce that we stir into the gnocchi.

Stack Them

Placing ingredients in a single layer on your sheet pan isn't your only option; they can also be stacked one on top of the other. To make **Roasted Pork Chops and Vegetables with Parsley Vinaigrette**, we place the chops on top of the hearty vegetables (potatoes, carrots, and fennel), allowing them to stay juicy without one side overcooking.

Protect in a Foil Pouch

For **Foil-Roasted Potatoes**, we encase red potatoes in a foil pouch on the sheet pan, which allows them to steam until their interiors are meltingly tender and the exteriors lightly browned. Adding butter and herbs to the foil pouch infuses the potatoes with flavor as they cook. This approach is hands-off and supereasy; plus, it makes cleanup a breeze. For **Lemon-Poached Halibut with Roasted Fingerling Potatoes**, we put the fish in a foil packet and the potatoes on the pan for crispy potatoes and moist fish.

Use Both Ends and the Middle

For **Curry Salmon with Sweet Potato Wedges and Asparagus**, the sweet potato wedges, spread across the sheet alone, roast for 25 minutes. Then, we push them to the center of the pan (where they will be exposed to less heat) and add the salmon on one side and the asparagus on the other. This way, the potatoes don't overcook and the salmon and asparagus, which need the same amount of cooking time, are done in just 10 minutes.

Keep Texture in Mind

Spiced Chicken Breasts with Squash, Caramelized Shallots, and Crispy Kale features paprika and oil-rubbed chicken with crispy skin. We toss the massaged kale with oil, too, which helps it break down. When added to the pan, it becomes crispy, providing a nice foil to the tender squash. Many of our recipes, such as **Miso Salmon with Kabocha and Cabbage**, combine browned or charred ingredients with raw, crunchy ones. In addition to the cabbage there is a crisp cucumber and edamame salad.

Raise Them Up

Placing a wire rack snugly in a sheet pan to cook breaded chicken parts or pork chops keeps their surfaces crisp and golden all the way around. We also use it for proteins such as fish, steak, and chicken when we want to make sure the air circulates around them evenly. And since even lean cuts of meat release juices as they cook, the juices drip through the rack, flavoring whatever is in the pan below. A rack is also handy when we want to get the protein closer to the heating element and to make certain it does not sit in its own juices.

A Sheet-Pan Dinner, Illustrated

Think of your sheet pan as a blank canvas, one that will be transformed as you add your ingredients. That said, there is also a science to cooking on a sheet pan. Paramount is how (and when) you arrange your chosen ingredients.

Here is visual step-by-step view of **Coffee and Chili–Rubbed Steaks with Sweet Potato Wedges and Scallions** (page 121), showing the strategies behind how we arranged everything on the pan.

1 Give sturdy vegetables, like sweet potatoes, a head start by roasting them on their own until they begin to soften.

2 While the vegetables cook, prepare the remaining ingredients.

3 Arrange more delicate vegetables, such as scallions, on top of partially cooked sturdy vegetables.

4 Placing the meat directly on the hot sheet pan jump-starts browning. Continue roasting until the meat is done and the vegetables are fully tender, rotating the sheet halfway through roasting.

5 Transfer the meat to a cutting board to rest before slicing. Leave the vegetables on the baking sheet to keep warm until ready to serve.

1

2

3

4

5

Essential Tips for Sheet-Pan Success

Making a sheet-pan meal requires that you mind the details. Everything from how vegetables are cut, to where they and a protein are positioned on the sheet, to cooking times and more really plays a role in the success of a final dish. Here's what you need to know:

one

Pay Attention to Oven Temperatures

In general, for sheet-pan cooking we used a hot oven (450 or even 500 degrees) because our aim was often to maximize browning, so higher oven temps were our friend. But some ingredients of the meal benefit from low and slow cooking, which is why you may find that things start in a very hot oven and then the heat is lowered dramatically. Consider **Salmon Tacos with Roasted Pineapple Slaw**; here we roast pineapple wedges in a 500-degree oven to caramelize the edges and then we lower the heat to 275 degrees and add the gutsy spice-rubbed salmon.

two

Preheat the Sheet Pan to Jump-Start Browning

When you place a sheet pan in the oven while it preheats (to a high temp), you suddenly have a hot surface that can accelerate browning, charring, or caramelizing. For **Lemon-Thyme Chicken with Ratatouille**, we place bone-in chicken skin side down on one half of an oil-slicked pan and arrange the vegetables on the other half; the chicken gets some crisping and the vegetables brown.

three

Cover the Entire Sheet Pan with Foil for Steam-Cooking or Braising

We learned that yes, you can actually braise using a sheet pan. For **Loukaniko and Lemony Potatoes with Feta-Dill Sauce**, we add broth, lemon juice, and garlic to the pan; cover it with foil; and braise the potatoes until they're soft and highly flavored. Covering the sheet pan with foil allows you to conveniently steam-cook rice, too. Plus, using this method makes it is easier to flavor the rice at the same time. This is true for **Mexican Rice with Spiced Tilapia**.

four

Stagger When Ingredients Hit the Pan

Sheet-pan cooking can be a juggling act sometimes, so you may need to move the pan in and out of the oven to add more ingredients or remove something that is already cooked. For **Old Bay Halibut with Red Potatoes, Corn, and Andouille**, the cooked corn is removed first and then the halibut is placed on the now-empty side of the sheet. Now everything on the pan cooks for just another 10 minutes.

five

Place Vegetables (and More) Cut Side Down for Browning

We pay special attention to how we cut vegetables as well as how we place them on the sheet pan. For instance, for **Garlic-Sage Chicken Leg Quarters with Cauliflower and Shallots,** we cut the cauliflower into wedges so that they can lie flat on the pan and thus become deeply burnished. The shallots are halved so they too have a flat side and can benefit from browning.

six

Make Salad Components While You're at It

While building our sheet-pan meals, we were inspired to incorporate interesting salads by using a vegetable also roasted on the pan as a component. For **Coffee and Fennel–Rubbed Boneless Short Ribs with Celery Root Salad**, we roast pieces of celery root on an upper rack until velvety as the base of an unusual salad with parsley leaves, pomegranate seeds, and a lemony dressing.

seven

Use the Microwave to Line Up Cooking Times

The microwave allows you to combine quick-cooking ingredients with those that need more time or lower heat. For **Herbed Roast Beef with Root Vegetables**, we cook the roast low and slow and give the dense vegetables a head start by microwaving them until nearly tender before placing them alongside the beef.

eight

Rotate the Sheet Pan

Ovens can have hot spots which will cause uneven cooking. To avoid this, the easy solution is to rotate the sheet pan during cooking.

nine

Switch Oven Racks Midstream

When your oven preheats, it will be consistently hotter at the top because of simple physics. The middle of your oven provides the most even cooking or baking. The bottom rack, since it's closest to the heat source, is ideal for getting great color on the bottom of your food.

If you are using two sheet pans, as some recipes specify, switching the pans from the top rack to a lower rack partway through cooking helps ensure perfectly cooked ingredients. And if you are using just one sheet pan, sometimes switching rack positions makes sense for the same reason.

ten

Use the Broiler for Quick Browning

Many recipes in the book use the broiler at one point (often at the end of the cooking time) for browning or to get an appealing char, or to cook a vegetable so it takes on some browning but remains crisp-tender. This is the case for **Mustardy Apple Butter–Glazed Pork Chops with Broccoli Rabe**. It is also integral to **Lime-Glazed Salmon and Crispy Rice Salad**, where we broil everything in the time it takes for the salmon to cook through and the rice to turn crispy.

Ways to Build Flavor Easily

When you are using just a sheet pan to create a meal, suddenly the flavor-building techniques you normally rely on when using a skillet, for instance, just don't work. Why? You have only ONE pan and it goes only in the oven; this requires a radical reinvention of many classical techniques. Take browning skin-on chicken thighs. The flavorful brown bits that stick to the skillet are pure gold and when you deglaze them with wine or broth, you have achieved flavor nirvana, the bedrock of flavor building. But we've come up with our own ways to build flavor, some of them quite radical, which deliver outstanding results and make the difference between a meal that is good and one that is great.

Brown for Flavor and Eye Appeal

Many of our recipes boost flavor and color by browning or charring. There are several avenues to this: preheating the baking sheet, adding glaze with sugar or honey, roasting cut side down, and using the broiler. For **Roasted Tofu and Sweet Potato Bowls with Snap Pea Salad**, the potato rounds hit the pan first when the oven is very hot. Then we toss the tofu with a mix of soy sauce, honey, sesame oil, and sambal; flip the potatoes and add the tofu to the pan; and brush more honey-soy mixture on everything partway through cooking. This results in tofu that is caramelized with a crisp exterior and tender interior and in potatoes with big flavor and deep browning on each side.

Make the Most of Spice Rubs

One of the easiest ways to add flavor to a protein is applying a spice rub. To add pizzazz to a flank steak dinner, **Spice-Rubbed Flank Steak with Toasted Corn and Black Bean Salad**, a rub with a decidedly Mexican flavor sets the tone for the meal. When the meat and corn hit the preheated sheet pan slicked with oil, the sizzling starts immediately, blooming the spices and toasting the corn for our salad.

Use Aromatics Many Ways

Don't be shy about aromatics. We load them up in rubs, marinades, glazes, relishes, and vinaigrettes. No flavor profile is off-limits here. For **Coriander-Cumin Butterflied Leg of Lamb with Radicchio Salad and Herb-Shallot Relish**, the flavoring starts with a spiced oil bloomed on the sheet pan. We place the lamb right on top of it, which seasons the lamb through and through as it cooks. When strained, this oil does double duty: We use it as part of a relish, which also includes some of the lamb juices left behind on the sheet pan. Some of the relish is incorporated into a vinaigrette that we toss with the radicchio, date, and orange salad.

Add Instant Flavor with Glazes

Traditionally, glazes are reduced on the stovetop. Without that option we have several workarounds. A good example is **Hoisin Pork Tenderloins with Green Beans, Potatoes, and Chive Butter**, as the hoisin itself is the glaze. Many other glazes are made by thickening the ingredients in the microwave so they won't slide off the food and burn on the pan.

Make the Most of Sauces and Vinaigrettes

Sometimes vinaigrettes are used more than once in a recipe: tossed with a protein or vegetable at the start and then used again toward the end of cooking for a hit of brightness. They are tailor-made for drizzling too. For **Chicken Souvlaki**, a dressing delivers a flavor triple play. And our homemade tzatziki sauce, slathered on the pitas, completes this vibrant meal; no opportunity for adding flavor was overlooked.

Use Those Meaty Juices

You cannot make a pan sauce on a sheet pan but what you can do is make the most of the juices left behind on the pan after roasting. How handy, right? For **Goat Cheese–Stuffed Chicken with Roasted Carrots**, while the chicken is resting we roll the roasted carrots around in the juices left on the sheet. No one will call these carrots boring. They are both caramelized and infused with the chicken juices.

Sheet-Pan Magic in Action

Baharat Chicken with Potatoes and Herb-Date Salad (page 94) illustrates several clever ways to layer flavor into a sheet-pan meal, in this case, crisp chicken and potatoes topped with a vibrant salad. Serve this and guests will think there is a pile of dirty dishes in the kitchen (that is, unless you want to bring this dish to the table right on the sheet pan).

Start the Chicken Skin Side Down on the Pan

In order to ensure that the chicken thighs become crispy (no one likes rubbery skin) without a hot skillet, place them skin side down at the start. Exposing the skin to the heat of the pan allows it to render its fat and become deliciously crispy.

Roast the Chicken Skin Trimmings

Don't throw these flavor bombs away. Put them on the sheet pan first and roast until crisp and fat has coated the sheet, delivering a deep flavor base. Discard the trimmings and add the potatoes to the sheet. We guarantee that these potatoes are like no others you've made.

Assemble an Herb-Forward Salad for a Huge Hit of Flavor

Whisk together a lemony dressing. Combine olives, sweet dates, shallot, and blood orange segments with the dressing, whole parsley leaves, more herbs, and fennel slivers for a bold and colorful accompaniment, the perfect foil for the spiced chicken and crispy potatoes.

Use a Potent Spice Rub

To flavor the thighs, sprinkle with some of the baharat, then slash the skin and add more to infuse the chicken with a Middle Eastern spice flavor throughout.

Add Instant Flavor with a Glaze-Ready Ingredient

Brush the chicken with potent sweet-savory pomegranate molasses at the end and roast once more briefly. This adds another layer of deep flavor to the chicken and turns it glossy and gloriously browned.

Drizzle It

Make a fragrant coriander–Aleppo pepper oil and drizzle it over everything, then calm the heat by drizzling yogurt for one last layer of flavor.

Pushing the Limits of What a Sheet Pan Can Do

These six techniques show how a sheet pan makes it easy to create meals, often eliminating steps, time, pots or skillets, and casserole dishes. Harness its powers with creative techniques and you'll feel like you have your own sous chef in the kitchen.

Elevate Your Salmon Game

It's easy to get into a salmon rut but the salmon recipes in this book will change that. Our **Lime-Glazed Salmon and Crispy Rice Salad**, inspired by the crispy rice salads of Thailand and Laos, is a gorgeous sheet-pan meal. Starting with cooked rice, spread across the pan, ensures that everything is ready at the same time. A fragrant chili-lime sauce is both a glaze for the salmon and a drizzling sauce at the end.

Create a Deli Classic

No one can resist a cheesy, saucy meatball sub on a crispy roll, but who makes this at home? Forget Friday night takeout and let your sheet pan do all the work to make **Meatball Subs with Roasted Broccoli**. The meatballs are tender and browned and the broccoli wedges are addictively caramelized. Your family will thank you.

Build a Noodle Dish

With a sheet pan, the Cantonese favorite **Singapore Noodles with Chicken and Shrimp** is appealingly hands-off. A medley of vegetables roasts on one side of the pan as char siu sauce–coated chicken thighs roast on the other, placed in a simple tray fashioned from foil, which makes it easy to remove them. The noodles just need some soaking before they roast briefly above the other ingredients; we nestle shrimp on top of everything at the end and give them a quick broil, which also makes the noodles a bit crispy.

Consider Big-Batch Breakfasts

Making breakfast for multiple guests requires the skills of a diner cook hustling to get brunch served. The sheet pan makes it far easier to serve four or more like **One Big Pancake**, **Sweet Potato and Poblano Frittata**, and **Huevos Rancheros**.

Make a Luscious Soup

Yes, you can make soup on a sheet pan! For **Zucchini, Leek, and Pea Soup with Crispy Prosciutto**, you can forget the chopping and simmering and let the oven and blender do all the work. First, use the sheet pan to transform sliced prosciutto into a crispy garnish. Then, roast halved zucchini and leeks with a few cloves of garlic and blend with hot broth and thawed frozen peas. The addition of basil and lemon zest rounds out the flavors and makes this pretty green puree sing.

Create a Fancy Salad

Charred Broccoli Caesar Salad with Chicken breaks all the rules. Where's the lettuce, you ask? We skipped it and opted for deeply caramelized broccoli. The chicken goes into the oven first, and while it rests, we crank up the oven temp for gorgeous charring on the broccoli wedges. Panko and Parmesan stand in for croutons. And a craveable dressing earns this recipe its Caesar moniker.

Sheet-Pan Improv: Make It Your Way!

A good sheet-pan meal takes some thought and planning, which is why we've provided you with two charts, one for vegetables that work well on a sheet pan and one for proteins. The cooking times and instructions will guide you as you put together your special meal. Here are the highlights of what you should consider before you start. Go bold, we say, and make it your own.

Five Steps to Sheet-Pan Success

one

Prepare Your Ingredients

- Be sure to cut your ingredients according to the chart.
- Marinate your protein if desired; even a short marinating time can add flavor.

two

Add Flavor at the Start

- Seasoning can be as simple as oil, salt, and pepper.
- Give your dish a distinct direction for flavoring. Take inspiration from a cuisine or flavor profile you like; this will inform all your choices.
- Consider using a spice rub.
- Add hearty herbs such as fresh rosemary, sage, and thyme.

three

Arrange Your Chosen Ingredients

- Place vegetables cut side down for better browning.
- Don't overcrowd the pan.
- Make sure there is some space between ingredients so heat can circulate.
- Place heartier ingredients, or any you want to crisp up, around the edges of the pan, and place easy-to-overcook items like fish and chicken breasts in the center of the pan.

four

Stagger Based on Times in the Chart

- Cooking times can vary widely so don't assume you can add everything at once. Use our charts on the next page as a guide.
- Flip and toss ingredients when necessary for browning or even cooking.
- Use the broiler especially for last-minute crisping or browning; your sheet pan should be 6 inches away from the heating element.

five

Now Is Your Chance to Get Creative with Fresh Flavors

- Simply squeezing an acid like lemon, lime, or orange juice can add both flavor and brightness.
- Drizzle a sauce over everything to give your dish an identity.
- Shower with chopped herbs for color and a burst of flavor.
- Add toppings that offer texture, creaminess, and eye appeal: cheese, plain yogurt, nuts, seeds, toasted panko, or crispy shallots. Consider fruit and vegetables such as sliced chiles, sliced snap peas, herb salads, and chopped orange pieces.

DIY Sheet-Pan Meals

Here are some useful sheet-pan cook times for proteins and vegetables. All ingredients bake in a 450-degree oven with the oven rack set to the lower-middle position.

Choose Your Protein

Protein	Preparation	Cook Time (Min.)	Doneness Temp. (°F)	Special Notes
Poultry				
Chicken Breast, Boneless	trimmed, pounded to even thickness	15-20	160°	
Chicken Breast, Bone-in	trimmed	35-40	160°	roast skin side up
Chicken Thigh, Boneless	trimmed	15-20	175°	
Chicken Thigh, Bone-in	trimmed	35-40	175°	
Beef				
Beef, Steak Tips	trimmed and cut into 2-inch pieces	10-15	125°	flip halfway through
Beef, Short Ribs	trimmed and cut into 2-inch pieces	10-15	125°	flip halfway through
Pork				
Pork Chop, Boneless	trimmed, 2 slits cut through fat on edges	10-15	140°	
Pork Chop, Bone-in	trimmed, 2 slits cut through fat on edges	15-20	140°	
Pork Tenderloin, Whole	trimmed	20-25	140°	
Tofu				
Tofu, Planks	1 inch thick, patted dry	12-17	n/a	
Seafood				
Salmon Fillet	1½ inches thick	15-20	125°	
Flaky White Fish, Thick	1½ inches thick	15-20	135°	
Firm White Fish, Thick	1½ inches thick	15-20	130°	

Three Sheet-Pan Formulas to Get You Started

Here are a few simple sheet-pan dinners we mapped out to show you how easy it is to build your own. Follow the chart for prep information, cook times, and other information.

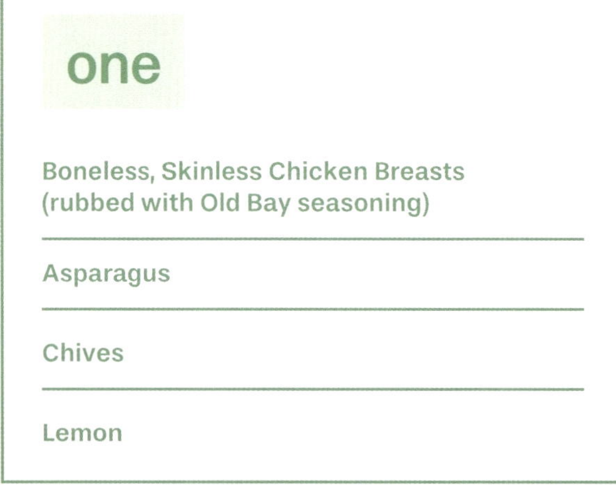

one

Boneless, Skinless Chicken Breasts (rubbed with Old Bay seasoning)

Asparagus

Chives

Lemon

Choose Your Vegetables

Vegetable	Preparation	Cook Time (Min.)	Special Notes
Asparagus	trimmed	10-15	
Beets	peeled and cut into 1-inch pieces or wedges	20-25	
Bell Peppers	stemmed, seeded, and sliced 1 inch thick	8-10	stir halfway through
Broccoli	cut into 1-inch florets	8-10	
Brussels Sprouts	trimmed and halved	8-10	arrange cut side down on sheet
Butternut or Other Winter Squash	peeled, seeded, and cut into 1-inch pieces	35-40	stir halfway through
Cabbage	trimmed and cut into 2-inch pieces	8-10	stir halfway through
Carrots	peeled and halved lengthwise	20-25	arrange cut side down on sheet
Cauliflower	trimmed and cut into 1-inch florets	10-15	
Celery Root	peeled and cut into 1-inch pieces	40-45	stir halfway through
Cherry Tomatoes	left whole	20-25	
Delicata Squash	trimmed, halved lengthwise, seeded, and sliced crosswise ½ inch thick	30-35	stir halfway through
Eggplant	cut into 1-inch pieces	25-30	stir halfway through
Fennel	stalks discarded, bulbs halved, cored, and sliced into 1-inch-thick wedges	30-35	
Green Beans	trimmed	20-25	stir halfway through
Mushrooms	trimmed and left whole if small, halved if medium, or quartered if large	40-45	stir halfway through
Potatoes	cut into 1-inch-thick pieces or wedges	35-40	arrange cut side down on sheet
Sweet Potatoes	cut into 1-inch-thick pieces or wedges	35-40	arrange cut side down on sheet
Zucchini or Summer Squash	halved lengthwise and sliced 1 inch thick	20-30	stir halfway through

two

Bone-in Pork Chops (rubbed with smoked paprika)

Potato and Broccoli Wedges

Creamy Mustard Sauce

three

Salmon

Green Beans

Lemon Vinaigrette

Finish with Fresh Herbs

Calling All Sheet Pans

Rimmed baking sheets, also called half-sheet pans, are true workhorses in the test kitchen. We have stacks of them that we use every day. For this book, we searched for new and innovative ways to use our sheet pans, primarily with the aim of turning out spectacular meals without any other pans. A high bar for sure, and for this challenge, we used the pan our testing team deemed the very best. You should have at least two sheet pans in your kitchen to take advantage of all our recipes.

Which One Is Best?

Our favorite rimmed baking sheet is the **Nordic Ware Baker's Half Sheet** (18 by 13 inches). It bakes and roasts food beautifully and is affordable, lightweight, very durable, and easy to handle. To maximize its use, especially when making sheet-pan meals, we recommend getting a wire rack for it.

Consider the Handy Quarter-Sheet Pan

If you regularly cook for just one or two people, we also recommend buying a quarter-sheet pan (13 by 9 inches). It is just the right size for our **Sweet Potato and Poblano Frittata** and **Nutella Bread Pudding**, both of which serve four. We use it to store prepped but not cooked foods in the fridge, for salting proteins, to hold mise en place items, to organize the cooking tools we may need for a recipe, and much more. We guarantee that you'll find lots of handy uses for it in your kitchen.

Wire Racks: The All-Important Sidekick

The success of many of our sheet-pan recipes depends on a wire rack to elevate the food for ideal crispness. Elevating the food allows air to circulate around it, meaning that both sides cook evenly and the underside is not soggy. A good rack should be sturdy and able to withstand a hot broiler, it should clean up without warping or damage, and it must fit inside a standard 18 by 13-inch rimmed baking sheet. Our winning model aced every test and features a grid small enough to keep food from falling through.

Our favorite half sheet–size wire rack is the **Checkered Chef Cooling Rack**. It's sturdy and fits nicely inside our favorite rimmed baking sheet. If you'd like a wire rack that fits inside a quarter-sheet pan, we also recommend the smaller version of our favorite, the **Checkered Chef Quarter Sheet Cooling/Baking Rack**

They Get Better with Age

If your pan doesn't look shiny and new anymore, is it actually bad? To find out, we made a bunch of different foods in shiny new pans, then in dull and darkened pans. Surprisingly, the dull and darkened pans actually browned better than the shiny new ones. This is because darker colors absorb heat more efficiently than lighter colors.

To make sure we weren't imagining things, we put shiny new sheet pans and dull older ones in the oven with temperature trackers attached to record the rates at which they heated. Sure enough, the older sheets heated faster, hitting just over 400 degrees in 15 minutes. The shiny new sheets only reached 350 degrees.

Our favorite rimmed baking sheet, the **Nordic Ware Baker's Half Sheet**

Can You Put Baking Sheets in the Dishwasher?

Aluminum baking sheets should not go in the dishwasher because uncoated aluminum reacts with harsh detergents, which can cause permanent discoloration and damage the texture of the baking sheet's surface. We recommend washing them by hand instead. Washing fully clad cookware in the dishwasher, including baking sheets, can degrade the inner layer of aluminum due to the high heat and harsh detergents, leaving sharp edges of steel at the perimeter of the pan.

The Sheet Pan as Kitchen Helper

We keep our sheet pans (both half- and quarter-size) in a convenient spot since we reach for them even when we are not cooking. And here are some of the reasons why.

Mise en place organizer

This French term for "everything in its place" is one that chefs live by. A prepped and organized cook is a better cook. To get organized, we like to array our ingredients in small prep bowls on a quarter-sheet pan.

Serve from it.

Bring the entire sheet pan to the table. It will make an impression.

Freeze ingredients such as berries, pieces of fruit, or nuts on it so you can transfer them to zipper-lock bags more easily.

Smash garlic or nuts with it.

Use it for raw and cooked proteins.

When cooking in batches, keep raw and cooked proteins separate for safety by designating one side of a wire rack (placed in a rimmed baking sheet) for each.

Keep things warm in the oven.

Use it for soaking skewers.

Frost a cake.

Place a cardboard cake round on an overturned sheet pan and place your first layer on top. Frost each layer as you go along and then frost the top and the sides. You don't have to worry about cleaning up stray bits of frosting, as they will all land on the sheet pan. To get the cake off the pan you can use a cake lifter or two long spatulas on either side to lift the cake.

Turn it into a drying rack for dishes.

Dish racks take up a lot of valuable space on the counter and can get moldy, but a sheet pan can be repurposed for this task when not being used for cooking. (You must use a wire rack in a sheet pan for this.)

Cool rice and grains faster.

For salads that use grains such as farro, quinoa, or rice, you need to cool the cooked grain before you make the salad. The easiest way to do this is to drain the grain, if needed, and spread it out over the sheet pan to cool.

Put a cutting board in it to carve juicy meats and roasts.

Open raw protein packages on it to keep your counter clean and sanitary.

Use it as a drip catcher (in the oven or under a cooling rack).

Pizza stone or pizza peel replacement

If you don't have a baking stone, you can use a preheated overturned baking sheet instead. If you don't have a baking peel, use an overturned sheet pan to slide the pizza onto the baking stone.

Use it as a drying rack for fruit, particularly berries and grapes.

Washing fruit is essential. but when it comes to smaller items like berries, it is just not effective to leave them on top of one another in a colander. Lay a clean dish towel on the sheet and scatter fruit over top.

Salt proteins in it or refrigerate them in it.

An inverted sheet pan makes a handy trivet for hot pots or pans. (Use a quarter-sheet pan.)

Spice Rubs, Sauces + Toppings

The sheet pan allows you to add flavor at various points along the way. But spice rubs and pastes like baharat and harissa can add deep seasoning to food before it goes into the oven, while sauces add a dramatic final touch when drizzled over an entire dish or dolloped around ingredients. Here are many sauces and seasonings that are supereasy to assemble and so versatile. In some cases, these define the cuisine the dish represents. Toppings can be as simple as peanuts or pomegranate seeds or more complex, like crispy shallots or quick pickles.

Harissa

Makes about ½ cup
Total Time 15 minutes

Harissa is a traditional Tunisian condiment that is great for flavoring soups, sauces, and dressings or dolloping on lamb, hummus, eggs, and sandwiches. We use it as a fantasic spice rub for many of our sheet-pan meals, If you can't find Aleppo pepper, you can substitute ¾ teaspoon paprika and ¾ teaspoon finely chopped red pepper flakes.

- 6 tablespoons extra-virgin olive oil
- 6 garlic cloves, minced
- 2 tablespoons paprika
- 1 tablespoon ground coriander
- 1–3 tablespoons ground dried Aleppo pepper
- 1 teaspoon ground cumin
- ¾ teaspoon caraway seeds
- ½ teaspoon table salt

Combine all ingredients in bowl and microwave until bubbling and very fragrant, about 1 minute, stirring halfway through microwaving; let cool completely. (Harissa can be refrigerated in airtight container for up to 4 days.)

Baharat

Makes about ½ cup
Total Time 10 minutes

"Baharat," the Arabic word for "spice," is the name of a spice blend found in dishes across North Africa and the Middle East. It's often also called seven spice blend, and the seven spices featured in our blend are those most commonly found, though there are regional variations. This warm blend has an intense profile that befits meat dishes, legumes, and hearty vegetables.

- 3 (3-inch) cinnamon sticks, broken into pieces
- 4¾ teaspoons cumin seeds
- 1½ tablespoons coriander seeds
- 1 tablespoon black peppercorns
- 2 teaspoons whole cloves
- 1 tablespoon ground cardamom
- 2 teaspoons ground nutmeg

Process cinnamon sticks in spice grinder until finely ground, about 30 seconds. Add cumin seeds, coriander seeds, peppercorns, and cloves and process until finely ground, about 30 seconds. Transfer to bowl and stir in cardamom and nutmeg. (Baharat can be stored in airtight container at room temperature for up to 1 month.)

Pesto

Makes 1½ cups
Total Time 10 minutes

We like to drizzle a little pesto over roasted root vegetables or lean proteins such as fish or chicken. This classic pesto also tastes great slathered on a wrap or panini or used as a base for bruschetta.

- 4 cups fresh basil leaves
- ¼ cup fresh parsley leaves
- 6 garlic cloves, smashed and peeled
- ½ cup pine nuts, toasted
- 1 cup extra-virgin olive oil
- 1 ounce Parmesan cheese, grated fine (½ cup)

1 Place basil and parsley in 1-gallon zipper-lock bag. Pound bag with flat side of meat pounder or with rolling pin until all leaves are bruised.

2 Process garlic, pine nuts, and herbs in food processor until finely chopped, about 1 minute, scraping down sides of bowl as needed. With processor running, slowly add oil until incorporated. Transfer pesto to bowl, stir in Parmesan, and season with salt and pepper to taste. (You can refrigerate this pesto in airtight container for up to 2 days or freeze it for up to 3 months. To prevent browning, press plastic wrap flush to the surface, or top the pesto with a thin layer of olive oil.)

Tzatziki Sauce

Makes about 1 cup
Total Time 20 minutes, plus 30 minutes chilling

This sauce pairs well with souvlaki, falafel, gyros, Greek salads, and grilled meats.

- ½ cucumber, peeled, halved lengthwise, seeded, and shredded
- ¼ teaspoon table salt
- ½ cup plain whole-milk Greek yogurt
- 1 tablespoon extra-virgin olive oil
- 1 tablespoon minced fresh mint and/or dill
- 1 small garlic clove, minced

1 Toss cucumber with salt in strainer and let drain for 15 minutes.

2 Whisk yogurt, oil, mint, and garlic together in bowl, then stir in cucumber. Cover and refrigerate for at least 30 minutes to allow flavors to meld. Season with salt and pepper to taste. (Tzatziki can be refrigerated in airtight container for up to 2 days.)

Lemon-Herb Sauce

Makes about ½ cup
Total Time 5 minutes

Serve with any dish that deserves the addition of an herby, creamy sauce. This sauce is extremely versatile.

- 6 tablespoons mayonnaise
- 2 scallions, minced
- 3 tablespoons chopped fresh parsley
- 1 tablespoon lemon juice

Whisk all ingredients together in bowl. Season with salt and pepper to taste. (Sauce can be refrigerated for up to 3 days.)

Avocado Crema

Makes about ½ cup
Total Time 5 minutes

We use this sauce for spiced chicken dishes and anything with a Mexican profile.

- ½ avocado, chopped coarse
- ¼ cup chopped fresh cilantro
- 3 tablespoons water
- 1 tablespoon lime juice
- 1 tablespoon plain yogurt

Process all ingredients in food processor until completely smooth, about 1 minute, scraping down sides of bowl as needed. Season with salt and pepper to taste. (Crema can be refrigerated with plastic wrap pressed flush to surface for up to 2 days.)

Lime Crema

Makes ½ cup
Total Time 5 minutes

This crema is wonderful with fish sandwiches and salmon burgers and is also a good way to jazz up roasted fish.

- ½ cup Mexican crema or sour cream
- ¼ teaspoon table salt
- 1 teaspoon grated lime zest plus 2 tablespoons juice

Combine all ingredients in small bowl. (Crema can be refrigerated in airtight container for up to 3 days.)

Creamy Apple-Mustard Sauce

Makes about ½ cup
Total Time 5 minutes

This easy, elegant sauce is the perfect accompaniment to cuts of pork. Applesauce tempers the mustards' bite with a touch of sweetness.

- ¼ cup whole-grain mustard
- 3 tablespoons unsweetened applesauce
- 2 tablespoons Dijon mustard
- 4 teaspoons cider vinegar
- 1 tablespoon honey
- 1 tablespoon minced fresh chives (optional)
- ¼ teaspoon table salt

Stir all ingredients (including chives, if using) in bowl until combined. (Sauce can be refrigerated in airtight container for up to 3 days.)

Ten-Minute Tomato Salsa

Makes 3 cups
Total Time 10 minutes

For bright, fresh salsa that requires about as much effort as opening a jar, we turn to the food processor to give us delicious flavor in record time.

- ½ small red onion, cut into 1-inch pieces
- ½ cup fresh cilantro leaves
- ¼ cup jarred sliced jalapeños
- 2 tablespoons lime juice
- 2 garlic cloves, chopped
- ½ teaspoon table salt
- 1 (28-ounce) can diced tomatoes, drained

Pulse onion, cilantro, jalapeños, lime juice, garlic, and salt in food processor until coarsely chopped, about 5 pulses, scraping down sides of bowl as needed. Add tomatoes and pulse until combined, about 3 pulses. Drain salsa briefly in fine-mesh strainer, then transfer to bowl and season with salt and pepper to taste. (Salsa can be refrigerated in airtight container for up to 2 days.)

Crispy Shallots

Makes ½ cup
Total Time 10 minutes

You can double this recipe for a big batch; increase the initial microwaving time to 5 to 10 minutes.

- 3 shallots, sliced thin
- ½ cup vegetable oil, for frying

Combine shallots and oil in medium bowl. Microwave until beginning to turn golden, 2 to 5 minutes. Stir and continue to microwave in 30-second increments until deep golden brown (30 seconds to 2 minutes). Using slotted spoon, immediately transfer shallots to paper towel–lined plate; season with salt to taste. Let drain and crisp, about 5 minutes. (Shallots can be stored in an airtight container for up to 1 month. Shallot oil can be refrigerated in airtight container for up to 1 month.)

Quick Sweet and Spicy Pickled Red Onion

Makes 1 cup
Total Time 5 minutes, plus 45 minutes pickling

These pickles pack serious sweet and spicy flavor with very little effort and they're equally at home on a taco as they are sprinkled over a roasted cauliflower main dish. Give them a try and you'll see that the opportunities are endless. If you're spice-averse, you can skip the jalapeños.

- 1 cup red wine vinegar
- ⅓ cup sugar
- ¼ teaspoon table salt
- 1 red onion, halved and sliced thin
- 2 jalapeño chiles, stemmed, seeded, and cut into thin rings

Microwave vinegar, sugar, and salt in bowl until steaming, 1 to 2 minutes. Stir in onion and jalapeño and let sit, stirring occasionally, for 45 minutes. Drain vegetables in colander. Serve. (Drained pickled onion can be refrigerated in airtight container for up to 1 week.)

Sumac Onion

Makes 1 cup
Total Time 10 minutes, plus 1 hour sitting

- 1 red onion, halved and cut through root end into ¼-inch-thick slices
- 2 tablespoons lemon juice
- 2 tablespoons red wine vinegar
- 1 tablespoon extra-virgin olive oil
- 1 tablespoon ground sumac
- ½ teaspoon sugar
- ¼ teaspoon table salt

Combine all ingredients in bowl. Let sit, stirring occasionally for 1 hour. (Onion can be refrigerated in airtight container for up to 1 week.)

CHAPTER ONE

Sandwiches, Tacos + Pizza

Cheddar-Crusted Grilled Cheese

Serves 4 | **Total Time** 50 minutes

- 4 teaspoons mayonnaise
- 8 slices hearty white sandwich bread
- 2 tablespoons unsalted butter, cut into 4 pieces
- 4 slices deli American cheese (2 ounces)
- 8 ounces white sharp cheddar cheese, shredded (2 cups), divided

Why This Recipe Works Golden brown, crunchy-edged, molten-gooey, and gilded with a lacy, crispy sharp cheddar crust: This is the ultimate grilled cheese sandwich. And it's made in the ultimate way. While grilled cheese cooking is straightforward—add the sandwich to a hot buttered skillet, flip, and eat—it makes just one basic sandwich. Here we assemble and cook all four on a preheated sheet pan. They're filled with cheddar cheese for sharp flavor, a little American cheese for meltiness, and a spread of mayo for extra richness. After we bake them until golden on both sides, we create the crust by placing sandwich-size piles of cheddar on the (now-empty) sheet, melting them, and then putting the sandwiches back down on top of the cheese to fuse the two. Buy the American cheese at the deli counter, not presliced cheese. We developed this recipe using Arnold Country Style White Bread; you may achieve more or less browning depending on the amount of sugar in the bread you use.

1 Adjust oven rack to middle position. Place rimmed baking sheet on rack and heat oven to 450 degrees.

2 Spread mayonnaise evenly on 1 side of each slice of bread, ½ teaspoon per slice. Remove hot sheet from oven and place on wire rack. Add butter to preheated sheet and spread to coat pan. Place bread mayonnaise side up on sheet to coat other side in butter. Layer 1 slice American cheese and ¼ cup cheddar on mayonnaise side of each of 4 slices of bread. Top with remaining 4 slices of bread, mayonnaise side down.

3 Bake sandwiches until just beginning to brown on first side, about 3 minutes. Flip sandwiches and bake until golden brown on second side, 4 to 6 minutes. Transfer sheet to wire rack and move sandwiches to plate.

4 Sprinkle four ¼-cup portions of remaining cheddar into piles in each quadrant of sheet, then spread into rectangles just larger than slices of bread, about 6 by 4 inches. Bake until cheese is melted and bubbly but not browned, about 2 minutes.

5 Remove sheet from oven. Place sandwiches, lighter side up, directly on top of melted cheddar. Return sheet to oven and cook until edges of cheddar are beginning to turn golden brown, 3 to 5 minutes. (If bread browns faster than cheese, cover bread with squares of aluminum foil.) Slide spatula underneath sandwiches and transfer, cheddar crust side up, to rack. (Do not slide spatula under sandwiches before cheddar is beginning to brown; it will pull cheddar and ruin crust.) Let sandwiches sit for 5 minutes to allow cheese to set. Transfer sandwiches to cutting board and cut diagonally. Serve.

VARIATIONS

Cheddar-Crusted Grilled Cheese with Tomato and Bacon

Omit butter. Line rimmed baking sheet with aluminum foil before placing in oven. Before cooking sandwiches, add 4 slices bacon to prepared sheet and roast until crispy, 6 to 10 minutes. Using slotted spoon, transfer bacon to paper towel–lined plate and discard foil, reserving fat. Add 2 tablespoons fat to sheet (or add vegetable oil to measure 2 tablespoons). Add 2 slices tomato and 1 piece crispy bacon, cut in half, to each sandwich after adding cheese in step 2.

Cheddar-Crusted Grilled Cheese with Turkey and Peppadew Peppers

Toss ½ cup thinly sliced peppadew peppers with 1 cup of the shredded cheddar; use to fill the sandwiches in step 2. Cut 4 slices deli turkey (3 ounces total) into rough 1½-inch pieces, then scatter over cheese-peppadew mixture in step 2.

Ultimate Roasted Vegetable Sandwich

Serves 4 to 6 | **Total Time** 55 minutes

- 1 pound eggplant, sliced into ½-inch-thick rounds
- 1 teaspoon table salt, divided
- ½ cup chopped fresh basil
- ⅓ cup mayonnaise
- ⅔ ounce Pecorino Romano cheese, grated (⅓ cup)
- 2 tablespoons capers, rinsed and chopped
- ¾ teaspoon pepper, divided
- 6 tablespoons extra-virgin olive oil
- 5 garlic cloves, minced
- ¼ teaspoon red pepper flakes
- 1 (8-ounce) zucchini, halved crosswise and sliced lengthwise into ½-inch-thick planks
- ½ small red onion, sliced ½ inch thick
- 1 tablespoon balsamic vinegar
- 1 (1-pound) loaf ciabatta, halved horizontally
- 8 ounces fresh mozzarella cheese, sliced into ¼-inch-thick rounds
- 1 cup jarred roasted red peppers, patted dry and sliced into 1-inch-thick strips

Why This Recipe Works Piling four meaty roasted vegetables and generous slabs of mozzarella cheese onto crusty ciabatta surely makes this one of the most satisfying sandwiches you will eat all summer. Serve on the patio for company or pack for the best beach lunch. Roasting the vegetables with a quick garlic-chile oil (infused in the microwave) makes them hyper-flavorful, as does tossing the vegetables with balsamic vinegar while they're still warm from roasting so they drink it up. For richness, we complement the savory qualities of this sandwich with a piquant mayonnaise made with fragrant basil, sharp Pecorino cheese, and briny capers. Be sure to use fresh bread here; once ciabatta becomes stale, the crust becomes tough and the sandwiches will be difficult to eat.

1 Arrange eggplant slices on paper towel–lined rimmed baking sheet and sprinkle all over with ½ teaspoon salt. Let sit for 15 minutes, then thoroughly pat dry with paper towels.

2 Adjust oven rack 6 inches from broiler element and heat broiler. Combine basil, mayonnaise, Pecorino, capers, and ½ teaspoon pepper in bowl; set aside.

3 Combine oil, garlic, pepper flakes, remaining ½ teaspoon salt, and remaining ¼ teaspoon pepper in large bowl. Microwave until bubbling and fragrant, about 75 seconds. Add eggplant, zucchini, and onion to bowl and toss to coat. Spread vegetables in even layer over aluminum foil–lined sheet and broil until softened and spotty brown, 5 to 7 minutes, rotating sheet halfway through broiling. Flip vegetables and repeat. Return vegetables to now-empty bowl and toss gently with vinegar. Discard foil on sheet.

4 Using your hands, hollow out ciabatta by removing inner crumb, leaving ¼-inch border on sides and bottom. Place ciabatta on now-empty sheet and broil until lightly toasted, about 1 minute per side.

5 Spread reserved mayonnaise mixture inside ciabatta. Build sandwich by layering mozzarella on bottom, followed by eggplant and zucchini, and finally roasted red pepper and onion. Scrape any remaining garlic oil in bowl over top, then cap with ciabatta top. Slice and serve.

Oven-Fried Chicken Sandwiches

Serves 4 | **Total Time** 45 minutes

- 1¼ cups panko bread crumbs
- 2 tablespoons extra-virgin olive oil
- 1 large egg
- 2 teaspoons all-purpose flour
- ½ teaspoon garlic powder
- ⅛ teaspoon plus ¼ teaspoon table salt, divided
- 2 (6- to 8-ounce) boneless, skinless chicken breasts, trimmed
- ¼ cup mayonnaise
- 4 hamburger buns, toasted

Dill Pickle Mayonnaise

Makes 1 cup
Total Time 5 minutes

- ½ cup dill pickle chips, patted dry and chopped fine, plus 1 teaspoon pickle brine
- ½ cup mayonnaise
- 1 tablespoon yellow mustard
- ½ teaspoon pepper

Combine all ingredients in bowl. (Sauce can be refrigerated in an airtight container for up to 2 days.)

Why This Recipe Works Fried foods are delightful, but making them can be messy and wasteful, and they might fall outside nutritional goals when eaten often. Our oven-fried recipe avoids all of that while delivering a delightfully crispy-coated result. Panko bread crumbs give the chicken crunch without the deep fry. Browning takes longer in the oven, without the aid of screaming-hot oil, so we pretoast the panko in the microwave so we don't overcook the chicken. A swoosh of mayo is the simplest condiment for this fried chicken sandwich, but if you're looking for something a little punchier, try Dill Pickle Mayonnaise instead. For a buffalo chicken variation, we add a lot of hot sauce, even to the chicken's dredge. If you'd like more funky heat, you can try our kimchi variation.

1 Adjust oven rack to middle position and heat oven to 400 degrees. Set wire rack in rimmed baking sheet and spray rack with vegetable oil spray.

2 Toss panko with oil in bowl until evenly coated. Microwave, stirring frequently, until light golden brown, 2 to 4 minutes. Transfer to shallow dish and let cool slightly. Whisk egg, flour, garlic powder, and ⅛ teaspoon salt together in second shallow dish.

3 Halve each breast crosswise and pound between 2 sheets of plastic wrap to uniform ½-inch thickness. Pat chicken dry with paper towels and sprinkle with remaining ¼ teaspoon salt. Working with 1 piece of chicken at a time, dredge in egg mixture, letting excess drip off, then coat with panko mixture, pressing gently to adhere. Arrange breaded pieces on prepared rack, spaced evenly apart. Bake until chicken registers 160 degrees, 18 to 22 minutes.

4 Spread mayonnaise evenly over bun bottoms, then top with 1 piece chicken and bun tops. Serve.

VARIATIONS

Buffalo Oven-Fried Chicken Sandwiches

Add 2 tablespoons Frank's RedHot Original Cayenne Pepper Sauce to egg mixture in step 2; add 2 tablespoons Frank's to mayonnaise before spreading over buns in step 4; and drizzle chicken with 2 tablespoons Frank's before topping with bun top. Add ½ cup crumbled blue cheese and 2 cups shredded iceberg lettuce to sandwiches before serving.

Spicy Kimchi Oven-Fried Chicken Sandwiches

Add 1 tablespoon kimchi juice to egg mixture in step 2, add 1 tablespoon gochujang to mayonnaise before spreading over buns in step 4, and add ¼ cup chopped cabbage kimchi to sandwiches before serving.

Chicken and Parsnip Shawarma

Serves 4 | **Total Time** 1 hour

- 12 ounces parsnips, peeled and trimmed
- 1 teaspoon table salt
- 1 teaspoon ground allspice
- 1 teaspoon ground ginger
- 1 teaspoon garlic powder
- 1 teaspoon ground coriander
- ½ teaspoon pepper
- ½ teaspoon ground turmeric
- ¼ teaspoon ground cinnamon
- ¼ teaspoon ground cardamom
- ¼ teaspoon cayenne pepper
- 2 tablespoons extra-virgin olive oil
- 4 (5- to 7-ounce) bone-in chicken thighs, trimmed
- 1 recipe Tahini-Garlic Sauce
- 4 (12 by 9-inch) lavash
- 8 kosher dill pickle spears

Why This Recipe Works Shawarma—arguably one of the most beloved street foods—is usually made with warmly spiced, slow-roasted chicken, lamb, or beef. Across the Arab world, restaurants and street vendors cook the meats on slow-rotating vertical spits and then shave off juicy, tender pieces to order. To make a chicken shawarma wrap into a filling dinner, we fold vegetables into the wrap. Parsnips have a dense texture and a penchant for soaking up seasoning. We jump-start juicy chicken thighs (on the outskirts of the sheet, where they're most exposed to the oven's heat) and then add the quicker-cooking parsnips halfway through cooking. Both chicken and vegetables get a thick coating of highly spiced oil to mimic the flavor and unctuousness of authentic shawarma, and the high-heat oven gives them the requisite char. Spreading tahini-garlic sauce on the lavash lends the wrap nutty flavor and creaminess, while folding pickle spears into the wrap adds substantial crunch and welcome tang.

1 Adjust oven rack to upper-middle position and heat oven to 450 degrees. Spray rimmed baking sheet with vegetable oil spray. Cut each parsnip to separate bulbous end from thinner end. Cut bulbous ends into ¼-inch-wide planks, then cut planks lengthwise into ¼-inch-wide batons. Repeat with thinner ends, halving planks crosswise so batons are no longer than 3 inches. Combine salt, allspice, ginger, garlic powder, coriander, pepper, turmeric, cinnamon, cardamom, and cayenne in medium bowl. Whisk in oil to make loose slurry. Microwave spice slurry, covered, until fragrant, about 30 seconds.

2 Toss parsnips with 1 tablespoon spice slurry in bowl; set aside. Pat chicken dry with paper towels, then brush all over with spice slurry. Place chicken, skin side up, in corners of prepared sheet and brush any remaining slurry in bowl on top of chicken.

3 Transfer sheet to oven and roast for 15 minutes. Add parsnips to center of sheet and continue to roast until chicken registers at least 195 degrees and parsnips are tender, 10 to 15 minutes.

4 Transfer chicken to cutting board and let rest until cool enough to handle. Toss parsnips with juices on pan. Once cool enough to handle, remove skin from chicken, chop it and add it to the parsnips. Using your hands to separate meat from bones, shred chicken fine (aim for strips no more than ¼ inch wide) and add to pan with parsnips, discarding bones. Toss to combine.

5 Working with 1 lavash at a time, lay on clean counter with short edge parallel to counter edge. Spread 3 tablespoons tahini-garlic sauce evenly over lavash, leaving ½-inch border around perimeter. Arrange one-fourth chicken-parsnip mixture in even layer over bottom third of lavash, then top with pickles. Fold bottom of lavash up and over filling, then fold in sides and roll tightly away from you around filling. Serve.

Tahini-Garlic Sauce

Makes 1 cup
Total Time 10 minutes

Look for molasses without additives.

- ⅓ cup tahini
- 3 tablespoons plain yogurt
- 2 tablespoons lemon juice
- 2 tablespoons water
- 2 teaspoons pomegranate molasses
- 1 garlic clove, minced
- ½ teaspoon table salt

Whisk all ingredients together in bowl. Season with salt and pepper to taste. (Sauce can be refrigerated in airtight container for up to 3 days. Thin with water as needed.)

Meatball Subs with Roasted Broccoli

Serves 4 | **Total Time** 55 minutes

- 1½ pounds broccoli crowns
- 2 tablespoons extra-virgin olive oil
- 1 teaspoon table salt, divided
- 1 teaspoon pepper, divided
- ½ teaspoon sugar
- ¾ cup panko bread crumbs
- 2 large eggs, lightly beaten
- 1 teaspoon garlic powder
- 1½ pounds 85 percent lean ground beef
- 2 teaspoons lemon juice
- 1⅓ cups marinara sauce
- 4 (8-inch) Italian sub rolls, split lengthwise and toasted
- 4 slices deli provolone cheese (4 ounces)

Why This Recipe Works We kept the mainstays of all successful weeknight dinners (easy, fast, complete, and minimally messy) in mind when streamlining the classic meatball sub. We love roasting meatballs to avoid the slow-cooking and stovetop splatter; plus, it encourages even browning. Sometimes a sandwich isn't enough, and roasting lets us use the rest of our sheet for a simultaneously cooked side. Broccoli wedges take about 25 minutes to roast; we remove the meatballs from the oven when they're cooked through and give the broccoli a few more minutes to brown and crisp. Halving and then saucing the meatballs makes them easy to stuff into rolls, which, once filled, we return to the oven so the sandwiches get warm and further toasted and the cheese melts. If you can't find 8-inch sub rolls, you could also try ciabatta rolls; 6-inch sub rolls will be too small to fit the meatballs.

1 Adjust oven rack to lowest position and heat oven to 450 degrees. Line rimmed baking sheet with aluminum foil and spray with vegetable oil spray.

2 Cut broccoli crowns into 4 wedges if 3 to 4 inches in diameter or 6 wedges if 4 to 5 inches in diameter. Toss broccoli with oil, ½ teaspoon salt, ½ teaspoon pepper, and sugar on sheet, then spread broccoli cut side down across half of prepared sheet.

3 Using fork, mash panko and eggs into paste in bowl. Stir in garlic powder, remaining ½ teaspoon salt, and remaining ½ teaspoon pepper. Add ground beef and knead mixture with your hands until well combined. Pinch off and roll into sixteen 1¾-inch-wide meatballs and arrange on empty half of sheet. Sheet will be crowded; rearrange broccoli and meatballs as needed to leave some space between each meatball. Roast until meatballs register at least 160 degrees, 15 to 20 minutes.

4 Transfer meatballs to plate and spread broccoli, cut side down, over entire sheet. Return sheet to oven and roast until broccoli is tender, 5 to 10 minutes. Toss broccoli with lemon juice, then season with salt and pepper to taste. Transfer broccoli to serving platter and cover with foil to keep warm.

5 Halve meatballs, then toss gently with marinara sauce in bowl. Remove foil from now-empty sheet, then arrange toasted rolls directly on sheet. Divide meatballs evenly among rolls, shingling meatball halves as needed and spooning any remaining sauce in bowl evenly over top. Lay 1 slice provolone over each sandwich, tearing slices as needed to cover meatballs completely. Bake until cheese is melted and sauce is warmed through, about 5 minutes. Serve meatball subs with broccoli.

Pork and Broccoli Rabe Sandwiches

Serves 4 | **Total Time** 1 hour

- 1 (1-pound) pork tenderloin, trimmed
- 6 tablespoons extra-virgin olive oil, divided
- 1 tablespoon minced fresh rosemary
- 1 tablespoon fennel seeds
- ¾ teaspoon table salt, divided
- ¾ teaspoon pepper, divided
- 1 pound broccoli rabe, trimmed and cut into 1-inch pieces
- 4 garlic cloves, minced
- 1 teaspoon red pepper flakes
- 2 red bell peppers, stemmed, seeded, and sliced thin
- 4 (6- to 8-inch) Italian sub rolls, split lengthwise
- 4 slices deli provolone cheese (4 ounces)
- 2 tablespoons red wine vinegar

Why This Recipe Works The underdog rival for the title of Philly's best sandwich loads up a hoagie roll with juicy pork, garlicky broccoli rabe, melty provolone, and vinegary hot peppers: a feast in a bun. Sandwich shops prepare each component separately, hours in advance; but for a streamlined home version, we roast the meat, greens, and peppers side by side on the sheet pan. We skip the standard roasted pork shoulder (too big, too slow) in favor of pork tenderloin. To ensure that it's flavorful and juicy, we season it heavily with rosemary and fennel seeds, roast it until just cooked through, and then shave it as thin as possible to mimic shreds of long-cooked pork shoulder. Tossing the slices with some oil and vinegar punches up the flavor and keeps the pork moist.

1 Adjust oven rack to middle position and heat oven to 450 degrees. Rub tenderloin with 2 tablespoons oil, then sprinkle with rosemary, fennel, ½ teaspoon salt, and ½ teaspoon pepper. Place on 1 side of rimmed baking sheet and roast for 10 minutes.

2 Toss broccoli rabe with 2 tablespoons oil, garlic, and pepper flakes in bowl. Toss bell peppers with 1 tablespoon oil, remaining ¼ teaspoon salt, and remaining ¼ teaspoon pepper in second bowl. Remove sheet from oven and flip pork. Spread broccoli rabe and bell peppers on hot sheet next to pork. Roast until pork registers 145 degrees and broccoli rabe and bell peppers are browned, about 20 minutes.

3 Remove sheet from oven. Transfer pork to cutting board, tent with aluminum foil, and let rest for 5 minutes. Transfer vegetables to bowl and cover with foil to keep warm. Wipe sheet clean with paper towels, arrange rolls directly on sheet, and cover interior of rolls completely with cheese, tearing slices as needed. Bake until bread is lightly toasted and cheese is melted, about 5 minutes.

4 Slice pork as thin as possible, transfer to clean bowl, and toss with remaining 1 tablespoon oil and vinegar. Nestle pork, broccoli, and bell peppers into warm rolls. Serve.

Pork Gyros

Serves 8 | **Total Time** 1¾ hours, plus 1 hour marinating

- ½ cup plus 1 tablespoon extra-virgin olive oil, divided
- 6 garlic cloves, minced
- 1½ tablespoons dried oregano
- 1½ tablespoons kosher salt for the marinade
- 1 tablespoon ground coriander
- 1 tablespoon paprika
- 2 teaspoons pepper
- 1 (4-pound) boneless pork butt roast, trimmed
- 8 (8-inch) pitas
- 1 romaine lettuce heart (6 ounces), sliced thin
- 1 small red onion, halved and sliced thin
- ½ English cucumber, halved lengthwise, seeded, and sliced thin
- 1 recipe Tzatziki Sauce (page 25)
- Lemon wedges

Why This Recipe Works A Greek gyro typically involves a towering vertical spit packed with layers of marinated meat. Flames lick the meat as the spit turns, slowly rendering the fat in each layer to create juicy, charred meat flavored with plenty of garlic and oregano. We managed to turn out juicy, charred, and flavorful pork with just the sheet pan and our oven. First we elevate marinated steaks of pork butt on a wire rack, cover them with foil, and steam them in a 350-degree oven. Uncovering the pork and continuing to roast it helps dry out its exterior. Finally, a stint under the broiler gives the meat a crisp, well-charred crust. While the meat rests, we toast the pitas that wrap a cooling homemade tzatziki sauce; crisp, thinly sliced romaine lettuce and red onion; and slices of rich, flavorful, juicy pork. You'll need half a cucumber for the Tzatziki Sauce and the other half for the sandwiches.

1 Combine ½ cup oil, garlic, oregano, salt, coriander, paprika, and pepper in 1-gallon zipper-lock bag. Slice pork lengthwise into 4 equal steaks, about 1 inch thick (if steaks are thicker than 1 inch, press them with your hand to 1-inch thickness), then add to bag with marinade. Seal bag and turn to distribute marinade evenly. Refrigerate for at least 1 hour or up to 24 hours.

2 Adjust oven rack 6 inches from broiler element and heat oven to 350 degrees. Set wire rack in rimmed baking sheet lined with aluminum foil. Remove pork from marinade and place on prepared rack; discard marinade.

3 Cover sheet tightly with foil and transfer to oven. Roast until pork registers 100 degrees, about 40 minutes. Remove sheet from oven and carefully remove foil so steam escapes away from you. Return sheet to oven and continue to roast until pork registers 160 degrees, 20 to 25 minutes longer.

4 Leave sheet in oven and turn on broiler. Broil until pork is well browned on top side only, about 10 minutes. Transfer pork to carving board and let rest for 5 minutes.

5 Brush 1 side of pitas with remaining 1 tablespoon oil. Place 4 pitas oiled side up on now-empty rack. Broil until pitas are soft and lightly toasted, about 1 minute. Repeat with remaining 4 pitas. Slice pork crosswise very thin. Toss pork with accumulated juices on carving board. Divide pork evenly among pitas and top with lettuce, onion, sliced cucumber, and tzatziki. Serve with lemon wedges.

Onion Sliders

Serves 6 (makes 12 sliders) | **Total Time** 45 minutes

Sauce

- 3 tablespoons mayonnaise
- 1 tablespoon ketchup
- 2 teaspoons sweet pickle relish
- ¼ teaspoon pepper

Sliders

- 1½ pounds 90 percent lean ground beef
- 1 onion, finely chopped
- 1 teaspoon vegetable oil
- ⅛ teaspoon plus ¼ teaspoon table salt, divided
- Pinch plus ⅛ teaspoon pepper, divided
- 6 slices deli American cheese (4 ounces)
- 12 (2½-inch) slider buns or soft dinner rolls

VARIATION

Bacon and Onion Sliders

Add 4 finely chopped slices bacon to onion mixture in step 3 and cook until bacon fat is rendered and bacon is beginning to crisp, increasing roasting time to 16 minutes. Substitute cheddar cheese for American cheese.

Why This Recipe Works These fast-food sliders are a regional treat that feature a juicy beef patty embedded with finely chopped onion, covered in melted cheese, and sandwiched in a soft steamed (mini) bun. In lieu of a restaurant griddle, we get quite crafty and make it all happen in the oven on a sheet pan. We start by roasting some onions on our sheet and then dividing them into 12 piles. To shape each slider-size patty, we press 2 ounces of ground beef into the roasted onion piles. Returning them to the hot oven for a mere 7 to 8 minutes gives us nicely cooked-through sliders that are perfectly tender and require minimal monitoring. Once the patties are cooked, we put cheese on the patties; stack the buns on top; and return the sheet pan to the oven to melt the cheese, warm the buns, and meld the flavors. A simple, classic burger sauce seals the deal, literally.

1 For the sauce Whisk all ingredients together in bowl; set aside for serving.

2 For the sliders Divide beef into twelve 2-ounce portions, then roll into balls. (Balls can be shaped up to 24 hours in advance.)

3 Adjust oven rack to lowest position and heat oven to 450 degrees. Combine onion, oil, ⅛ teaspoon salt, and pinch pepper on rimmed baking sheet, then spread into even layer. Roast until onions are softened, 10 to 12 minutes, stirring onions and redistributing into even layer at least 3 times during roasting.

4 Arrange onions into 12 piles evenly spaced across sheet. Sprinkle meat balls with remaining ¼ teaspoon salt and remaining ⅛ teaspoon pepper. Place balls on top of onion piles. Using bottom of greased drinking glass or meat pounder, firmly smash each ball until about 3½ inches in diameter. Return sheet to oven and cook until edges of patties are set and tops are still slightly pink, 7 to 8 minutes.

5 Stack cheese slices and cut into quarters (you will have 24 pieces). Remove sheet from oven. Top each patty with 2 pieces of cheese. Place bun bottoms on top of cheese and stack bun top on top of bun bottoms. Return to oven and cook until buns are warmed through, about 2 minutes.

6 Remove sheet from oven and remove bun tops. Transfer burgers to platter, carefully flipping each as you go so bun bottoms are underneath burgers and onions are on top of burgers. Top with reserved sauce and bun tops. Serve.

How to Build the Sheet Pan

Smash the meat on top of the onion piles and cook for 7 to 8 minutes. Place the cheese on the burgers, then place the bun bottoms on top of the cheese and cover with a bun top; heat through. Flip the burgers to transfer them to a platter and top them with sauce.

Salmon Burgers with Asparagus

Serves 4 | **Total Time** 45 minutes

- 1 slice hearty white sandwich bread, torn into 1-inch pieces
- 1 pound skinless salmon fillet, cut into 1-inch pieces
- 2 tablespoons mayonnaise
- 2 tablespoons chopped fresh parsley
- 1 tablespoon Dijon mustard
- 2 teaspoons capers, rinsed and minced
- 1 scallion, minced
- ½ teaspoon table salt, divided
- ⅛ teaspoon plus ¼ teaspoon pepper, divided
- 1 pound asparagus, trimmed
- 1 teaspoon extra-virgin olive oil
- 4 hamburger buns, toasted if desired
- 1 recipe Lemon-Herb Sauce (page 25)
- 1 small head Bibb lettuce, leaves separated

Why This Recipe Works A good salmon burger is elusive. And no wonder! There are so many ways they can go off the rails. Canned salmon? Never. Leftover salmon? Not a good idea. Store-bought bread crumbs? No, make your own. These easy salmon burgers use ingredients we bet you already have. The food processor also turns torn pieces of bread into crumbs for the binder. We use it again to make quick work of chopping chunks of salmon into the right size for burgers. We broil the burgers on a sheet pan along with asparagus for a hands-off dinner.

1 Adjust oven rack 4 inches from broiler element and heat broiler. Line rimmed baking sheet with aluminum foil. Pulse bread in food processor to fine crumbs, about 4 pulses; transfer to large bowl. Working in 2 batches, pulse salmon in now-empty food processor until coarsely ground, about 4 pulses; transfer to bowl with bread crumbs and toss to combine. Add mayonnaise, parsley, mustard, capers, scallion, ¼ teaspoon salt, and ⅛ teaspoon pepper and gently fold into salmon mixture until well combined.

2 Divide salmon mixture into 4 equal portions and gently pack into 1-inch-thick patties, about 3½ inches wide. Place patties on half of prepared sheet. Toss asparagus with oil, remaining ¼ teaspoon salt, and remaining ¼ teaspoon pepper and spread in single layer on other half of sheet. Broil until burgers are lightly browned on top, 4 to 6 minutes. Flip burgers and asparagus and continue to broil until burgers register 125 degrees (for medium-rare) and asparagus is lightly browned and tender, 3 to 6 minutes.

3 Transfer burgers and asparagus to serving platter. Top bun bottoms with lemon-herb sauce, burgers, lettuce, and bun tops. Serve with asparagus.

White Bean and Sun-Dried Tomato Patties with Lemony Spinach Salad

Serves 4 | **Total Time** 45 minutes

- ½ cup plain Greek yogurt
- 3 tablespoons plus ¼ cup chopped fresh basil, divided
- ⅓ cup oil-packed sun-dried tomatoes, chopped fine, plus 2 tablespoons packing oil, divided
- ⅛ teaspoon plus ½ teaspoon table salt, divided
- 2 (15-ounce) cans cannellini beans, rinsed, divided
- 1 large egg
- ⅓ cup panko bread crumbs
- 3 tablespoons extra-virgin olive oil, divided, plus extra for drizzling
- 3 ounces feta cheese, cut into ½-inch pieces
- 1 small red onion, halved and sliced ¼ inch thick
- 1½ tablespoons lemon juice
- 5 ounces (5 cups) baby spinach

Why This Recipe Works Bean burgers and other vegetarian burgers are notorious for easily falling apart. Our sheet-pan method, however, is hands-off, so the patties make it from pan to plate without issue. We start these savory cannellini bean burgers on a sheet pan preheated on the lower rack of a hot oven, which gives the bottom of the patties a nice crust. Then, instead of flipping the patties, we simply move the pan to a higher rack and broil them for a few minutes to brown the tops. With the extra space on the sheet, we roast some feta and onion to dress up a quick spinach side salad. Drain the beans thoroughly after rinsing. If you don't have sun-dried tomato packing oil, you can substitute vegetable oil.

1 Adjust 1 oven rack to lowest position and second rack 6 inches from broiler element. Place rimmed baking sheet on lower rack and heat oven to 450 degrees. Combine yogurt, 3 tablespoons basil, 1 tablespoon tomato packing oil, and ⅛ teaspoon salt in bowl; season with salt and pepper to taste and set yogurt sauce aside.

2 Place half of beans in large bowl and mash with potato masher. Add remaining beans and mash until partially broken down. Whisk egg, remaining 1 tablespoon tomato packing oil, and remaining ½ teaspoon salt together in separate bowl. Stir egg mixture, panko, sun-dried tomatoes, and remaining ¼ cup basil into mashed beans until well combined. Divide mixture into 4 equal portions and lightly pack into ¾-inch-thick patties. Transfer patties to large plate and refrigerate for 10 minutes.

3 Add 2 tablespoons olive oil to hot sheet, tilting to coat. Arrange patties on half of sheet and add feta and onion to other half of sheet. Roast on lower rack until patties are browned on bottoms, about 8 minutes. Remove sheet from oven and heat broiler. Brush tops of burgers with remaining 1 tablespoon olive oil. Return sheet to upper rack and broil until patties are lightly browned on top, about 2 minutes.

4 Toss lemon juice with feta, onion, and spinach in large bowl. Serve salad with patties and yogurt sauce.

Chicken Tacos with Salsa Verde

Serves 4 to 6 | **Total Time** 40 minutes, plus 30 minutes marinating

- ¼ cup vegetable oil, divided
- 3 tablespoons lime juice (2 limes), divided, plus lime wedges for serving
- 2 tablespoons water
- 1 teaspoon plus pinch sugar, divided
- 2 teaspoons table salt, divided
- ½ teaspoon pepper
- 3 garlic cloves, minced, divided
- 1 pound boneless, skinless chicken breasts, trimmed
- 8 ounces tomatillos, husks and stems removed, rinsed well, dried, and halved, divided
- ½ onion, peeled and cut into 1½-inch pieces
- ½ jalapeño chile, stemmed and seeded
- 1 cup chopped fresh cilantro, divided
- 12 (6-inch) corn tortillas, warmed
- 1 avocado, halved, pitted, and sliced thin
- 4 radishes, trimmed and sliced thin

Why This Recipe Works Here, flavorful shredded chicken meets a homemade salsa verde for weeknight tacos you can proudly serve up with all the fixings. To make them as satisfying as tacos made with braised meat, we give the chicken 30 minutes in a lime-garlic marinade, which amps up the flavor quotient. The gutsy salsa verde includes tomatillos, onion, and jalapeño, which take on flavor as they roast on one side of the sheet pan while the chicken is on the other. We blend all the roasted vegetables in a food processor along with raw tomatillos, which bring a fresh tanginess to the mix for a salsa with textural contrast and more nuanced flavor with a hit of brightness. Along with the shredded chicken and vibrant salsa verde, we serve the tacos with crisp radish, herbal cilantro, and, for necessary richness, sliced avocado.

1 Whisk 3 tablespoons oil, 1 tablespoon lime juice, water, 1 teaspoon sugar, 1½ teaspoons salt, pepper, and half of garlic together in medium bowl. Pound chicken breasts to uniform thickness. Add chicken to marinade; cover; and refrigerate, turning chicken occasionally, for 30 minutes.

2 Adjust oven rack to upper-middle position and heat oven to 450 degrees. Line rimmed baking sheet with aluminum foil. Toss half of tomatillos, onion, and jalapeño with remaining 1 tablespoon oil and ¼ teaspoon salt on prepared sheet, then arrange into even layer on half of sheet. Remove chicken from marinade, letting excess marinade drip off, then place chicken on empty side of sheet.

3 Roast until chicken registers 160 degrees and vegetables are tender, 15 to 20 minutes, rotating sheet halfway through roasting. Transfer chicken to cutting board and let rest while preparing salsa.

4 Pulse roasted vegetables, ½ cup cilantro, remaining 2 tablespoons lime juice, remaining pinch sugar, remaining ¼ teaspoon salt, remaining garlic, and remaining tomatillos in food processor until slightly chunky, 16 to 18 pulses. Season with salt and pepper to taste.

5 Shred chicken into bite-size pieces using 2 forks, then serve with tortillas, tomatillo salsa, avocado, radishes, lime wedges, and remaining ½ cup cilantro.

Steak Fajitas

Serves 4 to 6 | **Total Time** 45 minutes

- 5 radishes, trimmed and sliced thin
- 1 shallot, sliced thin
- ¼ cup lime juice (2 limes), plus lime wedges for serving
- 1 teaspoon sugar
- ⅛ teaspoon plus 2 teaspoons table salt, divided
- 2 red bell peppers, stemmed, seeded, and sliced thin
- 2 poblano chiles, stemmed, seeded, and sliced thin
- 2 tablespoons vegetable oil, divided
- 1 tablespoon chili powder, divided
- 1½ teaspoons ground cumin, divided
- 1 (1½-pound) flank steak, trimmed
- 1 teaspoon pepper
- ½ teaspoon baking soda
- 12 (6-inch) flour tortillas, warmed

Why This Recipe Works Fajitas can be a sizzling spectacle, but we wanted a recipe that was more about flavor than theater. A sheet pan lets us cook all of the components on one pan and to the perfect degree—which is much more appealing to us. We preheat the baking sheet before placing the flank steak in the center and scattering the peppers around it. There's a sizzle and then we turn on the broiler to achieve browning on both the steak and peppers. A potent spice rub augments the steak's flavor, color, and texture even further while a bit of baking soda aids in browning. Serve the fajitas as is or with salsa, guacamole, shredded cheese, and sour cream.

1 Adjust oven racks to middle position, place rimmed baking sheet on rack, and heat oven to 450 degrees. Combine radishes, shallot, lime juice, sugar, and ⅛ teaspoon salt in bowl; cover and refrigerate until ready to serve.

2 Toss bell peppers and poblanos with 1 tablespoon oil, 1 teaspoon chili powder, ½ teaspoon cumin, and ½ teaspoon salt in bowl. Pat steak dry with paper towels. Combine pepper, baking soda, remaining 1½ teaspoons salt, remaining 2 teaspoons chili powder, and remaining 1 teaspoon cumin together in small bowl, then rub thoroughly over steak.

3 Add remaining 1 tablespoon oil to hot sheet, tilting to coat. Lay steak in center of sheet, then scatter bell peppers and poblanos around steak. Heat broiler and broil until steak and peppers are lightly browned and steak registers 120 to 125 degrees (for medium-rare), 6 to 10 minutes, flipping steak halfway through broiling.

4 Remove sheet from oven. Transfer steak to cutting board, tent with aluminum foil, and let rest for 5 minutes. Leave vegetables on sheet, season with salt and pepper to taste, and tent with foil to keep warm.

5 Slice steak against grain ¼ inch thick and transfer, along with vegetables, to platter. Serve with tortillas, pickled radish mixture, and lime wedges.

Salmon Tacos with Roasted Pineapple Slaw

Serves 4 to 6 | **Total Time** 55 minutes

- 3 cups shredded cabbage
- ½ red onion, sliced thin
- ¼ cup minced fresh cilantro
- ½ jalapeño, seeded and chopped fine
- 3 tablespoons lime juice, plus lime wedges for serving
- ¼ teaspoon plus ⅛ teaspoon table salt, divided
- ¼ teaspoon pepper, divided
- ½ pineapple, peeled, cored, and cut lengthwise into 4 wedges
- 2 tablespoons unsalted butter, melted
- 1 teaspoon smoked paprika
- ¼ teaspoon ground coriander
- ⅛ teaspoon cayenne pepper
- 2 (6- to 8-ounce) skin-on salmon fillets, 1 inch thick
- 1 teaspoon vegetable oil
- 12 (6-inch) corn tortillas, warmed

Why This Recipe Works Salmon used to be an outlier in the world of fish tacos but not anymore. And you don't need to go to a pricey seafood restaurant to get them because they are so easy to make at home: no battering, no frying, no mess. Not only are salmon tacos fresher and healthier, they also open up a brave new world of pairings. Here a sweet-savory pineapple-cabbage slaw (with attitude) is a perfect match for rich, meaty salmon. Since we crave a bit of a crust on any fish used for tacos, we coat the salmon fillets with a spice rub before roasting them. Cooking them skin side down on a sheet pan ensures that they hold together and emerge perfectly moist inside—it's then supereasy to lift the salmon from the skin and sheet. Since we're already using the oven, we roast large wedges of pineapple until caramelized; this coaxes out a deep flavor and gives the pineapple some sophistication. Then we toss with the cabbage (in a mix of onion, cilantro, and lime juice). If using wild salmon, cook it until it registers 120 degrees.

1 Adjust oven rack to lowest position, place rimmed baking sheet on rack, and heat oven to 500 degrees. Toss cabbage, onion, cilantro, jalapeño, lime juice, ¼ teaspoon salt, and ⅛ teaspoon pepper in bowl; set aside.

2 Toss pineapple with melted butter in bowl, then arrange over half of hot sheet, spacing wedges evenly apart. Roast until pineapple is browned at edges, about 15 minutes, flipping wedges halfway through cooking.

3 Meanwhile, combine paprika, coriander, cayenne, remaining ⅛ teaspoon salt, and remaining ⅛ teaspoon pepper in bowl. Pat salmon dry with paper towels, rub with oil, and sprinkle evenly with spice mixture.

4 Reduce oven temperature to 275 degrees. Arrange fillets skin side down on empty half of sheet, spacing fillets evenly apart. Roast salmon until center is still translucent when checked with tip of paring knife and registers 125 degrees (for medium-rare) and pineapple is browned, 9 to 11 minutes, rotating sheet halfway through cooking.

5 Transfer pineapple to cutting board and chop into ½-inch pieces. Add to bowl with reserved cabbage mixture, tossing to combine. Flake salmon into rough 1-inch pieces (discarding skin if desired). Serve salmon on tortillas with pineapple slaw and lime wedges.

Black Bean and Sweet Potato Tacos

Serves 4 to 6 | **Total Time** 45 minutes

- 3 tablespoons extra-virgin olive oil
- 3 garlic cloves, minced
- 1½ teaspoons ground cumin
- 1½ teaspoons ground coriander
- 1 teaspoon minced fresh oregano or ¼ teaspoon dried
- 1 teaspoon table salt
- ½ teaspoon pepper
- 1 pound sweet potatoes, peeled and cut into ½-inch pieces
- 4 poblano chiles, stemmed, seeded, and cut into ½-inch-wide strips
- 1 large onion, halved and sliced ½ inch thick
- 1 (15-ounce) can black beans, rinsed
- ¼ cup chopped fresh cilantro
- 12 (6-inch) corn tortillas, warmed
- 1 recipe Avocado Crema (optional) (page 25)
- 1 recipe Quick Sweet and Spicy Pickled Red Onion (optional) (page 27)

Why This Recipe Works Tacos are often focused on rich proteins, but this plant-based version combines the right ingredients for a satisfying dinner from the pantry. Roasted sweet potatoes and onion, which we season with fragrant garlic, cumin, coriander, and oregano, make an inspiring filling. We add canned black beans for some more substance with ease. A topping of avocado crema, made by quickly blending avocado, cilantro, lime juice, and yogurt in the food processor, gives the dish welcome richness. You can skip the avocado crema and top the tacos with avocado and/or sour cream or store-bought Mexican crema if you prefer.

1 Adjust oven racks to upper-middle and lower-middle positions and heat oven to 450 degrees. Line 2 rimmed baking sheets with aluminum foil. Whisk oil, garlic, cumin, coriander, oregano, salt, and pepper together in large bowl. Add potatoes, poblanos, and onion to oil mixture and toss to coat.

2 Spread vegetable mixture in even layer over prepared sheets. Roast vegetables until tender and golden brown, about 30 minutes, stirring vegetables and switching and rotating sheets halfway through roasting.

3 Return vegetables to now-empty bowl, add black beans and cilantro, and toss gently to combine. Divide vegetables evenly among warm tortillas and top with avocado crema and pickled onions, if using. Serve.

Chipotle Mushroom and Cauliflower Tacos

Serves 4 to 6 | **Total Time** 1 hour

- 1¼ pounds cremini mushrooms, trimmed and quartered
- 1¼ pounds cauliflower florets, cut into 1-inch pieces
- ¼ cup vegetable oil
- 2 teaspoons table salt, divided
- 2-4 tablespoons minced canned chipotle chile in adobo sauce, divided
- ½ red onion, sliced thin
- ½ cup distilled white vinegar
- 2 tablespoons sugar
- ⅔ cup Mexican crema
- 3 cups thinly sliced red cabbage
- 12 (6-inch) corn tortillas, warmed

Why This Recipe Works Meaty roasted mushrooms and creamy cauliflower make an unexpectedly delicious and hearty taco filling. Roasting the mushrooms and cauliflower creates flavorful browning and varied textures; adding canned chipotle in adobo for the last few minutes of roasting contributes heat and depth to the vegetables. We love perking up the filling with a fresh, crunchy cabbage topping—it makes these tacos stunning and tasty. The microwave makes quick work of pickling red onion, to which we add the cabbage. Finally, a cool crema brings everything in this vegetarian taco together. You can make our Lime Crema (page 26) but store-bought is fine. Garnish with fresh cilantro leaves and serve with lime wedges, if desired.

1 Adjust oven rack to lowest position and heat oven to 500 degrees. Toss mushrooms, cauliflower, oil, and 1½ teaspoons salt together on rimmed baking sheet. Spread into even layer and roast until liquid has mostly evaporated, 23 to 25 minutes. Stir in 3 tablespoons chipotle and continue to roast until lightly browned, 3 to 5 minutes longer.

2 Meanwhile, combine onion, vinegar, sugar, and remaining ½ teaspoon salt in large bowl. Microwave, covered, until hot, about 2 minutes. Combine crema and remaining 1 tablespoon chipotle in small bowl.

3 Stir cabbage into onion mixture. Divide mushroom mixture, crema, and cabbage mixture evenly among tortillas. Serve.

Cheese Quesadillas

Serves 4 | **Total Time** 40 minutes

- 12 ounces Monterey Jack cheese, shredded (3 cups)
- 4 (10-inch) flour tortillas

Why This Recipe Works Quesadillas are the ultimate crowd-pleaser and yet not suited for more than one person when cooked in a skillet. To make four at a single go, we bake them on the sheet pan. To prevent the cheese from liquefying and running onto the sheet, we add it only after the first side of each tortilla has been adequately browned. We purposefully position the rounded edge of the tortillas toward the center of the baking sheet to best fit four large quesadillas at once. A variation with chicken and another with black beans make the quesadillas more filling for a handheld dinner. Letting the quesadillas cool before cutting them prevents the molten cheese from oozing out. If you're serving quesadillas for a party, you can double the recipe and spread the quesadillas across two sheet pans. Bake the quesadillas on the upper-middle and lower-middle racks and switch and rotate the pans halfway through cooking in step 3. Serve with your favorite accompaniments.

1 Adjust oven rack to middle position and heat oven to 450 degrees. Spray rimmed baking sheet with vegetable oil spray. Fold tortillas in half. Arrange folded tortillas in single layer on prepared sheet with rounded edges facing center of sheet.

2 Bake until tortilla tops and edges begin to turn spotty brown, 4 to 6 minutes. Remove sheet from oven. Flip tortillas over. Using tongs, open each tortilla and fill each with equal amount of Monterey Jack, leaving 1-inch border. Close tortillas and press firmly with spatula to compact.

3 Return quesadillas to oven and continue to bake until crisp around edges and golden brown on second side, 4 to 6 minutes longer. Remove from oven and press quesadillas gently with spatula to deflate any air bubbles. Transfer to wire rack and let cool for 5 minutes. Slice each quesadilla into 4 wedges, and serve.

VARIATIONS

Black Bean and Jalapeño Quesadillas

Reduce Monterey Jack to 2 cups. Drain and rinse 1 (15-ounce) can black beans. Using potato masher, mash half of beans in large bowl. Toss mashed beans, remaining black beans, and ¼ cup minced jarred jalapeños with Monterey Jack before filling tortillas in step 2.

Chicken and Herb Quesadillas

Reduce Monterey Jack to 2 cups. Toss 2 cups shredded rotisserie chicken, ¼ cup minced fresh cilantro, 2 thinly sliced scallions, and ⅛ teaspoon table salt with Monterey Jack before filling tortillas in step 2.

How to Build the Sheet Pan

Arrange the folded tortillas on the sheet with the rounded edge facing the center. Flip the tortillas once they're spotty brown. Open each tortilla with tongs and fill it with cheese. Bake until melty.

Chorizo, Corn, and Tomato Tostadas

Serves 4 | **Total Time** 45 minutes

- 1 (14-ounce) bag green coleslaw mix
- 1 tablespoon finely chopped jarred jalapeños, plus ¼ cup brine, divided
- 8 ounces Spanish-style chorizo sausage, halved lengthwise and sliced crosswise ¼ inch thick
- 4 ears corn, kernels cut from cobs
- 1 tablespoon vegetable oil
- 1 (15-ounce) can black beans, rinsed
- ¼ cup vegetable broth
- 12 (6-inch) corn tostadas
- 6 ounces cherry tomatoes, quartered
- 1 tablespoon lime juice
- 1 recipe Lime Crema (page 26)
- 4 ounces queso fresco or feta cheese, crumbled (1 cup)
- ¼ cup fresh cilantro leaves

Why This Recipe Works These meal-size tostadas pile on the veggies and spicy chorizo. The more toppings, the more work, so we streamline the process with the sheet pan. We roast the chorizo (Spanish-style smoked chorizo, so we don't need to take out a skillet) and corn until browned; meanwhile, we warm tostadas, spread with a flavorful black bean–jalapeño mixture, directly on the oven rack below. Using jarred jalapeños means we can toss some of their brine with the beans for added flavor, and some with coleslaw mix for a quick-pickled cabbage topping. Fresh cherry tomatoes and lime juice add freshness and tang, and an easy crema provides richness. Sprinkled with queso fresco and cilantro, our stacked tostadas hit all of our tastebuds. Look for tostadas next to the taco kits at most supermarkets.

1 Adjust oven racks to upper-middle and lower-middle positions, place rimmed baking sheet on upper rack, and heat oven to 450 degrees. Toss coleslaw mix with 3 tablespoons brine in bowl and season with salt and pepper to taste; set aside for serving.

2 Combine chorizo, corn, and oil in second bowl and spread in single layer on hot sheet. Cook until browned, about 15 minutes.

3 Meanwhile, combine beans, broth, jalapeños, and remaining 1 tablespoon brine in clean bowl and microwave until warm, about 2 minutes. Mash beans with potato masher until spreadable, season with salt and pepper to taste, and spread evenly over tostadas. During final 5 minutes of roasting chorizo, place tostadas directly on lower oven rack to warm through.

4 Remove sheet from oven, transfer chorizo-corn mixture to large bowl, and stir in tomatoes and lime juice. Divide mixture evenly among warmed tostadas. Top tostadas with slaw, lime crema, queso fresco, and cilantro. Serve.

Pepperoni Pan Pizza

Serves 4 to 6 | **Total Time** 2½ hours

Dough

- 3 cups (15 ounces) all-purpose flour
- 2 teaspoons instant or rapid-rise yeast
- 2 teaspoons sugar
- 1⅓ cups water, room temperature
- 1 teaspoon table salt
- ¼ cup extra-virgin olive oil

Sauce

- 1¼ cups canned crushed tomatoes
- 2 tablespoons extra-virgin olive oil
- 2 garlic cloves, minced
- 3 anchovy fillets, minced
- 1½ teaspoons dried oregano
- 1 teaspoon sugar
- ½ teaspoon red pepper flakes, plus extra for sprinkling
- ½ teaspoon table salt

Toppings

- 1 ounce Parmesan cheese, grated (½ cup), plus extra for sprinkling
- 12 ounces whole-milk block mozzarella cheese, shredded (3 cups)
- 4 ounces thinly sliced pepperoni

Why This Recipe Works This pizza is one of our favorites—and one of the easiest—in our repertoire, with an airy, focaccia-like crust and ultracrispy edges. Sheet-pan pizza requires minimal shaping, which means we can make a highly hydrated dough (for a light and tender crust) without worrying about how to roll or shape it. After stretching the dough across the sheet, we top the pie with a stir-together tomato sauce, generous amounts of Parmesan and mozzarella (all the way to the sides for crispy, lacy edges), and pepperoni, and bake on a preheated stone. We prefer to buy link pepperoni and slice it thin rather than using presliced pepperoni. Avoid preshredded cheese; it contains added starch, which gives the melted cheese a drier, chewier texture.

1 For the dough Whisk flour, yeast, and sugar together in bowl of stand mixer. Using dough hook on low speed, slowly add water to flour mixture and mix until cohesive dough starts to form and no dry flour remains, 2 to 4 minutes, scraping down sides of bowl as needed. Cover bowl and let rest for 10 minutes.

2 Add salt and mix on medium speed until dough forms satiny, sticky ball that clears sides of bowl, 6 to 8 minutes. Lightly spray rimmed baking sheet with vegetable oil spray. Rub bottom and sides of pan with oil. Using dough scraper or your greased hands, transfer dough to oiled sheet and turn to coat. With your greased hands, stretch dough into rough 12 by 8-inch rectangle of even thickness.

3 Cover sheet with plastic wrap and let rise until puffed and nearly doubled in volume, about 1 hour. Meanwhile, adjust oven rack to lowest position, place baking stone on rack, and heat oven to 500 degrees.

4 For the sauce Combine all sauce ingredients in bowl. (Sauce can be refrigerated for up to 24 hours.)

5 Using your greased hands, gently stretch dough to corners of sheet, pressing lightly with your fingertips to deflate dough and carefully lifting corners and edges of dough to pull toward edges of sheet. (It's OK if dough shrinks back slightly from corners of sheet at this point.) Cover loosely with plastic and let rest until slightly puffed, about 20 minutes.

6 Using your greased hands, press dough all the way to edges and corners of sheet. Using your fingertips, pinch edges of dough against sides of sheet to form small lip. Spread sauce into thin layer over surface of dough, leaving ½-inch border. Sprinkle Parmesan evenly over sauce. Sprinkle mozzarella over entire surface of dough, making sure some cheese sits on edges of dough against sheet. Top with pepperoni.

7 Place sheet on stone and bake pizza until cheese is bubbly and well browned, about 15 minutes, rotating sheet halfway through baking. Run knife around edge of sheet to loosen pizza and transfer to wire rack. Let cool for 5 minutes. Slice and serve, sprinkled with extra Parmesan and pepper flakes if desired.

VARIATIONS

Caprese Pan Pizza

You can use homemade pesto (see page 25) or store-bought. You can find balsamic glaze alongside the vinegars at the supermarket.

While dough is rising in step 3, toss 10 ounces cherry tomatoes (sliced ¼ inch thick), ½ teaspoon table salt, ½ teaspoon sugar, and 1 minced garlic clove together in bowl. Transfer to colander set over bowl and drain. Omit sauce in step 4 and spread 1¼ cups pesto over surface of dough in step 6 instead. Omit Parmesan and pepperoni. Substitute 10 ounces fresh mozzarella (sliced into ¼-inch-thick rounds) for shredded whole-milk mozzarella. Sprinkle pizza with drained tomatoes, ½ teaspoon pepper, and ¼ teaspoon table salt. Before serving, top baked pizza with ½ cup shaved Parmesan, ⅓ cup torn fresh basil leaves, and 2 tablespoons balsamic glaze, if desired.

Pan Pizza with 'Nduja, Ricotta, and Cherry Peppers

While dough is rising in step 3, pulse ½ cup room temperature 'nduja with ½ cup whole-milk ricotta cheese in food processor until smooth, about 15 pulses; set aside at room temperature. Substitute additional ¼ cup room temperature 'nduja for olive oil and anchovies in sauce in step 4, using fork to mash 'nduja into sauce until uniform. Substitute Pecorino Romano for Parmesan. Omit pepperoni. Before serving, drop rough 2-teaspoon-size dollops of 'nduja-ricotta mixture evenly over baked pizza and lightly smear with back of spoon. Before serving, top baked pizza with ⅓ cup shredded fresh basil and ⅓ cup thinly sliced jarred hot cherry peppers.

Lavash Flatbreads with Romesco, Tomatoes, and Spinach

Serves 4 (makes 2 flatbreads) | **Total Time** 20 minutes

Romesco Sauce

- ⅔ cup jarred roasted red peppers, patted dry
- ¼ cup slivered almonds, toasted
- ¼ cup fresh parsley leaves
- 3 tablespoons extra-virgin olive oil
- 1 tablespoon sherry vinegar
- 1 garlic clove, minced
- ¼ teaspoon table salt

Flatbreads

- 10 ounces frozen spinach, thawed, squeezed dry, and chopped
- 5 ounces cherry or grape tomatoes, halved
- ½ cup pitted green olives, chopped
- ¼ cup extra-virgin olive oil, divided
- 1 garlic clove, minced
- ¼ teaspoon red pepper flakes
- ¼ teaspoon table salt
- ¼ teaspoon pepper
- 2 (12 by 9-inch) lavash breads
- Parmesan cheese, grated

Why This Recipe Works Lavash, a thin round or rectangular flatbread popular throughout the Middle East, makes a great sandwich wrap, but we discovered that it also bakes into a crisp, cracker-like crust for inventive pizza that takes just 20 minutes. Serve it as a snack or with a salad for a fun meal. We toast the lavash on sheet pans for a sturdy base. Then we spread them with romesco—a robust red pepper and almond sauce that works well with the wheaty lavash—and top them with a flavorful mixture of spinach (frozen works great), fresh cherry tomatoes, and fruity green olives before returning them to the oven. We finish the flatbreads with a sprinkle of grated Parmesan.

1 For the romesco sauce Process all ingredients in food processor until smooth, about 1 minute, scraping down sides of bowl as needed. Season with salt and pepper to taste. Set aside. (Sauce can be refrigerated for up to 2 days.)

2 For the flatbreads Adjust oven racks to upper-middle and lower-middle positions and heat oven to 475 degrees. Combine spinach, tomatoes, olives, 2 tablespoons oil, garlic, pepper flakes, salt, and pepper in bowl. Brush both sides of lavash with remaining 2 tablespoons oil, lay on 2 baking sheets, and bake until crisp and golden brown, about 4 minutes, switching and rotating sheets and flipping lavash halfway through baking.

3 Spread romesco evenly over each lavash, then top with spinach mixture. Bake until warmed through, about 4 minutes, switching and rotating sheets halfway through baking. Sprinkle flatbreads with Parmesan. Slice and serve.

CHAPTER TWO

Poultry

Charred Broccoli Caesar Salad with Chicken

Serves 4 | **Total Time** 50 minutes

- 6 tablespoons mayonnaise
- 1 ounce Parmesan cheese, grated (½ cup), divided, plus extra for serving
- 7 tablespoons plus 1 teaspoon extra-virgin olive oil, divided
- ½ teaspoon grated lemon zest and 1 tablespoon juice
- 2 teaspoons white wine vinegar
- 2 teaspoons Worcestershire sauce
- 2 teaspoons Dijon mustard
- 3 anchovy fillets, rinsed and minced (optional)
- 1 garlic clove, minced to paste
- ¾ teaspoon plus ⅛ teaspoon pepper, divided
- ½ cup panko bread crumbs
- ¾ teaspoon plus ⅛ teaspoon table salt, divided
- 1 pound boneless, skinless chicken breasts, trimmed
- 1¾ pounds broccoli
- ½ teaspoon sugar
- ⅛ teaspoon red pepper flakes

Why This Recipe Works This recipe breaks all the rules when it comes to Caesar salad thanks to two sheet pans. Where's the lettuce, you ask? We replaced it with deeply caramelized broccoli. And to make this a meal, we top it with tender shredded chicken (roasted on a sheet pan, no skillet needed). As for the broccoli, this is where the second sheet pan comes in; we preheat it to jump-start the roasting so the crowns and the stalks are gloriously charred in minutes. To justify the Caesar moniker, we make a craveable and savory Caesar dressing that we toss with the broccoli before roasting. A cheesy panko topping stands in for the usual croutons.

1 Adjust oven racks to middle and lowest positions, place rimmed baking sheet on lower rack, and heat oven to 400 degrees. Line second sheet with aluminum foil and set aside. Whisk mayonnaise; 6 tablespoons Parmesan; ¼ cup oil; lemon juice; vinegar; Worcestershire; mustard; anchovies, if using; garlic; and ½ teaspoon pepper in bowl until smooth; set aside. Toss panko with 1 teaspoon oil in bowl until evenly coated. Microwave, stirring frequently, until light golden brown, 2 to 4 minutes. Transfer to bowl; stir in remaining 2 tablespoons Parmesan, lemon zest, ⅛ teaspoon salt, and pinch pepper; and set aside.

2 Pound thicker end of chicken breasts between 2 sheets of plastic wrap to uniform thickness. Pat chicken dry with paper towels and sprinkle with ¼ teaspoon salt and ¼ teaspoon pepper. Place chicken on foil-lined sheet and bake on upper rack (leave other sheet in oven) until chicken registers 160 degrees, 10 to 15 minutes, flipping breasts halfway through roasting. Transfer chicken to cutting board, tent with aluminum foil, and let rest.

3 While chicken cooks, cut broccoli horizontally at juncture of crowns and stalks. Cut crowns into 4 wedges if 3 to 4 inches in diameter or 6 wedges if 4 to 5 inches in diameter. Trim tough outer peel from stalks, then cut into ½-inch-thick planks about 2 to 3 inches long. Combine remaining 3 tablespoons oil, sugar, remaining ½ teaspoon salt, remaining pinch pepper, and pepper flakes in large bowl. Add broccoli and toss to coat.

4 Increase oven temperature to 500 degrees. Once oven has reached temperature, working quickly, lay broccoli in single layer, flat sides down, on preheated sheet. Roast on lower rack until stalks and florets are well browned and tender, 9 to 11 minutes.

5 Using 2 forks, shred chicken into bite-size pieces, then toss with roasted broccoli and reserved dressing and divide among individual serving plates. Sprinkle with reserved panko mixture and extra Parmesan. Serve.

Chicken Souvlaki

Serves 4 | **Total Time** 25 minutes

- 6 tablespoons extra-virgin olive oil
- 1 teaspoon grated lemon zest plus 2 tablespoons juice
- 1 teaspoon honey
- 1 teaspoon dried oregano
- 1 teaspoon table salt
- ½ teaspoon pepper
- 1 pound boneless, skinless chicken breasts, trimmed and cut into 1-inch pieces
- 1 green bell pepper, cut into 1-inch pieces
- 1 small red onion, cut into 1-inch pieces
- 4 (8-inch) pitas, warmed
- 1 recipe Tzatziki Sauce (page 25)
- 2 tablespoons torn fresh mint

Why This Recipe Works If you want to be instantly transported to the tiny eateries lining the back streets of Athens, where souvlaki is king, try this version using a sheet pan—no grill, rotisserie, or fussy skewering required. We promise it will brighten your mood to serve this at your table, especially in the dead of winter. Bright lemon flavor and charred yet moist, evenly cooked meat are the hallmarks of good souvlaki, which is almost always made with chunks of boneless, skinless breasts. Here, using a sheet pan and the broiler gives you more control, ensuring that the chicken is spotty brown and tender and that the vegetables straddle the line between overcooked and crisp but appealingly charred. A quick toss in a flavorful marinade made with lemon zest, olive oil, herbs, and honey also helps eliminate the chance that the chicken will dry out; we set some aside to toss with the chicken just before wrapping it in pita.

1 Adjust oven rack 6 inches from broiler element and heat broiler. Spray rimmed baking sheet with vegetable oil spray. Whisk oil, lemon zest, honey, oregano, salt, and pepper together in large bowl. Measure out and reserve ¼ cup oil mixture, then whisk lemon juice into remaining oil mixture in bowl; set vinaigrette aside. Toss chicken, bell pepper, and onion with reserved oil mixture in bowl, then spread into even layer on prepared sheet.

2 Broil until chicken is spotty brown on first side, 4 to 6 minutes. Stir chicken and vegetables, then redistribute into even layer and continue to broil until chicken is spotty brown on second side and registers 160 degrees and vegetables are tender, 4 to 6 minutes.

3 Whisk reserved vinaigrette to recombine, then drizzle over roasted chicken and vegetables on sheet; toss to combine, scraping up any fond from sheet. Lay each pita on 12-inch square of foil. Divide tzatziki evenly among pitas, spreading over half of each pita, then place one-quarter chicken and vegetables in center of each pita. Sprinkle with mint, then roll into wrap, using foil to hold shape, and serve.

Chicken Chilaquiles Verdes

Serves 4 | **Total Time** 55 minutes, plus 30 minutes marinating

---

- ¼ cup vegetable oil, divided
- 2 tablespoons water
- 1 tablespoon lime juice, plus lime wedges for serving
- 3 garlic cloves (2 peeled, 1 minced), divided
- 2 teaspoons table salt, divided
- 1 teaspoon sugar
- ½ teaspoon pepper
- 1 pound boneless, skinless chicken breasts, trimmed
- 1½ pounds tomatillos, husks and stems removed, rinsed well, dried, and halved
- 1 large onion, peeled and cut into 1½-inch pieces
- 2 poblano chiles, stemmed, halved, and seeded
- 1 jalapeño chile, stemmed, halved, and seeded
- 1½ cups coarsely chopped fresh cilantro leaves and tender stems, divided
- ⅓ cup chicken broth
- 8 ounces tortilla chips
- 1 avocado, halved, pitted, and cut into ½-inch pieces
- 2 ounces cotija cheese, crumbled (½ cup)

Why This Recipe Works Using just a blender and a sheet pan, this streamlined chilaquiles recipe is a revelation, one that will put this Mexican comfort food favorite on your table again and again. Chilaquiles verdes offers layers of fried, cut-up tortillas and shredded marinated chicken, all bound by an aromatic, spicy tomatillo sauce and served with a whole host of toppings. (That's where the fun begins.) We wanted to avoid frying tortilla pieces, so we relied on a small bag of store-bought tortilla chips instead. And we took advantage of one of the sheet pan's great attributes: Its large surface area allows you to rotate ingredients on and off the pan as their cooking times demand. (Witness the chicken and the roasted vegetables for the sauce.) We think diced avocado and crumbled cotija are necessary toppings. But, really, the sky is the limit here; other great choices include sliced red onion, sliced radishes, and Lime Crema (page 26) or store-bought Mexican crema.

1 Whisk 3 tablespoons oil, water, lime juice, minced garlic, 1½ teaspoons salt, sugar, and pepper together in medium bowl. Pound thicker end of chicken breasts between 2 sheets of plastic wrap to uniform ½-inch thickness, if needed. Add chicken to marinade; cover; and refrigerate, turning occasionally, for 30 minutes.

2 Adjust oven rack to upper-middle position and heat oven to 450 degrees. Line rimmed baking sheet with aluminum foil. Toss tomatillos, onion, poblanos, jalapeño, and peeled garlic with remaining 1 tablespoon oil on prepared sheet. Arrange vegetables in even layer on two-thirds of sheet, placing chiles skin side up. Remove chicken from marinade, letting excess marinade drip off, and arrange on empty third of sheet. Roast until chicken registers 160 degrees and skins of jalapeno and poblano are browned, 18 to 23 minutes, rotating sheet halfway through roasting. Transfer chicken to cutting board and let rest while preparing sauce.

3 Remove charred skins from poblanos. Transfer vegetables, along with any accumulated juices, to blender. Add 1¼ cups cilantro, broth, and remaining ½ teaspoon salt to blender and process until smooth, about 30 seconds, scraping down sides of blender jar as needed. Using 2 forks, shred chicken into bite-size pieces. (If sauce has cooled, transfer to bowl and reheat in microwave at 50 percent power for 2 minutes.)

4 Discard foil from sheet and wipe clean with paper towels. Transfer half of sauce and half of chicken to large bowl, add half of chips, and toss to coat, being careful not to break chips. Spread into even layer in now-empty sheet. Repeat with remaining sauce, chicken, and chips. Sprinkle with avocado, cotija, and remaining ¼ cup cilantro. Serve immediately.

Chicken Packets with Fennel and Sun-Dried Tomatoes

Serves 4 | **Total Time** 1 hour, plus 1 hour chilling

- 5 tablespoons extra-virgin olive oil
- 6 garlic cloves, sliced thin
- 1 teaspoon minced fresh thyme
- ¼ teaspoon red pepper flakes
- 12 ounces Yukon Gold potatoes, unpeeled, sliced crosswise ¼ inch thick
- 1 fennel bulb, stalks discarded, bulb halved, cored, and cut into ½-inch-thick wedges, layers separated
- ½ large red onion, sliced ½ inch thick, layers separated
- ¼ cup oil-packed sun-dried tomatoes, rinsed, patted dry, and chopped fine
- ¼ cup pitted kalamata olives, chopped fine
- ¾ teaspoon table salt, divided
- 4 (6- to 8-ounce) boneless, skinless chicken breasts, trimmed
- ¼ teaspoon pepper
- 2 tablespoons balsamic vinegar
- 2 tablespoons sliced fresh basil

Why This Recipe Works For all of you who struggle to get a well-rounded dinner on the table every night of the week, give yourself a break and try this lovely meal arranged in individual foil packets (so everyone gets their own—kids love this). This crafty cooking method mirrors cooking en papillote but is easier, and delivers a meal of chicken and vegetables packed with savory flavors. And once you assemble the packets, they take less than a half hour in the oven. All you need is aluminum foil, a ruler, and a sheet pan and you will be in business. For deep flavor in the absence of browning, we toss our vegetables in a fragrant garlic oil. We layer the vegetables under the chicken in the packets, leaving space for steam to circulate, to protect quick-cooking but lean boneless chicken breasts from the pan's direct heat. Make sure to buy chicken breasts that are roughly the same size.

1 Spray centers of four 20 by 12-inch sheets of aluminum foil with vegetable oil spray. Microwave oil, garlic, thyme, and pepper flakes in large bowl until garlic begins to brown, about 1 minute. Add potatoes, fennel, onion, tomatoes, olives, and ½ teaspoon salt to bowl with garlic oil and toss to combine.

2 Pound thicker end of chicken breasts between 2 sheets of plastic wrap to uniform ½-inch thickness, if needed. Pat chicken dry with paper towels and sprinkle with pepper and remaining ¼ teaspoon salt. Position 1 piece of prepared foil with long side parallel to edge of counter. In center of foil, arrange one-quarter of potato slices in 2 rows perpendicular to edge of counter. Lay 1 chicken breast on top of potato slices. Place one-quarter of vegetables around chicken. Repeat with remaining prepared foil, remaining potato slices, remaining chicken, and remaining vegetables. Drizzle any remaining oil mixture from bowl over chicken.

3 Bring short sides of foil together and crimp to seal tightly. Crimp remaining open ends of packets, leaving as much headroom as possible inside packets. Refrigerate for at least 1 hour or up to 24 hours.

4 Adjust oven rack to lowest position and heat oven to 475 degrees. Place packets on rimmed baking sheet and bake until chicken registers 160 degrees, 18 to 23 minutes. (To check temperature, poke thermometer through foil of 1 packet and into chicken.) Let chicken rest in packets for 3 minutes.

5 Transfer chicken packets to individual serving plates, open carefully (steam will escape), and slide contents onto plates. Drizzle vinegar over chicken and vegetables and sprinkle with basil. Serve.

VARIATIONS

Chicken Packets with Potatoes and Carrots

Omit sun-dried tomatoes and olives. Substitute 2 carrots (peeled, quartered lengthwise and cut into 2-inch lengths) for fennel, lemon juice for balsamic vinegar, and chives for basil.

Chicken Packets with Sweet Potato and Radishes

Omit olives. Substitute 1 tablespoon grated fresh ginger for thyme, 12 ounces sweet potato (peeled and sliced ¼ inch thick) for Yukon Gold potatoes, 4 radishes (trimmed and quartered) for fennel, 2 celery ribs (quartered lengthwise and cut into 2-inch lengths) for tomatoes, unseasoned rice vinegar for balsamic vinegar, and cilantro for basil.

Chicken Parmesan with Pizza-Shop Salad and Garlicky Toast

Serves 4 | **Total Time** 1¼ hours

- 2 cups panko bread crumbs
- 5½ tablespoons extra-virgin olive oil, divided
- 2 large eggs
- 4 teaspoons all-purpose flour
- 1½ teaspoons garlic powder
- 1 teaspoon dried oregano
- 1 teaspoon table salt, divided
- 1 teaspoon pepper, divided
- 1½ ounces Parmesan cheese, grated (¾ cup), divided
- 4 (6- to 8-ounce) boneless, skinless chicken breasts, trimmed
- 2 red onions, halved and sliced ½ inch thick
- 6 ounces whole-milk block mozzarella cheese, shredded (1½ cups)
- 8 (½-inch-thick) slices ciabatta bread
- 1 garlic clove, peeled and halved
- 1 small head (8 ounces) romaine lettuce, torn into bite-size pieces
- 1 tablespoon lemon juice
- ½ cup jarred marinara sauce, warmed
- ¼ cup chopped fresh basil

Why This Recipe Works Can you really make chicken Parmesan with only a sheet pan? That sounded heretical to us since normally we crisp the breaded chicken first in a skillet. To test the limits, we transferred the operation to the oven, while streamlining every step. To ensure browning without pan-frying, we pretoast the crispy panko coating in the microwave; we add Parmesan to the crumbs to get the dish's namesake in every bite. Flour and spices get whisked into the eggs to reduce three dredging steps to two. We bake the chicken, topping each breast with mozzarella to melt in the final 4 minutes. Meanwhile, on a separate sheet, we roast some red onions to make a quick pizza shop–style salad—you know, the kind with refreshing romaine lettuce and a bright recognizable dressing. While the chicken rests, we quickly toast some bread under the broiler, rub it with garlic, and sprinkle it with more Parmesan. That's three dishes easily juggled with two hands. If your loaf of bread is larger than 5 inches wide, you may need more Parmesan to cover each slice. You can use Italian bread if you can't find ciabatta.

1 Adjust oven racks to upper-middle and lower-middle positions and heat oven to 400 degrees. Line rimmed baking sheet with aluminum foil.

2 Toss panko with 2 tablespoons oil in bowl until evenly coated. Microwave, stirring occasionally, until deep golden brown, 5 to 6 minutes; let cool slightly. Whisk eggs, flour, garlic powder, oregano, ¼ teaspoon salt, and ¼ teaspoon pepper together in shallow dish. Combine cooled panko mixture and ½ cup Parmesan in second shallow dish.

3 Pound thicker end of chicken breasts between 2 sheets of plastic wrap to uniform ½-inch thickness, if needed. Pat chicken dry with paper towels and sprinkle with ½ teaspoon salt and ½ teaspoon pepper. Working with 1 breast at a time, dredge in egg mixture, letting excess drip off, then coat with panko mixture, pressing gently to adhere. Arrange chicken breasts in single layer on prepared sheet.

4 Toss red onions with 1 tablespoon oil, remaining ¼ teaspoon salt, and remaining ¼ teaspoon pepper on second rimmed baking sheet, spreading into even layer. Place sheet with chicken on upper rack and place sheet with onions on lower rack; roast until chicken registers 160 degrees and onions are browned, 20 to 25 minutes, switching and rotating sheets halfway through baking.

5 Remove sheets from oven. Transfer red onion to bowl and set aside to cool while finishing chicken and garlic bread. Sprinkle chicken, still on sheet, with mozzarella, then bake on upper rack until cheese is melted, about 4 minutes. Transfer to platter and let rest while making garlic bread.

6 Heat broiler. Brush bread slices with 1 tablespoon oil and place on now-empty second baking sheet. Broil on upper rack until edges of bread are lightly browned, about 2 minutes, flipping slices halfway through. Rub 1 side of bread slices with halved garlic clove and sprinkle with remaining ¼ cup Parmesan cheese. Return sheet to upper rack and broil until cheese is melted, about 1 minute. Add romaine, lemon juice, and remaining 1½ tablespoons oil to bowl with cooled onions, tossing to combine, then season with salt and pepper to taste. Top chicken with warmed marinara sauce and sprinkle with basil. Serve with salad and garlic bread.

Oven-Fried Chicken

Serves 4 | **Total Time** 1¼ hours, plus 2 hours marinating

Chicken

- ½ cup plus 2 tablespoons table salt for brining
- ¼ cup sugar for brining
- 2 tablespoons paprika
- 3 heads garlic, cloves separated, smashed, and peeled
- 3 bay leaves, crumbled
- 7 cups buttermilk for brining
- 4 (10-ounce) chicken leg quarters, trimmed, separated into drumsticks and thighs, and skin removed

Coating

- ¼ cup vegetable oil
- 1 box (5 ounces) plain Melba toasts, crushed
- 2 large eggs
- 1 tablespoon Dijon mustard
- 1 teaspoon dried thyme
- ¾ teaspoon table salt
- ½ teaspoon pepper
- ½ teaspoon dried oregano
- ¼ teaspoon garlic powder
- ¼ teaspoon cayenne pepper (optional)

Why This Recipe Works We thought the satisfying, audible crunch that comes with the first bite of a piece of chicken hot from the frying oil was impossible to capture in the oven. Until now. Our formula for oven-fried chicken has serious crunch without the mess and stress. Elevating the chicken from the sheet pan on a wire rack lets hot air circulate all around it so no side gets soggy. What provides the crunch? We tried a lot of coatings and found that pulverized Melba toasts make the crispiest shell. Chicken skin is only crispy if its fat is completely rendered—a slow process in the oven. Removing it removes this step and prevents the crunch from the Melba coating from being diminished. If you don't want to buy whole chicken legs and cut them into drumsticks and thighs, simply buy four drumsticks and four thighs. To make Melba toast crumbs, place the toasts in a heavy-duty zipper-lock freezer bag, seal, and pound with a meat pounder or other heavy blunt object. Leave some crumbs in the mixture the size of pebbles, but most should resemble coarse sand.

1 For the chicken Combine salt, sugar, paprika, garlic cloves, and bay leaves in large bowl or container, then stir in buttermilk until salt and sugar are completely dissolved. Submerge chicken in brine and refrigerate for 2 to 3 hours.

2 For the coating Adjust oven rack to upper-middle position and heat oven to 400 degrees. Toss oil and Melba toast crumbs together in shallow dish. Whisk eggs; mustard; thyme; salt; pepper; oregano; garlic powder; and cayenne, if using, together in second shallow dish.

3 Rinse chicken well, then pat dry with paper towels; place on wire rack set in aluminum foil–lined rimmed baking sheet.

4 Working with 1 piece at a time, coat chicken on both sides with egg mixture, letting excess drip off, then coat with Melba crumb mixture, pressing gently to adhere. Return chicken to rack, rearranging pieces on rack as needed to space evenly over sheet. Bake until chicken is deep nutty brown and registers 175 degrees, about 40 minutes. Serve.

Goat Cheese-Stuffed Chicken with Roasted Carrots

Serves 4 | **Total Time** 1 hour

- 4 ounces goat cheese, softened (1 cup)
- 3 tablespoons extra-virgin olive oil, divided
- 2 teaspoons minced fresh thyme
- 1 garlic clove, minced
- 1 teaspoon grated lemon zest
- 1 teaspoon table salt, divided
- 1 teaspoon pepper, divided
- 4 (12-ounce) bone-in split chicken breasts, trimmed
- 1½ pounds carrots, peeled and sliced ½ inch thick on bias
- 1 tablespoon packed brown sugar

Why This Recipe Works Do you remember the goat cheese–stuffed chicken of the 1990s? It was considered the height of dinner party food back then and was on every holiday buffet. Could we bring it back and make it better? We think this recipe does that in spades. To make it a one-pan meal, we roast sliced carrots on the same sheet pan with the chicken. The trick with goat cheese stuffing is to doctor it up with extra-virgin olive oil, fresh thyme, garlic, and lemon zest, which infuses not only the cheese but also the chicken breasts with bright flavor; plus, it makes the cheese easier to spread under the chicken skin. These impressive yet easy stuffed chicken breasts roast alongside the carrots in the exact same amount of time. Tossing the caramelized carrots with the chicken juices on the sheet pan after roasting makes them a sweet-savory, satisfying accompaniment.

1 Adjust oven rack to middle position and heat oven to 475 degrees. Combine goat cheese, 1 tablespoon oil, thyme, garlic, lemon zest, ¼ teaspoon salt, and ¼ teaspoon pepper in bowl.

2 Pat chicken dry with paper towels. Using your fingers, carefully loosen center portion of skin covering each breast. Place about 1½ tablespoons cheese mixture under skin, directly on meat in center of each breast half. Gently press on skin to spread out cheese mixture. Brush chicken skin with 1 tablespoon oil, then sprinkle chicken with ½ teaspoon salt and ½ teaspoon pepper.

3 Place chicken skin side up on half of rimmed baking sheet. Toss carrots with sugar, remaining 1 tablespoon oil, remaining ¼ teaspoon salt, and remaining ¼ teaspoon pepper. Spread carrots in single layer on other half of sheet. Roast until chicken registers 160 degrees, 35 to 40 minutes, rotating sheet halfway through roasting.

4 Transfer chicken to serving platter, tent with aluminum foil, and let rest for 5 minutes. Toss carrots with juices on sheet, season with salt and pepper to taste, and transfer to platter with chicken. Serve.

Lemon-Thyme Chicken with Ratatouille

Serves 4 | **Total Time** 1 hour

- 1 (14.5-ounce) can diced tomatoes, drained
- 12 ounces eggplant, cut into ½-inch pieces
- 2 small zucchini (6 ounces each), cut into ½-inch pieces
- 3 tablespoons extra-virgin olive oil, divided
- 1 tablespoon minced fresh thyme or 1 teaspoon dried, divided
- 2 garlic cloves, minced
- 1 teaspoon table salt, divided
- ¾ teaspoon pepper, divided
- 4 (12-ounce) bone-in split chicken breasts, trimmed
- 2 tablespoons minced fresh parsley
- Lemon wedges, for serving

Why This Recipe Works We love the result of reimagining ratatouille on the sheet pan for this chicken dinner. While the traditional method of stewing the summer vegetables gently brings out their flavors, it can also bring out their mushiness. Cooking them with dry heat allows their moisture to evaporate just enough and their flavors to really concentrate. It also allows us to complete the meal with golden-skinned chicken breasts. Preheating the baking sheet before placing the chicken and vegetables on it lets us crisp the skin. And when we flip the chicken, we stir the vegetables—the two cook in lockstep. For this recipe, we prefer small zucchini, which are less watery and have smaller seeds.

1 Adjust oven rack to upper-middle position, place rimmed baking sheet on rack, and heat oven to 450 degrees. Toss tomatoes, eggplant, and zucchini with 2 tablespoons oil, 1 teaspoon thyme, garlic, ½ teaspoon salt, and ¼ teaspoon pepper. Pat chicken dry with paper towels and sprinkle with remaining 2 teaspoons thyme, remaining ½ teaspoon salt, and remaining ½ teaspoon pepper.

2 Add remaining 1 tablespoon oil to hot sheet, tilting to coat. Place chicken skin side down on half of sheet and spread vegetables in single layer on other half. Roast until chicken releases from sheet and vegetables begin to wilt, about 10 minutes.

3 Flip chicken skin side up and continue to roast, stirring vegetables occasionally until chicken registers 160 degrees and vegetables are tender, 10 to 15 minutes.

4 Transfer chicken to plate, tent with aluminum foil, and let rest for 5 minutes. Toss vegetables with juices on sheet, and season with salt and pepper to taste. Return chicken to sheet, sprinkle parsley over vegetables and chicken, and serve with lemon wedges.

Spiced Chicken Breasts with Squash, Caramelized Shallots, and Crispy Kale

Serves 4 | **Total Time** 1 hour

- ½ cup extra-virgin olive oil
- 2 tablespoons minced fresh sage
- 2 teaspoons honey
- 1 teaspoon table salt
- ½ teaspoon pepper
- ¾ cup plain whole-milk yogurt
- 1 tablespoon water
- 7 garlic cloves, peeled (6 whole, 1 minced)
- 1 teaspoon grated orange zest
- 8 ounces kale, stemmed and cut into 2-inch pieces
- 2 pounds butternut squash, peeled, seeded, and cut into 1-inch pieces (6 cups)
- 8 shallots, peeled and halved
- ½ cup dried cranberries
- 2 teaspoons paprika
- 4 (12-ounce) bone-in split chicken breasts, trimmed and halved crosswise

Why This Recipe Works Chicken plus dark leafy greens plus starchy vegetable is an equation for a complete, satisfying, nutritious meal that the sheet pan is so successful at adding up. While we often stagger the cooking for multicomponent meals, we're able to roast these three very different ingredients together at the same rate thanks to the way we place them on the sheet. We mix the kale—massaged for tenderness—and squash with seasoned oil, halved shallots, bright dried cranberries, and whole garlic cloves. We spread the vegetables across the sheet and then place paprika-seasoned skin-on halved chicken breasts right on top of the vegetables to elevate them from the pan and to let their drippings flavor the veggies. Once everything is cooked, we toss the vegetables—the tender caramelized squash and shallots and the appealingly crispy kale—with the chicken juices and serve everything with a unifying yogurt sauce. Both curly and lacinato kale will work in this recipe.

1 Adjust oven rack to upper-middle position and heat oven to 475 degrees. Whisk oil, sage, honey, salt, and pepper in large bowl until well combined. In separate bowl whisk yogurt, water, minced garlic, orange zest, and 1 tablespoon oil mixture together; set yogurt sauce aside for serving.

2 Vigorously squeeze and massage kale with your hands in large bowl until leaves are uniformly darkened and slightly wilted, about 1 minute. Add squash, shallots, cranberries, whole garlic cloves, and ¼ cup oil mixture and toss to combine. Whisk paprika into remaining oil mixture, then add chicken and toss to coat.

3 Spread vegetables in single layer on rimmed baking sheet, then place chicken skin side up on top of vegetables. Roast until chicken registers 160 degrees, 25 to 35 minutes, rotating sheet halfway through roasting.

4 Remove sheet from oven, transfer chicken to plate, tent with aluminum foil, and let rest for 5 minutes. Toss vegetables with juices on sheet, season with salt and pepper to taste. Return chicken to sheet, drizzle ¼ cup yogurt sauce over chicken and serve, passing remaining yogurt sauce separately.

How to Build the Sheet Pan

Arrange the sweet potatoes around the perimeter of the sheet pan and the poblanos in the center. Arrange the chicken breasts over the poblanos. When the chicken is done, transfer it to a platter and let it rest; meanwhile, return the vegetables to the oven to continue browning.

Spiced Chicken Breasts with Sweet Potato-Poblano Salad

Serves 4 | **Total Time** 1¼ hours

Chicken and Vegetables

- 4 sweet potatoes (8 to 10 ounces each), peeled, halved lengthwise, and sliced crosswise ¾ inch thick
- 2 poblano chiles, stemmed, halved lengthwise, seeded, and cut crosswise into ½-inch-wide strips
- 3 tablespoons extra-virgin olive oil
- 1¾ teaspoons table salt, divided
- 2 teaspoons chili powder
- 2 teaspoons dried oregano
- 2 teaspoons ground cumin
- 1 teaspoon pepper
- 4 (12-ounce) bone-in split chicken breasts, trimmed
- 1 tablespoon honey
- 2 ounces cotija cheese, crumbled (½ cup)
- 2 tablespoons roasted, salted pepitas

Dressing

- ⅓ cup chopped fresh cilantro
- 2 tablespoons extra-virgin olive oil
- 2 garlic cloves, minced
- 1½ teaspoons grated lime zest plus 2 tablespoons juice
- ½ teaspoon table salt
- ½ teaspoon pepper

Why This Recipe Works This recipe makes magic of its three main ingredients for one of the most vibrant meals in our repertoire—on one sheet. First we arrange the sweet potatoes around the perimeter of the baking sheet for maximum browning, and we place the poblanos in the center to prevent burning. We position spice-rubbed chicken breasts on top of the poblanos, which shields the peppers from overcooking and flavors them with the same spices. When the chicken is done, we transfer it to a platter and let it rest; meanwhile, we return the vegetables to the oven to continue browning. We finish with more flavor, brightly dressing the vegetables and adding lots of richness with crumbled cotija cheese and crunchy toasted pepitas. Look for poblano chiles that are about 4 ounces each. If your chili powder is salt-free, increase the amount of salt on the chicken in step 2 to 2 teaspoons and decrease the amount of chili powder to 1½ teaspoons. You can substitute feta cheese for the cotija cheese, if desired.

1 **For the chicken and vegetables** Adjust oven rack to middle position and heat oven to 475 degrees. Spray rimmed baking sheet with vegetable oil spray. Toss potatoes, poblanos, oil, and ¾ teaspoon salt together on prepared sheet. Arrange sweet potatoes around perimeter of sheet and poblanos in center of sheet in even layer.

2 Combine chili powder, oregano, cumin, pepper, and remaining 1 teaspoon salt in bowl. Pat chicken dry with paper towels and place over poblanos on sheet. Sprinkle chicken all over with spice mixture. Roast, skin side up, until chicken registers 160 degrees, 35 to 40 minutes.

3 **For the dressing** While chicken and vegetables roast, whisk all ingredients together in bowl.

4 Remove sheet from oven and transfer chicken to large platter. Return vegetables to oven and continue to roast until potatoes are browned on bottom, 5 to 7 minutes longer. Let vegetables cool on sheet for 5 minutes. Toss vegetables with dressing and juices on sheet, then transfer to platter with chicken. Microwave honey until loose in texture, about 15 seconds, then brush over skin side of chicken. Sprinkle vegetables with cotija and pepitas. Serve.

Singapore Noodles with Chicken and Shrimp

Serves 4 | **Total Time** 1 hour

- 1 large carrot, peeled and cut into 2-inch-long matchsticks
- 1 onion, halved and sliced thin
- 1 red bell pepper, stemmed, seeded, and cut into 2-inch-long matchsticks
- 3 cups shredded green cabbage
- ¼ cup plus 4 teaspoons vegetable oil, divided
- 1½ teaspoons table salt, divided
- 12 ounces boneless skinless chicken thighs, trimmed and sliced into ¼-inch-thick strips
- 2½ tablespoons bottled char siu sauce
- 8 ounces rice vermicelli
- 1½ tablespoons curry powder
- 1 teaspoon sugar
- ¼ teaspoon white pepper
- 3 eggs, lightly beaten
- 5 scallions (3 cut into 2-inch lengths with white parts halved lengthwise, 2 sliced thin on bias)
- 8 ounces jumbo shrimp (16 to 20 per pound), peeled and deveined

Why This Recipe Works This Cantonese dish is a restaurant favorite, but honestly, it's easy to re-create at home and using a sheet pan makes the process appealingly hands-off. At first we thought that shifting the stir-fried noodle dish to the oven would be a nonstarter given how many different ingredients (and textures) are involved, but rotating the sheet pan in and out of the oven a few times in precise order makes it happen. A medley of vegetables roast on one side of the pan as char siu sauce–coated sliced chicken thighs roast on the other side, placed in a simple tray fashioned from foil. Containing the sauced chicken allows us to easily remove it when it's done and continue to cook (or rather, roast) the recipe's scrambled egg in the clearing. While all this is happening, we soak vermicelli noodles; then, we roast them on the pan briefly with the other ingredients to give them some browning. Finally, we nestle in juicy shrimp and run the pan under the broiler to cook the shrimp and create a top layer of crispy noodles. We used Lee Kum Kee brand char siu sauce when developing this recipe.

1 Adjust oven rack to upper-middle position and heat oven to 450 degrees. Line one-third of rimmed baking sheet with aluminum foil, folding sides up slightly to create small tray. Spray foil with vegetable oil spray.

2 Toss carrot, onion, bell pepper, cabbage, 1 tablespoon oil, and ¼ teaspoon salt in bowl, then spread into even layer over unlined portion of sheet. Pat chicken dry, then toss with char siu sauce. Transfer to prepared foil tray on sheet, spreading into even layer. Roast until vegetables are nearly crisp-tender and chicken is cooked through, about 15 minutes.

3 While chicken and vegetables cook, place noodles in large bowl, then pour boiling water over top to cover by 2 inches. Soak noodles for 5 minutes, stirring once halfway through, then drain and rinse with cold water. Using kitchen shears, cut vermicelli into 3- to 4-inch strands, then return noodles to strainer to continue to drain. Stir curry powder, sugar, white pepper, 3 tablespoons oil, and 1 teaspoon salt together in large bowl.

4 Transfer cooked chicken to bowl with curry mixture and cover to keep warm; discard foil from sheet. Drizzle 2 teaspoons oil evenly over now-empty portion of sheet. Using fork, whisk eggs and ⅛ teaspoon salt in bowl until thoroughly combined and mixture is pure yellow, then pour onto oiled part of sheet. Return sheet to oven and roast until eggs are opaque, 2 to 3 minutes. Using spatula, break up eggs into bite-size pieces, then scrape vegetables and eggs into bowl with chicken.

5 Add drained vermicelli and 2-inch lengths of scallions to bowl with chicken-vegetable mixture and toss until well combined. Transfer to now-empty sheet and spread into even layer. Roast for 5 minutes, then transfer sheet to wire rack. Using tongs, stir and toss noodles, then return to oven and roast for 5 minutes longer. Meanwhile, combine shrimp with remaining 2 teaspoons oil and remaining ⅛ teaspoon salt.

6 Return sheet to rack and heat broiler element. Nestle shrimp into noodle mixture, then return sheet to oven and broil until shrimp are opaque and top layer of noodles begins to brown and crisp in spots, 2½ to 3 minutes, rotating pan and flipping shrimp halfway through broiling. Sprinkle with thinly sliced scallions and serve.

How to Build the Sheet Pan

Roast the vegetables on one side and the chicken, in a foil tray, on the other. Transfer chicken to bowl with curry mixture; cook the eggs in the clearing; add eggs and vegetables to the bowl with the chicken. Transfer soaked vermicelli to the bowl and toss; add everything to the pan and roast. In the last 3 minutes add the shrimp and broil.

Teriyaki Chicken Thighs with Sesame Vegetables

Serves 4 | **Total Time** 1¼ hours

- 8 (5- to 7-ounce) bone-in chicken thighs, trimmed
- 2 tablespoons vegetable oil, divided
- 1 red bell pepper, stemmed, seeded, and cut into ¼-inch-wide strips
- 8 ounces shiitake mushrooms, stemmed and sliced thin
- 3 garlic cloves, minced, divided
- 1 tablespoon grated fresh ginger, divided
- 8 ounces snap peas, strings removed
- 5 tablespoons mirin
- 5 tablespoons soy sauce
- ¼ cup water
- 3 tablespoons sugar
- 2 teaspoons cornstarch
- ⅛ teaspoon red pepper flakes
- 1 tablespoon toasted sesame oil
- 1 tablespoon toasted sesame seeds
- ½ teaspoon table salt

Why This Recipe Works Sheet-pan roasting is a hands-off path to our teriyaki chicken ideal: crispy chicken in a sweet-sticky sauce. It allows us to crisp the chicken before applying a glaze, all while preparing a vegetable "stir-fry" in the same pan. We brown chicken thighs in the oven, slashing the skin and placing them on a wire rack to render and drain away the fat to leave behind a thin sheath of crackly skin. We toss sliced bell pepper and mushrooms with garlic and ginger and spread them alongside the chicken to roast. Snap peas go in 10 minutes later so they don't overcook. Briefly broiling everything crisps the thighs' skin further. We thicken our pantry teriyaki sauce in the microwave before brushing it on our never-soggy chicken. Depending on your wire rack, you may need to place parchment paper underneath the vegetables to prevent them from falling through. Serve with rice.

1 Adjust 1 oven rack to lower-middle position and second rack 8 inches from broiler element. Heat oven to 450 degrees. Set wire rack in rimmed baking sheet lined with aluminum foil. Make 3 diagonal slashes through skin of each thigh with sharp knife (do not cut into meat). Brush chicken with 1 tablespoon vegetable oil. Lay chicken skin side up on 1 half of prepared rack and roast on lower rack for 20 minutes.

2 Toss bell pepper and mushrooms with half of garlic, 1½ teaspoons ginger, and remaining 1 tablespoon vegetable oil. Spread vegetables over empty half of rack. Rotate sheet and continue to roast for 10 minutes. Sprinkle snap peas over vegetables and continue to roast until chicken registers 165 degrees and vegetables start to brown, about 10 minutes.

3 Remove sheet from oven and heat broiler. Place sheet on upper rack and broil until chicken and vegetables are well browned and chicken registers 175 degrees, 3 to 5 minutes. Meanwhile, combine mirin, soy sauce, water, sugar, cornstarch, pepper flakes, remaining garlic, and remaining 1½ teaspoons ginger in bowl and microwave, whisking occasionally, until thickened, 3 to 5 minutes.

4 Remove sheet from oven, brush chicken with 3 tablespoons of sauce, and let rest for 5 minutes. Transfer vegetables to clean bowl; toss with sesame oil, sesame seeds, and salt. Serve vegetables and chicken with remaining sauce.

Baharat Chicken with Potatoes and Herb-Date Salad

Serves 4 | **Total Time** 1¼ hours

Chicken and Potatoes

- 1 tablespoon Baharat (page 24)
- 1¾ teaspoons table salt, divided
- 8 (5- to 7-ounce) bone-in chicken thighs
- 1½ pounds small red or yellow potatoes, halved
- 4 teaspoons pomegranate molasses

Salad

- 4 teaspoons extra-virgin olive oil
- 1 tablespoon lemon juice
- ⅛ teaspoon table salt
- ½ fennel bulb, cored and sliced thin
- 1 cup coarsely chopped fresh parsley
- 1 cup coarsely chopped fresh dill
- 1 cup coarsely chopped fresh mint
- ½ cup pitted Castelvetrano olives, halved
- 3 ounces pitted dates, chopped (½ cup)
- 1 shallot, sliced thin
- 1 blood orange, peeled and segmented (optional)
- Coriander and Aleppo Pepper-Spiced Oil (optional)

Why This Recipe Works The humble bone-in chicken thigh will never let you down: You cannot overcook it. The skin is divine and easy to crisp up. And it takes on different flavor profiles easily. We have the sheet pan to thank for our creativity here. The potatoes, not only the chicken, will get your attention because they're tossed in the rendered fat left behind on the sheet pan after roasting the chicken skin trimmings. We guarantee these potatoes are like no others you've made. In the last minutes of cooking, the chicken gets a quick slather with some complementary sweet-tart pomegranate molasses. While the chicken and potatoes are roasting on your trusty sheet pan, put together an herb-forward salad with olives, jammy dates, crunchy fennel, and juicy oranges—a gorgeous and sunny-tasting salad that you'll sprinkle over and around the chicken for a stunning presentation. Use potatoes that are 1 to 2 inches in diameter. Pomegranate molasses with added sugar will brown faster in step 4. You can use our recipe for baharat or use store-bought. For a big burst of flavor, drizzle plain yogurt and Coriander and Aleppo Pepper-Spiced Oil over the entire dish before serving.

1 For the chicken and potatoes Adjust oven racks to upper-middle and lowest positions and heat oven to 450 degrees. Combine baharat and 1 teaspoon salt in bowl; set aside.

2 Use sharp knife to cut away any pockets of fat and any skin that extends beyond meat of chicken thighs and reserve trimmings. Pat chicken dry with paper towels, then sprinkle 2 teaspoons spice mixture over flesh side of thighs. Using tip of paring knife, poke skin of each thigh 8 to 10 times. Rub remaining spice mixture over skin.

3 Scatter reserved trimmings over surface of rimmed baking sheet. Roast on lower rack until trimmings are mostly crisped and fat is rendered, 8 to 10 minutes. Discard crisped trimmings, leaving fat behind.

4 Add potatoes and remaining ¾ teaspoon salt to fat on sheet and stir to coat. Arrange potatoes cut side down, in even layer over sheet, then nestle chicken skin side down between potatoes. Roast on lower rack until undersides of potatoes are starting to brown around edges, about 20 minutes. Flip potatoes cut side up, then arrange around perimeter of sheet, moving thighs, skin side up, to center of sheet. Roast on upper rack until chicken is browned and crisp and potatoes are golden, about 7 minutes. Brush chicken skin with pomegranate molasses, then return to oven and roast until skin is glossy and largest thigh registers at least 185 degrees, 1 to 3 minutes more. Transfer chicken and potatoes to platter.

5 For the salad Whisk oil, lemon juice, and salt together in medium bowl. Add fennel; parsley; dill; mint; olives; dates; shallot; and orange, if using, and gently toss to combine. Scatter salad around chicken and potatoes with salad, drizzling with yogurt and Coriander and Aleppo Pepper-Spiced Oil, if using.

Coriander and Aleppo Pepper-Spiced Oil

Makes ¼ cup
Total Time 5 minutes

- ¼ cup extra-virgin olive oil
- 1 tablespoon ground dried Aleppo pepper
- 2 teaspoons coriander seeds
- ⅛ teaspoon table salt

Microwave all ingredients until bubbly and fragrant, 1 to 2 minutes. (Oil can be stored in airtight container at room temperature for up to 1 week.)

Peruvian Chicken with Cauliflower and Sweet Potatoes

Serves 4 | **Total Time** 1½ hours, plus 1 hour marinating

- 6 tablespoons extra-virgin olive oil, divided
- ¼ cup fresh mint leaves
- 6 garlic cloves, peeled
- 3½ teaspoons pepper, divided
- 1 tablespoon ground cumin
- 1 tablespoon sugar
- 2 teaspoons grated lime zest plus ¼ cup juice (2 limes)
- 2 teaspoons table salt, divided
- 2 teaspoons smoked paprika
- 2 teaspoons dried oregano
- ½ habanero chile, stemmed and seeded
- 4 (10-ounce) chicken leg quarters, trimmed
- 1 small head cauliflower (1½ pounds), cored and cut into 1½-inch florets
- 1 pound sweet potatoes, peeled and cut into 1-inch pieces
- 1 small red onion, halved and sliced through root end into ½-inch-thick wedges
- 3 cups (3 ounces) baby arugula

Why This Recipe Works Peruvian chicken, pollo a la brasa, is one of the world's most revered chicken preparations for good reason—it's succulent, charred, and flavored with an incredible marinade. Without a rotisserie, we make an inspired recipe—along with sides—on the sheet pan by nailing a spicy (both hot and warm), herby, citrusy marinade. For the sides, roasted sweet potatoes fit the dish's Peruvian profile nicely. Roasted red onion wedges turn mellow and sweet to complement the potatoes, and roasted cauliflower adds deep, nutty complexity. Giving all the vegetables a head start in the oven means they can brown on the uncrowded sheet pan and then roast to perfect tenderness with the chicken. You can substitute 1 tablespoon of minced serrano chile for the habanero, if desired. Wear gloves when handling the chile.

1 Process 3 tablespoons oil, mint, garlic, 1 tablespoon pepper, cumin, sugar, lime zest and juice, 1½ teaspoons salt, paprika, oregano, and habanero in blender until smooth, 10 to 20 seconds. Transfer marinade to 1-gallon zipper-lock bag. Add chicken, seal bag, and turn to coat chicken with marinade. Refrigerate for at least 1 hour or up to 12 hours.

2 Adjust oven rack to middle position and heat oven to 425 degrees. Toss cauliflower, potatoes, onion, remaining 3 tablespoons oil, remaining ½ teaspoon pepper, and remaining ½ teaspoon salt together on rimmed baking sheet and spread into even layer. Bake until top edges of cauliflower and potatoes are lightly browned, about 15 minutes.

3 Remove sheet from oven. Using spatula, push vegetables to half of sheet (they will no longer be in single layer). Place chicken, skin side up, on now-empty half of sheet. Roast until chicken registers 175 degrees and vegetables are tender, about 40 minutes, rotating sheet halfway through roasting.

4 Transfer chicken to carving board and let rest for 5 minutes. Toss arugula with roasted vegetables, then transfer to platter. Separate leg quarters into thighs and drumsticks, then transfer to platter with vegetable mixture. Serve.

Garlic-Sage Chicken Leg Quarters with Cauliflower and Shallots

Serves 4 | **Total Time** 1 hour

- 1 head cauliflower (2 pounds), cored and cut into 8 wedges through stem
- 6 shallots, peeled and halved
- ¼ cup extra-virgin olive oil, divided
- 2 tablespoons chopped fresh sage or 2 teaspoons dried, divided
- 1 teaspoon table salt, divided
- 1 teaspoon pepper, divided
- 4 (10-ounce) chicken leg quarters, trimmed
- 2 garlic cloves, minced
- 1 teaspoon grated lemon zest, plus lemon wedges for serving
- 8 ounces grape tomatoes
- 1 tablespoon chopped fresh parsley

Why This Recipe Works We think chicken leg quarters give you a great bang for your dinner buck: They're meaty and rich, feel elevated, and are really hard to screw up. Here, some smart cuts ensure that the chicken and cauliflower cook at the same rate on the sheet pan. We make slashes in the chicken leg quarters to hasten their rendering. And we slice the cauliflower into big wedges to make sure they don't overcook in the same time—and to ensure flat surfaces for lots of browning to boot. We arrange the cauliflower wedges down the center of the sheet pan and the chicken leg quarters in each corner where they get exposed to the most heat. When it's time to use the broiler, we array the cherry tomatoes on top of the cauliflower; the chicken is gorgeously burnished by the broiler and the tomatoes wilt into the vegetables. Sage and garlic are refined flavors that enhance the delicate ingredients. Some leg quarters are sold with the backbone attached; removing it before cooking makes the chicken easier to serve. If you substitute cherry tomatoes for grape tomatoes, halve them before adding them to the pan.

1 Adjust 1 oven rack to lower-middle position and second rack 6 inches from broiler element. Heat oven to 475 degrees. Gently toss cauliflower and shallots with 2 tablespoons oil, 1 tablespoon sage, ½ teaspoon salt, and ½ teaspoon pepper on rimmed baking sheet. Arrange cauliflower pieces cut side down in single layer in center of sheet.

2 Pat chicken dry with paper towels. Make 4 diagonal slashes through skin and meat of each leg quarter with sharp knife (each slash should reach bone). Sprinkle chicken with remaining ½ teaspoon salt and remaining ½ teaspoon pepper. Place each piece of chicken skin side up in 1 corner of sheet; rest chicken directly on sheet, not on vegetables.

3 Whisk garlic, lemon zest, remaining 2 tablespoons oil, and remaining 1 tablespoon sage together in bowl. Brush skin side of chicken with seasoned oil mixture. Transfer sheet to lower rack and roast until chicken registers 175 degrees, cauliflower is browned, and shallots are tender, 25 to 30 minutes, rotating sheet halfway through roasting.

4 Remove sheet from oven and heat broiler. Scatter tomatoes over vegetables. Place sheet on upper rack and broil until chicken skin is browned and crisp and tomatoes have begun to wilt, 3 to 5 minutes.

5 Remove sheet from oven and let rest for 5 minutes. Sprinkle with parsley and serve with lemon wedges.

Harissa Wings with Cucumber-Tomato Salad

Serves 4 to 6 | **Total Time** 1½ hours

Chicken Wings

- 2 pounds chicken wings, halved at joints, wingtips discarded
- ¼ cup Harissa, divided (page 24)
- ¾ teaspoon table salt
- ¼ teaspoon pepper
- 1½ tablespoons honey
- 1 teaspoon lime zest, plus lime wedges for serving
- 2 tablespoons finely chopped fresh cilantro
- 1 scallion, sliced thin

Cucumber-Tomato Salad

- 1 English cucumber, quartered lengthwise and sliced crosswise ¼ inch thick
- 2 ripe tomatoes, cored and cut into ¼-inch pieces
- ½ teaspoon table salt, for salting vegetables
- ½ cup pitted green olives, chopped coarse
- ¼ cup fresh mint leaves, shredded
- 1 tablespoon extra-virgin olive oil
- 2 tablespoons lemon juice
- ½ teaspoon pepper

Why This Recipe Works Sheet pan suppers automatically have an element of fun with their robust flavor pairings and attractive serving opportunities, but we turn the interest up even more by cooking supercrispy wings, souped up with harissa, on the sheet. We start by roasting the wings with salt and pepper and harissa paste to achieve a layer of deep flavor and lacquering. We combine more harissa with honey (for some balance and requisite sticky goodness) and lime zest and toss the roasted wings in the pan. A final sprinkling of cilantro and scallions provides welcome freshness and an allium bite. Another necessary addition: the cooling counterpoint. A cucumber-and-tomato salad with chopped green olives, fresh mint, lemon juice, and olive oil does the trick and rounds out the plate. We prefer to buy whole chicken wings and butcher them ourselves because they tend to be larger than wings that come presplit. If you can find only presplit wings, opt for larger ones, if possible. We prefer to make our own harissa for this recipe, but you can use store-bought. The salad is best eaten within 1 hour of being dressed.

1 For the chicken wings Adjust oven rack to middle position and heat oven to 425 degrees. Line rimmed baking sheet with aluminum foil and spray with vegetable oil spray. Toss wings with 1 tablespoon harissa, salt, and pepper on prepared sheet, then arrange in single layer, fatty side up, on sheet. Roast until well browned, about 1 hour, rotating sheet halfway through roasting.

2 For the cucumber-tomato salad Meanwhile, toss cucumber, tomatoes, and salt together in colander set over bowl. Let drain for 15 minutes, then discard liquid. Transfer cucumber-tomato mixture to bowl. Add olives, mint, oil, lemon juice, and pepper and toss to combine. Season with salt and pepper to taste.

3 Combine honey, lime zest, and remaining 3 tablespoons harissa in large bowl. Transfer wings to bowl with harissa mixture and toss to combine. Transfer to serving platter and sprinkle with cilantro and scallion. Serve with lime wedges and salad.

Chili-Rubbed Chicken with Schmaltzy Vinegar Potatoes

Serves 4 | **Total Time** 1½ hours

- 1 tablespoon chili powder
- 1 tablespoon packed brown sugar
- 1½ teaspoons table salt, divided
- 1 teaspoon pepper
- ¼ teaspoon cayenne pepper
- 2 tablespoons vegetable oil, divided
- 1 (3½- to 4-pound) whole chicken, giblets discarded
- 2 pounds small red potatoes, unpeeled, halved
- 3 scallions, green parts only, sliced thin
- 2 teaspoons cider vinegar

Why This Recipe Works Let's admit it, this recipe is an excuse to eat your fill of schmaltzy potatoes with a hit of vinegar, a cousin to the beloved chips served in Great Britain with malt vinegar. But there is no deep frying required. The open expanse of a rimmed baking sheet allows you to put a chicken in the middle and the small potatoes around the perimeter. This arrangement encourages the potatoes to soak up the savory fat and juices from the chicken as it roasts. We butterfly the chicken (cut out the backbone so it can lie flat), so it cooks evenly and weeknight-quick. This also exposes all of the chicken skin to the high heat so it can render in a short time. We give it a chili-based spice rub that includes brown sugar (which helps in browning) and a small kick of cayenne. We add the puckery vinegar to the potatoes just before serving, plus more fat from the sheet pan along with aromatic scallions to cut the richness. Use small red potatoes measuring 1 to 2 inches in diameter. Note that you can often find butterflied chickens at the supermarket.

1 Adjust oven rack to lower-middle position and heat oven to 450 degrees. Spray rimmed baking sheet with vegetable oil spray. Combine chili powder, sugar, 1 teaspoon salt, pepper, and cayenne together in bowl, then stir in 1 tablespoon oil. With chicken breast side down, use kitchen shears to cut through bones on either side of backbone; discard backbone. Trim away excess fat and skin around neck. Flip chicken over and press on breastbone to flatten.

2 Pat chicken dry with paper towels and, using your fingers, carefully loosen skin covering breast and legs. Rub 2 teaspoons spice mixture underneath skin, then rub remaining spice mixture all over chicken.

3 Place chicken skin side up in center of prepared sheet. Toss potatoes with remaining ½ teaspoon salt and remaining 1 tablespoon oil and arrange cut side up on sheet around chicken. Roast until chicken skin is deep golden brown and breast registers 160 degrees and thighs register 175 degrees, 45 minutes to 1 hour, rotating sheet halfway through roasting. (If chicken begins to get too dark, cover loosely with aluminum foil.) Transfer chicken to carving board and let rest for 15 minutes. Using slotted spoon, transfer potatoes to serving bowl; add 1 tablespoon fat from sheet and cover to keep warm.

4 Carve chicken. Add scallion greens and vinegar to potatoes and gently toss to coat, then season with salt and pepper to taste. Serve with chicken.

VARIATIONS

Herbes de Provence Roast Chicken with Fennel

Substitute 4 teaspoons herbes de provence for chili powder, sugar, and cayenne and reduce pepper to ¼ teaspoon pepper; substitute 3 fennel bulbs (halved, cored, and sliced ½ inch thick) for potatoes; parsley for scallions; and 1 teaspoon sherry vinegar for cider vinegar.

Ras el Hanout Roast Chicken with Carrots

Substitute 2 teaspoons ras el hanout for chili powder, sugar, pepper, and cayenne; 1½ pounds carrots (peeled, halved lengthwise, and cut into 2-inch lengths) for potatoes; cilantro for scallions; and 1 teaspoon lemon juice for cider vinegar.

Garlic Roasted Chicken with Sweet Potatoes and Green Beans

Serves 4 | **Total Time** 1½ hours

- ⅓ cup roasted garlic
- 6 tablespoons unsalted butter, softened
- 1 tablespoon minced fresh thyme
- 1¼ teaspoons table salt, divided
- 4 small sweet potatoes (8 ounces each), unpeeled, each lightly pricked with fork in 3 places
- 1 (3½- to 4-pound) whole chicken, giblets discarded
- ½ teaspoon pepper, divided
- 1 pound green beans, trimmed
- 1½ teaspoons grated lemon zest plus 1 tablespoon juice
- 1 teaspoon minced fresh parsley
- ¼ cup sliced almonds, toasted

Why This Recipe Works We've all done it—throw a few garlic cloves, some fresh herbs, and maybe a cut lemon into the cavity of a chicken and hope for the best. But if you want a roast chicken that is heady with the flavor and aroma of garlic strong enough to perfume your house, you need a strategy. We also wanted to push the limits with this recipe by roasting whole sweet potatoes and green beans to perfection using one sheet pan. First, we butterfly the chicken so it lies flat on our pan and gives us easy access to rub the garlicky paste under all the skin. We give the sweet potatoes a head start in the microwave so they and the chicken are done at the same time as they roast in the oven. To make the most of the luscious juices pooled on the sheet pan, we toss the green beans in them (yum) and put the pan back in the oven for schmaltzy, garlicky beans to serve alongside the chicken and potatoes. To get a jump start on this dinner, roast the garlic up to a week ahead. Alternatively, you can use store-bought roast garlic. Note that you can often find butterflied chickens at the supermarket.

1 Adjust oven rack to lower-middle position and heat oven to 425 degrees. Line rimmed baking sheet with aluminum foil. Using fork, mash roasted garlic, butter, thyme, and ¼ teaspoon salt in bowl until smooth, about 30 seconds; set aside.

2 Place potatoes on large plate and microwave until potatoes yield to gentle pressure and centers register 200 degrees, 6 to 9 minutes, flipping potatoes every 3 minutes. Using tongs, transfer potatoes to half of prepared sheet.

3 With chicken breast side down, use kitchen shears to cut through bones on either side of backbone; discard backbone. Trim away excess fat and skin around neck. Flip chicken over and press on breastbone to flatten. Pat chicken dry with paper towels and, using your fingers, carefully loosen skin covering breast and legs. Rub butter mixture under skin, then sprinkle exterior of chicken with ½ teaspoon salt and ¼ teaspoon pepper.

4 Transfer chicken to empty half of sheet with potatoes. Roast chicken and potatoes until breast registers 160 degrees and thighs register 175 degrees, 45 to 60 minutes, rotating sheet halfway through roasting. Transfer chicken and potatoes to carving board and let rest while preparing green beans.

5 Add green beans, remaining ½ teaspoon salt, and remaining ¼ teaspoon pepper to now-empty sheet and toss in rendered chicken juices on sheet. Spread green beans into even layer over sheet, then roast until tender, 12 to 15 minutes, stirring halfway through roasting.

6 Carve chicken. Slit each potato lengthwise. Using clean dish towel, hold ends and squeeze slightly to push flesh up and out. Sprinkle with lemon zest and parsley. Toss green beans with lemon juice and sprinkle with almonds. Serve chicken with potatoes and green beans.

Roasted Garlic

Makes ⅓ cup
Total Time 1¼ hours, plus 20 minutes cooling

- 2 large garlic heads
- 2 teaspoons extra-virgin olive oil
- ⅛ teaspoon table salt

1 Adjust oven rack to middle position and heat oven to 425 degrees. Cut ½ inch off top of each garlic head to expose most of tops of garlic cloves. Place garlic heads, cut side up, in center of large piece of aluminum foil. Drizzle each with oil, sprinkle with salt, and gather foil tightly around garlic to form packet.

2 Place packet directly on oven rack and roast garlic for 45 minutes. Carefully open just top of foil to expose garlic and continue to roast until garlic is soft and golden brown, about 20 minutes.

3 Remove garlic from oven and let cool for 20 minutes. When cool, squeeze garlic from skins into bowl. (Roasted garlic can be refrigerated in airtight container for up to 1 week.)

Roast Chicken with Warm Bread Salad

Serves 4 | **Total Time** 1 hour, plus 24 hours salting

- 1 (3½- to 4-pound) whole chicken, giblets discarded
- 3¾ teaspoons kosher salt, divided
- 2 teaspoons plus ¼ cup extra-virgin olive oil, divided
- ½ teaspoon pepper, divided
- 2 tablespoons champagne vinegar
- 1 teaspoon Dijon mustard
- 3 scallions, sliced thin
- 2 tablespoons dried currants
- 8 ounces country-style bread, cut into ¾- to 1-inch pieces (5 cups)
- ¼ cup chicken broth
- 5 ounces (5 cups) baby arugula

Why This Recipe Works Until you make this recipe, you may be at a loss to understand why it became a cult favorite. The ingredient list is short and ordinary, the method is easy, but it's a recipe that is more than the sum of its parts. It was originally the hallmark of Judy Rogers' Zuni Café in San Francisco, and now, decades later, it still is. The chicken skin is bronzed, its meat juicy and well seasoned. And the bread? It's an irresistible mix of crunchy, chewy, and moist pieces, all tossed with savory chicken drippings. First, we salt a butterflied chicken a day in advance to ensure it's juicy and evenly cooked. We toss bread cubes with the fat and fond from roasting the chicken, along with broth to keep them moist; then, we roast them until crisp and ready to mingle with a peppery arugula salad. Note that you can often find butterflied chickens at the supermarket. Do not trim any excess fat or skin from the chicken.

1 With chicken breast side down, use kitchen shears to cut through bones on either side of backbone; discard backbone. Flip chicken over and press on backbone to flatten. Pat chicken dry with paper towels and, using your fingers, carefully loosen skin covering breast and legs. Rub ½ teaspoon salt under skin of each breast, ½ teaspoon under skin of each leg, and 1 teaspoon salt into bird's cavity. Place chicken on large plate and refrigerate, uncovered, for 24 hours.

2 Adjust oven rack to middle position and heat oven to 450 degrees. Pat chicken dry with paper towels and place skin side up on rimmed baking sheet. Brush 2 teaspoons oil over chicken skin, then sprinkle with ¼ teaspoon salt and ¼ teaspoon pepper. Roast chicken until skin is deep golden brown and breast registers 160 degrees and thighs register 175 degrees, 45 minutes to 1 hour, rotating sheet halfway through roasting. (If chicken begins to get too dark, cover loosely with aluminum foil.)

3 While chicken roasts, whisk vinegar, mustard, ¼ teaspoon salt, and remaining ¼ teaspoon pepper together in large bowl. Slowly whisk in remaining ¼ cup oil. Stir in scallions and currants and set aside.

4 Transfer chicken to carving board and let rest for 15 minutes. Meanwhile, pour fat left in sheet into bowl; measure out 2 tablespoons fat, discarding remainder (if you have less than 2 tablespoons fat, add oil to measure 2 tablespoons). Scrape off any fond from sheet and add to reserved oil. Toss bread with broth and remaining ¼ teaspoon salt, squeezing to help bread absorb broth. Add oil and fond mixture and toss to coat bread. Add bread to now-empty sheet, spreading into even layer, and roast until bread pieces are golden and crisp but not hard, 9 to 11 minutes, stirring halfway through. Carve chicken and whisk any accumulated juices into vinaigrette. Add bread and arugula to bowl with vinaigrette and toss to coat. Serve.

Bulgur Bowls with Chicken Meatballs and Sumac Kale

Serves 4 to 6 | **Total Time** 50 minutes

- 2 tablespoons Harissa (page 24)
- 2¼ teaspoons table salt, divided
- 3½ cups boiling water
- 1¾ cups fine-grind bulgur
- 4 teaspoons ground sumac, divided, plus extra for sprinkling
- 1 pound ground chicken
- 3 tablespoons plain whole-milk yogurt
- 3 tablespoons minced fresh parsley
- 2 garlic cloves, minced
- 1½ teaspoons ground cumin
- ¾ teaspoon ground coriander
- 1 pound curly kale, stemmed, leaves torn into 1½- to 2-inch pieces
- 5 tablespoons extra-virgin olive oil, divided
- 1 red onion, halved and sliced thin
- ¼ cup chopped pitted dates
- 1 tablespoon lemon juice
- 1 recipe Tahini-Garlic Sauce (page 37)
- ⅓ cup pomegranate seeds
- Pomegranate molasses

Why This Recipe Works Tired of grain bowls with shredded chicken and a mishmash of the usual salad bar ingredients? Elevate your bowl game and make this one with a sheet pan as your ally. Here the ingredients are cleverly infused with spices native to the Middle East. The grain, bulgur, pulls double duty: After soaking it in a harissa-spiked brew and seasoning it with tart sumac, we use a portion as a binder for the meatballs and broil the rest alongside them on the sheet pan. We use the same pan to roast kale with red onion and dates and then dress them in lemon juice and more sumac. We bowl everything up and drizzle it with rich tahini sauce and tangy pomegranate molasses. Be sure to use ground chicken, not ground chicken breast (also labeled 99 percent fat-free). You can use homemade or store-bought harissa.

1 Adjust oven rack 6 inches from broiler element and heat oven to 400 degrees. Whisk harissa, 1 teaspoon salt, and boiling water together in large bowl. Stir in bulgur, cover, and let sit until grains are tender, about 15 minutes.

2 Drain bulgur (if you don't have any excess liquid you can skip draining), then toss with 2 teaspoons sumac in bowl. Combine ¾ cup bulgur-sumac mixture, ground chicken, yogurt, parsley, garlic, cumin, coriander, and ½ teaspoon salt in separate bowl. Using your wet hands, pinch off and roll into sixteen 1½-inch-wide meatballs, each about 2 tablespoons; transfer to large plate and set aside.

3 Spread kale over rimmed baking sheet, then drizzle with 2 tablespoons oil and sprinkle with ½ teaspoon salt. Vigorously squeeze and massage kale with your hands until leaves are uniformly darkened and slightly wilted, about 1 minute. Toss onion and dates with 1 tablespoon oil and remaining ¼ teaspoon salt in bowl, then scatter over top of kale on sheet. Roast until kale and onion are tender, about 10 minutes. Transfer to bowl, stir in lemon juice and remaining 2 teaspoons sumac, and cover to keep warm. Wipe sheet clean, then spray with vegetable oil spray. Heat broiler.

4 Transfer remaining bulgur-sumac mixture to half of now-empty sheet, spreading into even layer. Transfer reserved meatballs to second half of sheet, then brush top of bulgur with remaining 2 tablespoons oil. Broil until top layer of bulgur is lightly browned and crisp in spots and meatballs are cooked through and lightly browned, 7 to 12 minutes, rotating sheet halfway through broiling. Divide bulgur among serving bowls, then top with reserved kale mixture and meatballs. Drizzle with tahini-garlic sauce and sprinkle with pomegranate seeds. Serve, drizzling with pomegranate molasses and extra sumac.

How to Build the Sheet Pan

Roast the kale mixture on the sheet pan and then remove and keep warm. Spread the soaked bulgur mixture over one half of the sheet pan in an even layer. Place the meatballs on the second half of the sheet pan and broil.

Mini Maple-Dijon Glazed Turkey Meatloaves with Broccoli

Serves 4 | **Total Time** 45 minutes

- 1 shallot, chopped coarse
- ¼ cup panko bread crumbs
- ½ teaspoon table salt, divided
- ¼ teaspoon pepper
- 1 pound 93 percent lean ground turkey
- ¼ cup milk
- 2 tablespoons unsalted butter, melted and cooled
- 1 tablespoon Worcestershire sauce
- 2 tablespoons Dijon mustard
- 1 tablespoon maple syrup
- 1½ teaspoons packed dark brown sugar
- 1 pound broccoli florets, cut into 1½-inch pieces
- 2 tablespoons extra-virgin olive oil, divided
- ¼ teaspoon lemon zest plus 1 tablespoon lemon juice

Why This Recipe Works We love individual meatloaves—they have a higher ratio of crust and tangy glaze to meaty interior, which makes them as flavorful as they are cute. It also makes them speedy. Mixing the turkey with bread crumbs and milk keeps the meat mixture moist as it cooks at high heat. Placing the loaves on a wire rack set in a rimmed baking sheet ensures that they cook evenly from all sides. We glaze the meatloaves twice with the tangy maple-Dijon glaze, first after shaping and then again when the meatloaves are mostly cooked. The first coating dries out in the oven, forming a sticky base that the remaining glaze clings to and really boosts the flavor of the turkey. We use the empty space on either side of the mini meatloaves to roast broccoli florets, and we dress them with lemon just before serving. If using whole broccoli, trim the stems from the florets and then peel the stems and slice ½ inch thick.

1 Adjust oven rack to middle position and heat oven to 400 degrees. Set wire rack in rimmed baking sheet and spray rack with vegetable oil spray. Process shallot, panko, ¼ teaspoon salt, and pepper in food processor, until shallot is finely ground, about 20 seconds, scraping down sides of processor bowl as needed. Add turkey, milk, butter, and Worcestershire and pulse until just combined, 8 to 12 pulses. Transfer to bowl, cover, and refrigerate until ready to use. Stir mustard, maple syrup, and sugar together in second bowl.

2 Divide ground turkey mix into 4 equal portions and shape each portion into 4½ by 3-inch oval. Arrange meatloaves in row down center of prepared rack, leaving about 3 inches of space on both sides for broccoli. Brush half of mustard mixture over meatloaves. Toss broccoli, 1 tablespoon oil, and remaining ¼ teaspoon salt in bowl until evenly coated. Arrange broccoli on both sides of meatloaves. Reserve bowl.

3 Bake until meatloaves register 130 to 135 degrees, 14 to 16 minutes. Brush with remaining mustard mixture and continue to cook until meatloaves register 160 to 165 degrees, about 5 minutes longer. Let meatloaves rest for 5 minutes. Meanwhile, return broccoli to bowl and toss with remaining 1 tablespoon oil and lemon zest and juice. Season with salt and pepper to taste. Serve.

Green Goddess Gnocchi with Spring Vegetables and Chicken Sausage

Serves 4 | **Total Time** 45 minutes

- 3 ounces cream cheese, softened
- ¼ cup chopped fresh parsley
- ¼ cup extra-virgin olive oil, divided
- 3 tablespoons water
- 1 tablespoon lemon juice, plus lemon wedges for serving
- 2 teaspoons dried tarragon
- 1 teaspoon dried dill
- 1 anchovy fillet, rinsed
- ¼ teaspoon onion powder
- ¼ teaspoon table salt, divided
- ¼ teaspoon pepper
- 1 pound shelf-stable potato gnocchi
- 1 pound asparagus, trimmed
- 12 ounces cooked chicken-garlic sausages
- 4 ounces sugar snap peas, strings removed

Why This Recipe Works If you haven't tried making dinner using those vacuum-sealed packages of gnocchi that you've been walking by for years, you are really missing out. But how can you cook them so it doesn't feel like you are eating starch bombs? First, get out your sheet pan—since roasting gnocchi can transform it, giving it a nutty taste and fluffy texture. Here a fresh, lightly creamy green goddess–style sauce ups the ante on flavor. To make it a complete dinner, we add asparagus and fresh sugar snap peas, plus precooked chicken-garlic sausages (which come in lots of flavors). We roast the asparagus and sausage and add the peas at the last minute. Be sure to use shelf-stable (not refrigerated) gnocchi in this recipe. Separate any stuck-together gnocchi before tossing with the oil in step 2. You can use precooked chicken or pork sausage in this recipe. As the gnocchi sits, it will continue to absorb the sauce; be prepared to serve it immediately or toss with additional hot water, 1 tablespoon at a time, until it reaches the desired consistency.

1 Adjust 1 oven rack to middle position and second rack 4 inches from broiler element. Heat oven to 500 degrees. Process cream cheese, parsley, 2 tablespoons oil, water, lemon juice, tarragon, dill, anchovy, onion powder, ⅛ teaspoon salt, and pepper in blender until smooth, about 1 minute, scraping down side of blender jar as needed. Set aside until ready to serve.

2 Toss gnocchi with 1 tablespoon oil on rimmed baking sheet, then spread into single layer over sheet. Roast on lower rack until gnocchi are golden brown on bottom, about 10 minutes.

3 Remove sheet from oven and heat broiler. Condense gnocchi into rough 10 by 6-inch rectangle in center of sheet, flipping browned side up. Place asparagus on top of gnocchi in center of sheet, then drizzle with remaining 1 tablespoon oil and sprinkle with remaining ⅛ teaspoon salt. Arrange sausages around perimeter of sheet. Place sheet on upper rack and broil until asparagus is beginning to brown, about 4 minutes, rotating sheet halfway through broiling.

4 Remove sheet from oven and flip asparagus and sausages. Scatter snap peas in open space around perimeter of sheet and broil until sausages are browned and snap peas are beginning to brown, about 4 minutes, rotating sheet halfway through broiling.

5 Transfer sausages and asparagus to serving platter. Toss gnocchi and snap peas with reserved green goddess sauce, season with salt and pepper to taste. Serve immediately with lemon wedges.

CHAPTER THREE

Beef, Pork + Lamb

Baharat-Rubbed Steak Tips with Lemony Spinach and Pear Salad

Serves 4 | **Total Time** 40 minutes

- ¼ cup extra-virgin olive oil, divided
- 1 tablespoon Baharat (page 24)
- 2 teaspoons honey
- 1¼ teaspoons plus ⅛ teaspoon table salt, divided
- 2 pounds sirloin steak tips, trimmed and cut into 2-inch pieces
- 1 tablespoon minced shallot
- 1 teaspoon minced fresh thyme
- ½ teaspoon grated lemon zest plus 1½ tablespoons juice
- ⅛ teaspoon pepper, divided
- 6 ounces (6 cups) baby spinach
- 1 ripe but firm pear, halved, cored, and sliced thin
- 3 tablespoons toasted and chopped pistachios
- 2 ounces goat cheese, crumbled (½ cup)

Why This Recipe Works A steak tip dinner with flair in less than an hour? This recipe has you covered. And best of all, it isn't shy on flavor—and it's easy to make indoors, great char included. While you preheat your broiler you have time to make a baharat and honey-based paste for the steak tips and get your sheet pan and rack set up. It's the intense heat of the broiler that allows for the perfect "sear," and placing the steak tips on a rack brings them just close enough to the broiler while allowing the fat to drip through to the pan. A bright salad topped with fresh sliced pear, toasted pistachios, and creamy goat cheese elevates this easy meal to company status. The sweetness of the pear balances the richness of the beef, while the nuts and cheese add welcome savory notes. Sirloin steak tips, also called flap meat, are sold as whole steaks, cubes, and strips. To ensure uniform pieces, we like to purchase whole steak tips and cut them ourselves. You can use our recipe for baharat or use store-bought.

1 Adjust oven rack 8 inches from broiler element and heat broiler. Line rimmed baking sheet with aluminum foil, set wire rack on sheet, and spray rack with vegetable oil spray.

2 Whisk 2 tablespoons oil and baharat in medium bowl. Microwave, covered, until bubbling, 1 to 2 minutes. Whisk in honey and 1¼ teaspoons salt and let cool for 5 minutes. Pat steak tips dry with paper towels, then add to bowl with spice paste, tossing to coat. Transfer steak tips to prepared rack, spacing evenly apart, and broil until browned and meat registers 130 to 135 degrees (for medium), flipping once halfway through broiling, 7 to 10 minutes. (If steak tips vary in size, start checking smaller pieces after 6 minutes of broiling.) Let steak tips rest on rack for 5 minutes.

3 Whisk shallot, thyme, lemon zest and juice, pepper, remaining 2 tablespoons oil, and remaining ⅛ teaspoon salt together in large bowl. Add spinach and pear and toss to combine. Season with salt and pepper to taste. Sprinkle with pistachios and goat cheese. Serve salad with steak tips.

Hoisin and Five-Spice Beef and Vegetable Kebabs

Serves 4 | **Total Time** 50 minutes

- 16 (6-inch) wooden skewers, soaked in water for at least 15 minutes
- 6 tablespoons hoisin sauce, divided
- 1 tablespoon vegetable oil
- ¾ teaspoon table salt, divided
- 16 (2- to 3-inch-wide) shiitake mushrooms, stemmed
- 2 zucchini (8 ounces each), sliced into ½-inch-thick rounds
- 1½ teaspoons five-spice powder
- ¾ teaspoon garlic powder
- ½ teaspoon cornstarch
- 1½ pounds sirloin steak tips, trimmed and cut into 1-inch pieces
- 1 teaspoon sesame seeds, toasted

Why This Recipe Works Steak tips are a chameleon: They easily take on the flavors of any given spice rub, paste, or marinade they meet. And they're a great choice for kebabs given that they are supereasy to cut into chunks perfect for skewering. The combo of a sheet pan and the broiler allows you to mimic the intensity of the grill, though getting it to all work out requires a few adjustments. While smoke coming from a grill is expected outdoors, we did not want to smoke out our kitchens or set off the fire alarm. To that end, our glaze for the beef is thickened with cornstarch to help it cling and keep excess liquid from dripping off the skewers and onto the pan. It is important to resist the urge to put meat and vegetables on the same skewer. Sure, skewers with both look pretty, but meat and vegetables cook at different rates; keeping them on separate skewers puts you in control of doneness. We get the veggie skewers cooking first before adding the meat skewers. The beef and vegetables take on depth and complexity from hoisin sauce, which we use two ways, as a component for the glaze for the meat—mixed with five-spice powder and garlic powder—and on its own for the vegetables. We reserve some glaze to brush on the meat skewers halfway through cooking, creating a more distinct crust. For the veggie skewers, we use tender and mild zucchini and savory, rich shiitakes. Sirloin steak tips, also called flap meat, are sold as whole steaks, cubes, and strips. To ensure uniform pieces, we like to purchase whole steak tips and cut them ourselves. Look for shiitake mushrooms that are 2 to 3 inches wide. We had better luck using wooden skewers here: You will need sixteen 6-inch wooden skewers. If your skewers are longer than 6 inches, be sure to trim them down to prevent scorched tips. Serve with rice.

1 Adjust oven rack to 6 inches from broiler element and heat broiler. Line rimmed baking sheet with aluminum foil, set wire rack, on sheet and spray rack with vegetable oil spray. Whisk 2 tablespoons hoisin, oil, and ½ teaspoon salt in large bowl. Add mushrooms and zucchini and toss to coat.

2 Pass two 6-inch skewers, spaced ¼ inch apart, vertically through 1 zucchini round, then thread 1 mushroom on top. Repeat with remaining vegetables, packing tightly so that vegetables fit across four sets of 6-inch skewers and making sure to keep ¼ inch space between skewers; set skewers aside. (Each set of skewers should contain approximately 4 mushrooms and 4 zucchini slices.)

3 Whisk five-spice powder, garlic powder, and cornstarch together in now-empty bowl. Whisk in remaining ¼ cup hoisin and remaining ¼ teaspoon salt. Measure out 1½ tablespoons hoisin mixture and set aside in small bowl, then add beef to remaining hoisin mixture and toss to coat.

4 Pass two 6-inch skewers, spaced ¼ inch apart, vertically through 1 piece beef. Repeat with remaining beef, packing tightly so that beef fits across four sets of 6-inch skewers and making sure to keep ¼ inch space between skewers; set skewers aside. (Each set of skewers should contain approximately 8 pieces beef.) If beef pieces are thinner than 1 inch, fold in half onto skewers to create more even shape.

5 Space vegetable skewers evenly apart on prepared rack. Broil for 4 minutes. Flip vegetable skewers. Add beef skewers, rearranging vegetable and beef skewers as needed so they're evenly spaced.

6 Broil until meat is browned on first side, 3 to 4 minutes. Flip beef skewers, brush second side with reserved 1½ tablespoons hoisin mixture, and broil until second side is browned and meat registers 130 to 135 degrees (for medium) and vegetables are tender and browned, 4 to 5 minutes longer. Transfer skewers to serving platter and let rest, covered, for 5 minutes. (Continue to broil vegetable skewers while beef rests if more browning is desired.) Sprinkle skewers with sesame seeds. Serve.

Coffee and Chili-Rubbed Steaks with Sweet Potato Wedges and Scallions

Serves 4 | **Total Time** 1 hour

- 10 radishes, trimmed and sliced thin
- 1 tablespoon lime juice, plus lime wedges for serving
- 1 tablespoon table salt, divided
- 1½ pounds sweet potatoes, unpeeled, cut lengthwise into 1-inch-wide wedges
- 2 tablespoons extra-virgin olive oil, divided
- 2¼ teaspoons pepper, divided
- 16 scallions, trimmed
- 2 tablespoons packed dark brown sugar
- 1 tablespoon finely ground coffee
- 1 tablespoon chili powder
- 2 (1-pound) boneless strip or rib-eye steaks, 1½ to 1¾ inches thick, trimmed

Why This Recipe Works Normally a combo of spice-rubbed steaks, wedges of browned sweet potatoes, and charred scallions would require the juggling skills of a sous chef. Enter the sheet pan, your key to doing it all with ease. We simulate pan-searing by arranging the steaks on an already hot sheet so they cook quickly. This produces a satisfying sizzle and, with an extra boost from a spice rub, a flavorful crust on one side of the steaks. Jump-starting the sweet potatoes while heating the pan for the steaks allows everything to come out of the oven and onto the serving platter at the same time. The scallions should be left whole; trim off only the small roots.

1 Adjust oven rack to lower-middle position and heat oven to 450 degrees. Toss radishes with lime juice and ¼ teaspoon salt in bowl; cover and refrigerate until ready to serve.

2 Toss potatoes with 1½ tablespoons oil, 1 teaspoon pepper, and 1 teaspoon salt on rimmed baking sheet, then arrange skin side down on half of sheet. Roast until potatoes begin to soften, about 25 minutes.

3 Meanwhile, toss scallions with ¼ teaspoon salt, ¼ teaspoon pepper, and remaining ½ tablespoon oil in bowl. Combine sugar, coffee, chili powder, remaining 1½ teaspoons salt, and remaining 1 teaspoon pepper in small bowl. Pat steaks dry with paper towels and rub with spice mixture.

4 Lay scallions on top of potatoes on sheet. Place steaks on empty half of sheet. Roast until steaks register 120 to 125 degrees (for medium-rare) and potatoes are fully tender, 12 to 15 minutes, rotating sheet halfway through roasting.

5 Remove sheet from oven. Transfer steaks bottom side up to cutting board, tent with aluminum foil, and let rest for 5 minutes. Leave vegetables on sheet and tent with foil to keep warm. Slice steaks ¼ inch thick and serve with potatoes, quick-pickled radishes, and lime wedges.

How to Build the Sheet Pan

Toss the beans, shallots, and olive oil together on the prepared sheet pan and then spread them across the sheet in an even layer. Set the wire rack on top of the beans in the sheet. Place the steak on the wire rack and then roast.

Flank Steak with Roasted White Bean and Arugula Salad

Serves 4 | **Total Time** 1¼ hours

- 2 (15-ounce) cans navy beans, rinsed
- 2 shallots, halved and sliced thin
- 2 tablespoons extra-virgin olive oil, divided
- 1 (1-pound) flank steak, 1 inch thick, trimmed
- ¾ teaspoon table salt, divided
- ½ teaspoon pepper, divided
- 2 tablespoons oil-packed sun-dried tomatoes, chopped coarse, plus 3 tablespoons tomato packing oil
- ½ teaspoon grated lemon zest plus 3 tablespoons juice
- 1 teaspoon minced fresh rosemary
- 4 ounces (4 cups) baby arugula
- ¼ cup chopped fresh parsley

Why This Recipe Works We understand that just the thought of a flank steak going in the oven might make you seriously anxious. But here's how to do it: Roast it in a very low oven (on a wire rack set atop a sheet pan) until it is succulently tender but not yet fully cooked, and then blast it with the heat from the broiler, which finishes the cooking. White beans and shallots roast below the wire rack (where we station the flank steak) until their edges turn golden and crisp, with the skins of the beans gently splitting to reveal their creamy interior. Then we toss the roasted beans and shallots with peppery arugula, sweet and tangy sun-dried tomatoes, some fresh rosemary, and a zesty lemon vinaigrette (using some of the sun-dried tomato packing liquid) for a warm, hearty salad that complements the steak perfectly. The combination is rustic yet vibrant—a balance of earthy flavors with fresh, herbal notes. If you don't have enough tomato packing oil, you can substitute extra-virgin olive oil. If your steak is thinner than 1 inch, check for doneness early; transfer the steak to a cutting board to rest but continue to roast the beans for the full amount of time in step 2.

1 Adjust 1 oven rack to middle position and second rack 6 inches from broiler element. Heat oven to 225 degrees. Line rimmed baking sheet with aluminum foil and spray with vegetable oil spray. Toss beans, shallots, and 1 tablespoon olive oil together on prepared sheet, then spread across sheet in even layer. Set wire rack on top of beans in sheet.

2 Cut steak in half with grain, then halve each piece against grain to create 4 steaks. Pat steaks dry with paper towels and sprinkle with ¼ teaspoon salt and ¼ teaspoon pepper. Brush steaks with remaining 1 tablespoon olive oil and place on wire rack. Place sheet on lower rack and roast until steaks register 125 degrees, 35 to 40 minutes. Remove sheet from oven and heat broiler.

3 Return sheet to oven on upper rack and broil until steaks register 130 to 135 degrees (for medium), 5 to 7 minutes. Transfer steaks to cutting board, tent with aluminum foil, and let rest for 5 minutes. Set sheet with beans aside while steaks rest.

4 Whisk tomato packing oil, lemon zest and juice, rosemary, remaining ½ teaspoon salt, and remaining ¼ teaspoon pepper together in large bowl. Add beans, arugula, parsley, and tomatoes and toss to combine. Season with salt and pepper to taste. Slice steaks thin against grain and serve with salad.

Spice-Rubbed Flank Steak with Toasted Corn and Black Bean Salad

Serves 4 to 6 | **Total Time** 45 minutes

- 1 tablespoon ground cumin
- 1 tablespoon chili powder
- 1 tablespoon packed dark brown sugar
- 1½ teaspoons ground coriander
- 1 teaspoon table salt, divided
- ¾ teaspoon plus ⅛ teaspoon pepper, divided
- ¼ teaspoon ground cinnamon
- ⅛ teaspoon red pepper flakes
- 1 (2-pound) flank steak, trimmed
- 3 ears corn, kernels cut from cobs (2 cups)
- 5 tablespoons vegetable oil, divided
- 2 tablespoons lime juice
- 2 scallions, sliced thin
- 1–2 teaspoons minced canned chipotle chile in adobo sauce
- 2 teaspoons honey
- 1 (15-ounce) can black beans, rinsed
- 1 red bell pepper, stemmed, seeded, and chopped fine
- ¼ cup minced fresh cilantro

Why This Recipe Works When you put a sheet pan in the oven as it preheats (here to a whopping 475 degrees), it helps to create browning on meat. In this case, we're talking about a big beefy flank steak that can serve up to six people. And for a bit of pizzazz, we concocted a bold spice rub to create a flavorful crust and to give our dinner an unmistakeable Mexican flair. But we didn't stop there. Keeping to this theme, we created a nearly no-cook salad to serve with the steak: a mix of canned black beans, minced bell pepper, roasted corn, and cilantro plus a lime-forward vinaigrette. When the oven is preheated we remove the hot sheet pan, slick it with oil by tilting it side to side, and add the steak on one side and the corn kernels on the other. The minute they hit the pan they both start sizzling beautifully, a great sign that our dinner is headed in a good direction. The corn takes a bit longer, so we give it more time while the meat rests on a cutting board. We prefer to use fresh corn here; however, 2 cups of thawed frozen corn can be substituted. For a spicier salad, use the larger amount of chipotle.

1 Adjust oven rack to lower-middle position, place rimmed baking sheet on rack, and heat oven to 475 degrees. Combine cumin, chili powder, sugar, coriander, ¾ teaspoon salt, ¾ teaspoon pepper, cinnamon, and pepper flakes in bowl. Pat steak dry with paper towels, then rub with spice mixture. Toss corn with 1 tablespoon oil, remaining ¼ teaspoon salt, and remaining ⅛ teaspoon pepper.

2 Working quickly, pour 2 tablespoons oil over hot sheet, tilting to coat, then place steak on half of sheet and corn on other half, spreading corn into even layer. Roast until steak registers 130 to 135 degrees (for medium), about 20 minutes, stirring corn halfway through roasting.

3 Meanwhile, whisk remaining 2 tablespoons oil, lime juice, scallions, chipotle, and honey together in large bowl. Stir in beans, bell pepper, and cilantro; set aside.

4 Transfer steak to cutting board, tent with aluminum foil, and let rest while finishing corn. Spread corn into even layer over sheet then return to oven and roast until lightly browned, 5 to 10 minutes.

5 Stir roasted corn into bowl with black beans and season with salt and pepper to taste. Slice steak thin against grain and serve with corn-bean salad.

Herbed Roast Beef with Root Vegetables

Serves 8 to 10 | **Total Time** 2 hours, plus 1 hour salting

Herb Paste and Butter

- ¼ cup minced fresh parsley
- 1 tablespoon minced fresh thyme
- 1 small shallot, minced
- 1½ tablespoons extra-virgin olive oil
- 1½ tablespoons Dijon mustard
- 4 tablespoons unsalted butter, softened

Roast

- 1 (3½- to 4-pound) boneless top sirloin roast, fat trimmed to ¼ inch
- 1½ tablespoons plus ½ teaspoon kosher salt, divided
- 1 tablespoon plus ¼ teaspoon pepper, divided
- 2 pounds carrots, peeled and cut into 2-inch lengths
- 2 pounds red potatoes, unpeeled, cut into 1½-inch pieces
- 3 tablespoons plus 1 teaspoon extra-virgin olive oil
- 1 tablespoon minced fresh thyme or 1 teaspoon dried

Why This Recipe Works When most people think of a beef roast, they picture a grand prime rib or an elegant tenderloin—both undeniably delicious, both undeniably expensive. We take a different approach, opting for a more affordable roast (top sirloin roast) that boasts rich marbling, deep beefy flavor, and a beautifully tender bite, without an all-day commitment. This is a roast beef dinner you can serve on a Sunday, but without the fuss. The secret? A humble sheet pan, which acts as both cooking vessel and searing surface. We start by butterflying the roast, opening it up like a book, and slathering the inside with a fragrant herb-mustard paste before rolling it back up. This little trick infuses the meat with flavor from the inside out, ensuring that every slice is deeply seasoned. From there, the oven does the heavy lifting. A low, gentle roast ensures even cooking, while carrots and potatoes—presoftened in the microwave—nestle alongside, soaking up all the meaty, savory drippings. As the beef nears its doneness, we blast the heat for the final 10 to 15 minutes of roasting, encouraging a beautifully burnished crust while at the same time turning the vegetables crisp and caramelized. And for the final flourish? A luscious herbed butter, sliced into neat coins, which melt over the warm beef slices, echoing the fragrant paste tucked within. It's comfort, elegance, and pure satisfaction—all from a single sheet pan. Top sirloin roast is also labeled top butt roast, center-cut roast, spoon roast, shell roast, or shell sirloin roast; do not confuse it with a whole top sirloin butt roast or top loin roast. Look for an evenly shaped roast with a ¼-inch fat cap. If your carrots are very thick, slice them in half lengthwise first to ensure even cooking. This recipe requires refrigerating the salted beef for at least 1 hour or up to 24 hours before cooking (a longer time is preferable). The coarse texture of kosher salt makes it easier to sprinkle evenly over the entire surface of a large roast; if you don't have kosher salt, you can substitute table salt, but reduce the amount to 1 tablespoon plus ¼ teaspoon.

1 For the herb paste and butter Combine parsley, thyme, and shallot in bowl. Transfer half of herb mixture to second bowl and stir in oil and mustard; set aside. Add softened butter to remaining herb mixture and mash with fork until combined. Lay 18 by 11-inch sheet of plastic wrap or parchment on counter with long side parallel to counter edge. Transfer butter mixture to center and shape into approximate 5-inch log with long side parallel to counter edge. Fold plastic over log and roll up. Pinch plastic at ends of log and roll on counter to form tight cylinder. Tuck ends of plastic underneath and refrigerate until needed.

2 For the roast Position roast fat side up on cutting board. Insert knife one-third of way up from bottom of roast along 1 long side and cut horizontally, stopping ½ inch before edge. Open up roast. Keeping knife parallel to cutting board, continue to cut through thicker portion of roast about halfway up from bottom of roast, keeping knife level with first cut and stopping about ½ inch before edge. Open up this flap. If uneven, cover with plastic wrap and use meat pounder to even out.

3 Sprinkle roast evenly, inside and out, with 1½ tablespoons salt and 1 tablespoon pepper. Spread herb-mustard mixture over interior of roast, fold roast back together, and tie securely with kitchen twine at 1½-inch intervals. Refrigerate, uncovered, for at least 1 hour or up to 24 hours.

4 Meanwhile, adjust oven rack to lower-middle position, and heat oven to 250 degrees. Spray rimmed baking sheet with vegetable oil spray. Microwave carrots, potatoes, and 3 tablespoons water in covered bowl, stirring occasionally, until vegetables are nearly tender, 15 to 20 minutes. Drain well, then toss with 3 tablespoons oil, thyme, remaining ½ teaspoon salt, and remaining ¼ teaspoon pepper.

5 Pat roast dry with paper towels, rub with remaining 1 teaspoon oil, and place fat side up on prepared sheet. Spread vegetables around roast. Roast until beef registers 110 degrees, 1¼ to 1¾ hours.

6 Remove sheet from oven and increase oven temperature to 500 degrees. Continue to roast until beef registers 120 to 125 degrees (for medium-rare) or 130 to 135 degrees (for medium), 10 to 15 minutes.

7 Transfer beef to carving board and let rest for 15 to 20 minutes. Meanwhile, if necessary, continue to roast vegetables until well browned, 10 to 20 minutes. Slice chilled herbed butter into coins. Remove twine from roast, slice ¼ inch thick, and serve with vegetables and butter.

Coffee and Fennel-Rubbed Boneless Short Ribs with Celery Root Salad

Serves 4 | **Total Time** 1 hour 5 minutes

- 3 pounds celery root, peeled and cut into ¾-inch pieces
- 5 tablespoons extra-virgin olive oil, divided
- 1½ teaspoons table salt, divided
- ¾ teaspoon pepper, divided
- 1 tablespoon ground fennel
- 2 teaspoons ground coffee
- 2 teaspoons packed brown sugar
- 1 teaspoon garlic powder
- 4 (6- to 8-ounce) boneless short ribs, 1½ to 2 inches thick and 4 to 5 inches long, trimmed
- 1 cup pomegranate seeds
- 1 cup fresh parsley leaves
- 1 tablespoon lemon juice

Why This Recipe Works Short ribs and slow braising? That's old news! Boneless short ribs roast up beautifully on a sheet pan, emerging from the oven tender, juicy, and packed with deep, beefy flavor. To match their richness, we go bold with a fennel-coffee rub, creating an irresistible crust. But why stop there? On another sheet pan, we roast pieces of celery root; its natural sweetness and velvety texture make the perfect counterpoint to the savory meat. Both pans slide into a blazing 450-degree oven, with the ribs getting a quick flip for even cooking. And the finishing touch? A scattering of pomegranate seeds and fresh parsley transforms the roasted celery root into a vibrant, refreshing salad—an effortlessly luxurious meal, all thanks to the sheet pan. Do not substitute bone-in English-style short ribs. Because they are cooked gently and not seared, the short ribs will be rosy throughout.

1 Adjust oven racks to upper-middle and lower-middle positions and heat oven to 450 degrees. Toss celery root, 3 tablespoons oil, ¾ teaspoon salt, and ¼ teaspoon pepper together in bowl, then arrange in single layer on rimmed baking sheet. Roast on upper rack for 30 minutes, stirring halfway through and redistributing into even layer.

2 Meanwhile, combine fennel, coffee, sugar, garlic powder, remaining ¾ teaspoon salt, and remaining ½ teaspoon pepper in small bowl. Pat ribs dry with paper towels, rub evenly with 1 tablespoon oil, and sprinkle with spice mixture. Arrange ribs on second sheet.

3 Stir celery root and redistribute into even layer. Place ribs on lower rack and roast until meat registers 120 to 125 degrees (for medium-rare) or 130 to 135 degrees (for medium) and celery root is tender and lightly browned, 10 to 15 minutes, flipping ribs halfway through roasting. Transfer ribs to cutting board, tent with aluminum foil, and let rest while preparing salad.

4 Remove sheet pan with celery root from oven and add pomegranate seeds, parsley, lemon juice, and remaining 1 tablespoon oil and toss to coat. Season with salt and pepper to taste. Slice ribs thin against grain and arrange on sheet pan with salad. Serve.

Zucchini Noodles with Pesto Meatballs

Serves 4 | **Total Time** 40 minutes

- ¾ cup panko bread crumbs
- ¾ cup milk
- ½ cup basil pesto (page 25), divided
- 1 teaspoon table salt, divided
- ¼ teaspoon red pepper flakes
- 1 pound 85 percent lean ground beef
- 3 zucchini (8 ounces each), ends trimmed
- 2 teaspoons extra-virgin olive oil
- ¼ teaspoon pepper
- 4 ounces cherry tomatoes, halved
- ¼ cup grated Parmesan cheese

Why This Recipe Works This spin on spaghetti and meatballs isn't a gimmick to get more vegetables on your plate (although we love that upshot). Roasting spiralized zucchini noodles is a lovely way to cook them—they're not bland like they are when boiled, and their flavor becomes more concentrated than when they're sautéed. Rather than a traditional marinara, we use richly flavored pesto that pairs well with the fresh flavor of the zucchini. Then we top the dish with cherry tomatoes as a nod to classic spaghetti and meatballs. A panade of panko bread crumbs and milk helps keep the meatballs tender, and for even more herbal flavor we incorporate some pesto into the meatballs. We prefer to spiralize our own zucchini; you can substitute 1 pound of store-bought spiralized zucchini, though it tends to be drier and less flavorful. Avoid buying large zucchini, which have thicker skins and more seeds. You can use our pesto recipe or any fresh store-bought variety here.

1 Adjust oven rack to middle position and heat oven to 375 degrees. Using fork, mash panko and milk into paste in large bowl. Stir in 5 tablespoons pesto, ¾ teaspoon salt, and pepper flakes, then add ground beef and knead mixture with your hands until well combined. Pinch off and roll mixture into 1½-inch meatballs (you should have 12 meatballs); set aside.

2 Using spiralizer, cut zucchini into ⅛-inch-thick noodles, then cut noodles into 12-inch lengths. Toss zucchini noodles with oil, pepper, and remaining ¼ teaspoon salt on rimmed baking sheet then spread into even layer over sheet. Roast for 5 minutes, then push zucchini to sides of sheet and arrange meatballs in center. Return to oven and roast until zucchini is tender and meatballs are cooked through, 10 to 15 minutes.

3 Remove sheet from oven. Transfer zucchini to colander and shake to remove any excess liquid. Toss zucchini with remaining 3 tablespoons pesto in bowl, then divide among individual serving bowls. Top with meatballs, tomatoes, and Parmesan. Serve.

Glazed Meatloaf with Lemon-Herb Potatoes and Brussels Sprouts

Serves 4 | **Total Time** 1¼ hours

- 35 square saltines
- 2 ounces Parmesan cheese, grated (1 cup)
- 2 large eggs
- ¼ cup milk
- ¼ cup soy sauce
- 1½ tablespoons minced fresh thyme or 1½ teaspoons dried
- 1½ teaspoons granulated garlic
- ¼ teaspoon red pepper flakes
- ¾ teaspoon table salt, divided
- ½ teaspoon pepper, divided
- 2 pounds 85 percent lean ground beef
- ½ cup ketchup
- 1 pound small red potatoes, unpeeled, halved
- 1 pound brussels sprouts, trimmed and halved
- 3 tablespoons extra-virgin olive oil, divided
- 1 tablespoon chopped fresh parsley
- ½ teaspoon grated lemon zest

Why This Recipe Works Who doesn't love to cozy up to a savory meatloaf, its crust slathered with enough tangy ketchup that you get some in every single bite? For a totally hands-off sheet-pan meal, we start by choosing straightforward meatloaf ingredients that don't require precooking. A panade of crushed saltines and milk keeps the ground beef moist in the oven. Soy sauce and grated Parmesan cheese add savory depth while fresh thyme, granulated garlic, and red pepper flakes add pep. We roast hearty small red potatoes and brussels sprouts alongside the meatloaf; they get better the longer they cook, turning creamy inside and deeply browned and crisp on the bottom. To brighten up the vegetables' deep roasted flavor, we give them a quick toss in a lemon-parsley oil just before serving. There are about 35 saltines in one sleeve of crackers. Use small red potatoes measuring 1 to 2 inches in diameter; if your potatoes are larger, cut them into 1-inch pieces to ensure that they cook through properly. Use brussels sprouts no bigger than golf balls, as larger ones are often tough and woody.

1 Adjust oven rack to lower-middle position and heat oven to 400 degrees. Spray rimmed baking sheet with vegetable oil spray.

2 Transfer saltines to 1-gallon zipper-lock bag, seal bag, and crush fine with rolling pin. Combine Parmesan, eggs, milk, soy sauce, thyme, granulated garlic, pepper flakes, ¼ teaspoon salt, ¼ teaspoon pepper, and saltine crumbs in large bowl. Mix until all crumbs are moistened and mixture forms paste. Add beef and mix with your hands to thoroughly combine.

3 Transfer meatloaf mixture to center of prepared sheet. Using your we hands, shape into 9 by 5-inch rectangle; top should be flat and meatloaf should be an even 1½ inches thick. Brush top and sides of meatloaf with ketchup.

4 Toss potatoes, brussels sprouts, 2 tablespoons oil, remaining ½ teaspoon salt, and remaining ¼ teaspoon pepper together in bowl, then arrange vegetables cut side down on sheet around meatloaf. Bake until meatloaf registers 160 degrees and vegetables are tender and browned on bottoms, 40 to 45 minutes, rotating sheet halfway through baking.

5 Transfer meatloaf to cutting board; let rest for 10 minutes. Transfer vegetables to bowl and stir in parsley, lemon zest, and remaining 1 tablespoon oil. Slice meatloaf and serve with vegetables.

Beef Kofte with Cucumber Salad

Serves 4 | **Total Time** 45 minutes, plus 1 hour chilling

- ½ cup pine nuts
- 5 garlic cloves, peeled
- 2 teaspoons hot smoked paprika
- 1 teaspoon table salt
- 2 teaspoons ground cumin
- ½ teaspoon pepper
- ¼ teaspoon ground coriander
- ¼ teaspoon ground cloves
- ⅛ teaspoon ground nutmeg
- ⅛ teaspoon ground cinnamon
- 1½ pounds 80 percent lean ground beef
- ½ cup grated onion, drained briefly
- ⅓ cup minced fresh parsley
- ⅓ cup minced fresh mint
- 1½ teaspoons unflavored gelatin
- 8 (6-inch) wooden skewers, soaked in water for at least 15 minutes
- 1 recipe Cucumber Salad
- 1 recipe Yogurt-Garlic Sauce

Why This Recipe Works Can you re-create boldly flavored Middle Eastern kofte using a sheet pan? Absolutely. These spiced, herb-packed ground meat kebabs usually hit the grill, but a few smart tweaks make them just as delicious made indoors. First, kneading the meat gives the kofte that signature sausage-like spring, while a touch of gelatin helps it hold firm. Skewers? Short and wooden is the way to go. Metal ones let the meat spin, messing with the even cooking, and long wooden skewers just fill the kitchen with smoke. To keep things clean and smoke-free, we set the kofte on a wire rack and place a crumpled piece of foil underneath to catch drippings while keeping the high heat in check. And for a fresh, vibrant side, we toss together a bright salad of parsley leaves and crisp cucumber slices. Pomegranate molasses and a sprinkle of pomegranate seeds add a pop of tartness to the salad that cuts through the rich, savory kofte. The final flourish is a creamy tahini-garlic sauce that brings everything together with a silky, complex finish. You will need eight 6-inch wooden skewers for this recipe. If your skewers are longer than 6 inches, be sure to trim them down. Serve with rice pilaf or make sandwiches with warm pita bread, sliced red onion, and chopped fresh mint.

1 Crumple 20-inch length of aluminum foil into loose ball. Uncrumple foil and place in rimmed baking sheet. Place wire rack on top of foil. Process pine nuts, garlic, paprika, salt, cumin, pepper, coriander, cloves, nutmeg, and cinnamon in food processor until coarse paste forms, 30 to 45 seconds. Transfer mixture to large bowl. Add beef, onion, parsley, mint, and gelatin; knead with your hands until thoroughly combined and mixture feels slightly sticky, about 2 minutes.

2 Divide mixture into 8 equal portions and pack into tight balls. Roll, squeeze, and shape each portion into 5-inch-long cylinder about 1 inch in diameter. Using eight 6-inch wooden skewers, thread 1 cylinder onto each skewer, reshaping as needed. Transfer skewers to prepared sheet, cover with plastic wrap, and refrigerate for at least 1 hour or up to 24 hours.

3 Adjust oven rack to upper middle position and heat oven to 500 degrees. Roast kofte until meat registers 160 degrees and top of kofte is browned, 15 to 18 minutes. Transfer to platter and let rest for 5 minutes. Serve kofte with cucumber salad and yogurt-garlic sauce.

Cucumber Salad

Serves 4
Total Time 10 minutes

- 1 tablespoon pomegranate molasses
- 1 tablespoon red wine vinegar
- ¼ teaspoon table salt
- ⅛ teaspoon pepper
- 3 tablespoons extra-virgin olive oil
- 3 cups fresh parsley leaves
- 1 English cucumber, halved lengthwise and sliced thin crosswise
- 1 cup pomegranate seeds

Whisk pomegranate molasses, vinegar, salt, and pepper together in large bowl. Whisking constantly, slowly drizzle in oil until emulsified. Add parsley leaves, cucumber, and pomegranate seeds and toss to coat. Season with salt and pepper to taste.

Yogurt-Garlic Sauce

Makes about 1 cup
Total Time 5 minutes

- 1 cup plain whole-milk yogurt
- 2 tablespoons lemon juice
- 2 tablespoons tahini
- 1 garlic clove, minced
- ½ teaspoon table salt

Whisk all ingredients together in bowl. Refrigerate until serving. (Sauce can be refrigerated in airtight container for up to 2 days.)

Mustardy Apple Butter-Glazed Pork Chops with Broccoli Rabe

Serves 4 | **Total Time** 1 hour

- 3 tablespoons apple butter
- 2 tablespoons maple syrup
- 1 tablespoon Dijon mustard
- 1 teaspoon soy sauce
- ½ teaspoon cider vinegar
- 1¾ teaspoons kosher salt, divided
- 4 (6- to 8-ounce) boneless pork chops, ¾ to 1 inch thick, trimmed
- 1 pound broccoli rabe
- 3 tablespoons extra-virgin olive oil, divided
- 1 garlic clove, minced
- ¼ teaspoon red pepper flakes
- 2 teaspoons minced fresh parsley

Why This Recipe Works The best way to produce tender, juicy chops with a stay-put glaze is to take it slow, or in other words, roast them in a low-temperature oven, which gives the glaze an opportunity to become tacky and cling to the meat. For the glaze, the classic pairings for pork—apples, maple syrup, and mustard—fit the bill along with soy sauce and cider vinegar, which keep things from veering into too-sweet territory. In addition to the slow roasting, giving the chops two separate applications of glaze plus a run under the broiler achieves gorgeous burnished glaze and perfectly done chops. For the broccoli rabe, a short stint under the broiler renders it tender to the bite and gives it a bit of browning. We like the consistency that Musselman's Apple Butter gives the glaze; if you're using another brand, you may need to thin the glaze with up to 1 tablespoon of water.

1 Adjust oven rack to middle position and heat oven to 275 degrees. Line rimmed baking sheet with aluminum foil and set wire rack in sheet. Spray rack with vegetable oil spray. Stir apple butter, maple syrup, mustard, soy sauce, and vinegar together in small bowl.

2 Sprinkle 1 teaspoon salt evenly over both sides of chops. Place chops on prepared rack and brush 1 teaspoon glaze on top and sides of each chop. Roast until meat registers 135 to 137 degrees, 40 to 45 minutes.

3 Meanwhile, trim and discard bottom 1 inch of broccoli rabe stems. Wash broccoli rabe with cold water, then dry with clean dish towel. Cut tops (leaves and florets) from stems, then cut stems into 1-inch pieces (keep tops whole). Drizzle 1 tablespoon oil over second rimmed baking sheet, then arrange broccoli rabe in even layer over sheet. Combine remaining 2 tablespoons oil, garlic, pepper flakes, and remaining ¾ teaspoon salt in bowl, then drizzle evenly over broccoli rabe on sheet and toss to combine; set aside.

4 Remove sheet from oven and heat broiler. Brush 1 tablespoon glaze on top and sides of each chop. Return sheet to oven and broil until glaze is bubbly and slightly charred in spots, 3 to 6 minutes. Transfer chops to large plate and let rest for 5 minutes.

5 While chops rest, adjust oven rack 4 inches from broiler element. Broil reserved broccoli rabe until half of leaves are well browned, about 2½ minutes. Using tongs, toss to expose unbrowned leaves, then return sheet to oven and broil until most leaves are lightly charred and stems are crisp-tender, about 2½ minutes. Sprinkle chops with parsley and serve with broccoli rabe.

Parmesan-Crusted Pork Chops with Winter Squash

Serves 4 | **Total Time** 1 hour

- 2 cups panko bread crumbs
- 3 tablespoons extra-virgin olive oil, divided
- ¼ cup all-purpose flour
- 2 large eggs
- 3 tablespoons Dijon mustard
- 2 ounces Parmesan cheese, grated (1 cup)
- ¼ cup minced fresh parsley
- 1¼ teaspoons table salt, divided
- ¾ teaspoon pepper, divided
- 4 (6- to 8-ounce) boneless pork chops, ¾ to 1 inch thick, trimmed
- 1 large acorn squash (2 pounds), sliced crosswise into ½-inch-thick rings and seeded
- 1 tablespoon plus 1 cup sugar, divided
- 12 ounces (3 cups) fresh or thawed frozen cranberries
- ¼ cup water
- ¼ teaspoon five spice powder

Why This Recipe Works Nothing says fall like pork chops and winter squash. Here we up the ante, aiming for Parmesan-crusted pork chops with sweet and savory rings of winter squash, and do it all on a sheet pan—with plenty of support from the microwave, which helps us out in several places. To give the chops maximum crunch, we coat them in Parmesan-seasoned panko. Pretoasting the panko in the microwave is the key to a well-browned crust, and elevating the pork on a wire rack ensures that the crust stays crunchy as the chops roast. We slice acorn squash into rings for a lovely scalloped shape and give them a head start in the microwave so they finish roasting at the same time as the pork. A sweet-tart cranberry sauce, which cooks entirely in the microwave, makes this autumnal meal feel special.

1 Adjust oven rack to middle position and heat oven to 425 degrees. Toss panko with 2 tablespoons oil in shallow dish until evenly coated. Microwave panko, stirring every 30 seconds, until light golden brown, about 5 minutes; let cool slightly. Spread flour in second shallow dish. Whisk eggs and mustard together in third shallow dish. Stir Parmesan, parsley, ½ teaspoon salt, and ¼ teaspoon pepper into cooled panko mixture until well combined.

2 Line rimmed baking sheet with aluminum foil and set wire rack in sheet. Spray rack with vegetable oil spray. Pat pork dry with paper towels, cut 2 slits, about 2 inches apart, through fat on edges of each pork chop, and sprinkle with ¼ teaspoon salt and ¼ teaspoon pepper. Working with 1 chop at a time, dredge in flour, dip in egg mixture, then coat with toasted panko mixture, pressing gently to adhere. Lay breaded chops on 1 half of prepared rack, spaced at least ¼ inch apart.

3 Place squash on large plate, brush with remaining 1 tablespoon oil, and sprinkle with ¼ teaspoon salt and remaining ¼ teaspoon pepper. Microwave until squash begins to soften but still holds its shape, 8 to 10 minutes.

4 Place squash on other half of rack opposite pork, slightly overlapping if needed, and sprinkle with 1 tablespoon sugar. Bake pork chops and squash until chops register 145 degrees and squash is tender, 20 to 30 minutes. Remove sheet from oven and let rest for 5 minutes.

5 While chops bake, combine cranberries, water, five-spice powder, remaining ¼ teaspoon salt, and remaining 1 cup sugar in bowl and microwave, stirring occasionally, until cranberries are broken down and juicy, about 10 minutes. Mash cranberries coarse with fork. Serve pork chops and squash with cranberry sauce.

Roasted Pork Chops and Vegetables with Parsley Vinaigrette

Serves 4 | **Total Time** 1 hour

- 1 pound Yukon Gold potatoes, unpeeled, halved lengthwise, and cut crosswise into ½-inch-thick slices
- 1 pound carrots, peeled and cut into 3-inch lengths, thick ends quartered lengthwise
- 1 fennel bulb, stalks discarded, bulb halved, cored, and cut into ½-inch-thick wedges
- 10 garlic cloves, peeled
- 2 teaspoons minced fresh rosemary or ¾ teaspoon dried
- ⅓ cup extra-virgin olive oil, divided
- 2 teaspoons table salt, divided
- 1½ teaspoons pepper, divided
- 1 teaspoon paprika
- 1 teaspoon ground coriander
- 4 (12-ounce) bone-in pork rib or center-cut chops, 1 to 1½ inches thick, trimmed
- 4 teaspoons red wine vinegar
- 2 tablespoons minced fresh parsley
- 1 small shallot, minced
- ⅛ teaspoon sugar

Why This Recipe Works If you want to sit down and enjoy a glass of wine after a hard day rather than race around your kitchen getting dinner underway, this recipe is the lazy person's route to a hearty pork chop dinner. And it's not just any dinner, because the pork chops get a vibrant spice rub and we toss the vegetables with whole garlic cloves and rosemary, while a red wine–parsley vinaigrette pulls it all together and looks gorgeous, too. To our amazement, roasting pork chops on a sheet pan instead of pan-searing them turned out tender, juicy meat and provided extra space to cook vegetables at the same time. Since pork chops cook relatively quickly, we partially roast the vegetables—a rustic mix of thick-sliced Yukon Gold potatoes, carrot spears, and fennel wedges—to give them a head start. Once the vegetables turn soft and take on some color, we add the pork chops, seasoned with a rub of pepper, salt, paprika, and coriander, for a deeply flavored crust.

1 Adjust oven rack to upper-middle position and heat oven to 450 degrees. Toss potatoes, carrots, fennel, garlic, rosemary, 1 tablespoon oil, ¾ teaspoon salt, and ¼ teaspoon pepper together in bowl, then spread in single layer on rimmed baking sheet. Roast until beginning to soften, about 25 minutes.

2 Meanwhile, combine 1 teaspoon salt, 1 teaspoon pepper, paprika, and coriander in bowl. Using sharp knife, cut 2 slits, about 2 inches apart, through fat on edge of each pork chop. Pat chops dry with paper towels, rub with 1 teaspoon oil, then sprinkle with spice mixture.

3 Arrange pork chops on top of vegetables and continue to roast until pork registers 145 degrees and vegetables are tender, 10 to 15 minutes, rotating sheet halfway through roasting.

4 Remove sheet from oven and let pork chops rest for 5 minutes. Whisk vinegar, parsley, shallot, sugar, remaining oil, remaining ¼ teaspoon salt, and remaining ¼ teaspoon pepper together in bowl. Drizzle vinaigrette over pork and vegetables. Serve.

Lemony Roasted Radicchio, Fennel, and Root Vegetables with Sausage

Serves 4 | **Total Time** 55 minutes

- 2 fennel bulbs, stalks discarded, bulbs halved, cored, and sliced into ½-inch wedges
- 1 pound red potatoes, unpeeled, cut into ¾-inch pieces
- 1 head radicchio (10 ounces), halved, cored, and cut into 2-inch wedges
- 8 shallots, peeled and halved
- ¼ cup extra-virgin olive oil, divided
- 6 garlic cloves, peeled
- 1 teaspoon minced fresh rosemary or ¼ teaspoon dried
- 1 teaspoon sugar
- ¾ teaspoon table salt
- ¼ teaspoon pepper
- 1 pound sweet or hot Italian sausage
- ¼ cup chopped fresh basil
- ¼ cup minced fresh chives
- 3 tablespoons lemon juice
- 1 tablespoon water

Why This Recipe Works Just mention radicchio and you can count us in. Bittersweet and beautiful, this multicolored lettuce cousin claims the spotlight here in the midst of a medley of vegetables and hearty Italian sausage. This recipe features a whole head of radicchio cut into substantial wedges plus peppery fennel, creamy potatoes, and aromatic shallots—an intriguing balance of flavors and textures. For the seasoning, we toss the vegetables with oil, whole garlic cloves, rosemary, and bit of sugar (to encourage browning). We realized our goal of roasting everything on one sheet pan by figuring out the timing and placement on the pan for each element. We roast the fennel, potatoes, and shallots first to give them a head start; then, we move them to the sides of the pan and place the radicchio in the empty center and the sausage on top of the vegetables. Arranging the radicchio in the center of the baking sheet, with the other vegetables around the perimeter, keeps it from charring in the hot oven. Placing smoky, herby Italian sausages on top of the vegetables allows the meat's flavorful juices to drip down so that the vegetables take on a savory richness. Once all the vegetables are perfectly tender and caramelized, we drizzle the whole shebang with a bright, lemony dressing that we enhance with the roasted garlic from our sheet pan (after smashing it into a paste); the stint in the oven gives the garlic a bracing aroma and sweetness, and for our dressing, a delicious complexity. When coring the radicchio, leave just enough core to hold each wedge together.

1 Adjust oven rack to middle position and heat oven to 450 degrees. Toss fennel, potatoes, radicchio, shallots, 1 tablespoon oil, garlic, rosemary, sugar, salt, and pepper together in bowl. Spray rimmed baking sheet with vegetable oil spray.

2 Spread vegetables, excluding radicchio, into single layer on prepared sheet. Roast for 10 minutes. Push vegetables to sides of sheet and arrange radicchio wedges, cut side down, in center. Place sausages on top of vegetables around perimeter of sheet and roast for 10 minutes. Rotate sheet; flip sausages; and continue to roast until sausages register 160 degrees and vegetables are tender and golden brown, 10 to 15 minutes longer.

3 Transfer sausages to cutting board and cut into 1-inch pieces; return to sheet. Transfer garlic cloves to cutting board and smash into paste using flat side of chef's knife. Whisk basil, chives, lemon juice, water, garlic paste, and remaining 3 tablespoons oil in bowl until combined. Drizzle half of dressing all over vegetables and sausages on sheet. Serve, seasoning with salt and pepper to taste, and passing remaining dressing separately.

Italian Sausage with Peppers, Onions, Tomatoes, and Polenta

Serves 4 | **Total Time** 1 hour

- ¼ cup extra-virgin olive oil, divided
- 12 ounces grape or cherry tomatoes
- 1 onion, halved and sliced thin
- 1 red bell pepper, stemmed, seeded, and cut into ¼-inch-wide strips
- 1 garlic clove, minced
- 1 teaspoon minced fresh rosemary
- ½ teaspoon table salt
- ¼ teaspoon pepper
- 1 pound sweet or hot Italian sausage
- 1 (18-ounce) tube cooked polenta, sliced in half lengthwise
- 1 ounce Parmesan cheese, grated (½ cup)
- 2 tablespoons sliced fresh basil

Why This Recipe Works We highly recommend making this dinner on a cold winter evening. It's pure comfort food, can be made quickly, and is almost entirely hands-off, thanks to the convenient polenta every grocery store sells in a tube. To streamline this classic combo and avoid multiple bubbling pots, we cook everything together on a sheet pan. A hot pan means that not only can we brown our sausages nicely but we can also give our onions and peppers the slightly charred edge that we love. To get our vegetables saucy quickly, we use grape tomatoes, which break down easily, giving the onions and peppers a bright, acidic finish to complement the sausages. For the log of polenta, we simply slice it in half horizontally so it warms all the way through. Since it doesn't brown up much by the time everything else is cooked, we flip it over, sprinkle it with some Parmesan, and broil the whole sheet to achieve good browning, not only on the polenta but on the sausages, onions, and peppers too, and then we sprinkle on fresh basil—a satisfying finish to our easy dinner.

1 Adjust oven rack to upper-middle position and heat oven to 450 degrees. Brush rimmed baking sheet with 1 tablespoon oil. Toss tomatoes, onion, bell pepper, garlic, rosemary, salt, pepper, and remaining 3 tablespoons oil together in bowl. Scatter tomato mixture evenly over half of prepared sheet. Place sausages and polenta, cut side down, on empty half of sheet.

2 Roast until sausages are browned and reach 160 degrees, 20 to 30 minutes, flipping halfway through roasting. Remove sheet from oven and heat broiler.

3 Turn polenta over and sprinkle cut side with Parmesan. Broil polenta and sausages until Parmesan is bubbly and beginning to brown, 3 to 5 minutes. Remove sheet from oven, transfer polenta to cutting board, and slice crosswise 1 inch thick. Sprinkle basil over polenta and serve with sausages and tomato mixture.

Loukaniko and Lemony Potatoes with Feta-Dill Sauce

Serves 4 | **Total Time** 1 hour

- 1¾ pounds Yukon Gold potatoes, peeled and cut lengthwise into ½- to ¾-inch-wide wedges
- 6 tablespoons extra-virgin olive oil, divided
- 4 garlic cloves, minced, divided
- 1 teaspoon grated lemon zest plus 6 tablespoons juice (2 lemons), divided, plus lemon wedges for serving
- ¾ teaspoon table salt, divided
- ¾ teaspoon pepper, divided
- 1 cup chicken broth
- 1½ pounds loukaniko (Greek pork sausage), halved lengthwise
- ¾ cup plain whole-milk Greek yogurt
- 2 ounces feta cheese, crumbled (½ cup)
- 2 tablespoons chopped fresh dill, divided
- 3 ounces (3 cups) baby arugula
- ½ English cucumber, halved lengthwise and sliced thin crosswise

Why This Recipe Works If you want to make something adventurous but easy, look no further than this Greek spin on meat and potatoes, elevated by a creamy yogurt-feta dill sauce. What could be more appealing than lemony roasted potatoes, a tzatziki-style sauce, and loukaniko (a traditional Greek pork sausage scented with orange and red wine), all served over a bed of fresh arugula and cucumber? And we learned that yes, you can actually braise using a sheet pan, which we do here with the potato wedges. They need a head start on the sausage, so we put them on the sheet pan first along with a combination of broth, lemon juice, and garlic and cover the pan with foil to cook. Once the potatoes are fully cooked, we remove the foil, add the loukaniko to the sheet, and roast the potatoes and sausages until the potatoes are lightly toasted and the sausages tender. The yogurt sauce, enriched with feta and dill, is a perfect foil for the meal's rich, earthy flavors. Loukaniko is available at specialty Greek markets and online (it may be spelled "locanico" or "loucanico"). If you can't find it, kielbasa, linguiça, and andouille are all good substitutes; if the sausages are longer than 6 inches, cut them crosswise into smaller lengths.

1 Adjust oven rack to middle position and heat oven to 450 degrees. Toss potatoes with ¼ cup oil, two-thirds garlic, lemon zest, ½ teaspoon salt, and ½ teaspoon pepper and arrange in even layer on rimmed baking sheet. Pour broth and ¼ cup lemon juice over potatoes; cover sheet tightly with aluminum foil; and roast until paring knife inserted into potatoes meets little resistance, 20 to 25 minutes.

2 Remove sheet from oven and discard foil. Arrange loukaniko cut sides down on clear areas of sheet (do not remove potatoes from sheet). Return sheet to oven and roast until potatoes are beginning to brown and loukaniko are browned on bottoms, 20 to 25 minutes.

3 Meanwhile whisk yogurt, feta, 1 tablespoon dill, remaining 2 tablespoons oil, remaining garlic, remaining 2 tablespoons lemon juice, remaining ¼ teaspoon salt, and remaining ¼ teaspoon pepper together in bowl until smooth; set aside. Toss arugula and cucumber together in deep serving platter.

4 Using spatula, carefully transfer potatoes and loukaniko to platter with arugula mixture. Drizzle any pan juices over top and sprinkle with remaining 1 tablespoon dill. Serve with feta-dill sauce and lemon wedges.

How to Build the Sheet Pan

Toss the potatoes, oil, garlic, lemon zest, salt, and pepper together on the sheet. Spread into an even layer then add broth and lemon juice. Cover the sheet with aluminum foil and roast until tender. Uncover the sheet, add the loukaniko, and roast until browned.

Bratwurst Sandwiches with Potato and Kale Salad

Serves 4 | **Total Time** 45 minutes

- 1 pound small red potatoes, unpeeled, halved
- 7 tablespoons extra-virgin olive oil, divided
- 1 teaspoon table salt, divided
- ½ teaspoon pepper, divided
- 2 red onions, halved and sliced ¼ inch thick
- 1½ pounds bratwurst
- ¼ cup whole-grain mustard, divided
- 2 tablespoons red wine vinegar
- 4 (6-inch) Italian sub rolls, split lengthwise and toasted
- 5 ounces (5 cups) baby kale
- 4 radishes, trimmed and sliced thin

Why This Recipe Works We don't think bratwurst sandwiches should be reserved for game day. Why not elevate them a bit using a sheet pan and assemble a delicious meal while you're at it? We start by roasting brats, potatoes, and onions all together on a preheated sheet pan. By selecting small red potatoes and cutting them in half, we can roast everything for the same amount of time, keeping the process supersimple. While the sausage and vegetables are cooking, we quickly whisk together a flavorful vinaigrette of whole-grain mustard, red wine vinegar, and olive oil. We spread the same whole-grain mustard into the toasty buns to match our vinaigrette's flavor profile. As soon as they hit the salad bowl, the warm potatoes absorb plenty of our zippy vinaigrette and, with the addition of baby kale and sliced radishes, provide the perfect side to serve with our brats. Use small red potatoes measuring 1 to 2 inches in diameter; if your potatoes are larger, cut them into 1-inch pieces to ensure that they cook through properly.

1 Adjust oven rack to middle position, place rimmed baking sheet on rack, and heat oven to 425 degrees. Toss potatoes with 2 tablespoons oil, ½ teaspoon salt, and ¼ teaspoon pepper in bowl. In separate bowl, toss onions with 1 tablespoon oil.

2 Place bratwurst on half of hot sheet and spread potatoes cut side down on other half. Scatter onions around bratwurst on sheet. Roast until sausages register at least 160 degrees and potatoes are tender, 25 to 30 minutes, flipping bratwurst halfway through roasting.

3 Meanwhile, whisk 2 tablespoons mustard, vinegar, remaining ¼ cup oil, remaining ½ teaspoon salt, and remaining ¼ teaspoon pepper together in large bowl; set aside.

4 Remove sheet from oven. Add potatoes to bowl with dressing and toss to coat. Transfer bratwurst to cutting board and cut into 2-inch lengths. Spread remaining 2 tablespoons mustard evenly into rolls, then top with bratwurst and onions. Add kale and radishes to potatoes and toss gently to combine. Serve immediately with sandwiches.

Hoisin Pork Tenderloins with Green Beans, Potatoes, and Chive Butter

Serves 4 | **Total Time** 1 hour

- 4 tablespoons unsalted butter, softened
- 2 tablespoons minced fresh chives
- 1 garlic clove, minced to paste
- 1 teaspoon pepper, divided
- ¾ teaspoon table salt, divided
- 1 pound green beans, trimmed
- 3 tablespoons extra-virgin olive oil, divided
- 1½ pounds fingerling potatoes, unpeeled, halved lengthwise
- 2 (12- to 16-ounce) pork tenderloins, trimmed
- ¼ cup hoisin sauce

Why This Recipe Works We often pan-roast pork tenderloins by browning them in a skillet and transferring the skillet to the oven. But if you roast them the entire time, you have an opportunity to cook a side dish right in the same pan. Since you don't get any browning on the pork this way, you need a spice rub or a glaze to add both appealing color and flavor to the lean and mild pork. Our solution? We brush the meat with dark, intensely flavored hoisin sauce. The spice notes of garlic, star anise, and chiles in the hoisin meld with the pork as it cooks, and the sauce gives the vegetables a subtle, almost unidentifiable sweetness. We pair the lean tenderloin with equally quick-cooking fingerling potatoes and green beans. To give the green beans a chance to steam, we lay the pork over them (which also insulates the pork and slows down the cooking) along the somewhat cooler center of the baking sheet, placing the potatoes closer to the pan's edge. An easy garlic-chive butter melts over the resting pork and adds richness to the vegetables. Buy tenderloins that are of equal size and weight so they cook at the same rate. A rasp-style grater makes quick work of turning the garlic into a paste.

1 Adjust oven rack to lower-middle position and heat oven to 450 degrees. Combine butter, chives, garlic, ¼ teaspoon pepper, and ¼ teaspoon salt in bowl; set aside for serving.

2 Toss green beans with 1 tablespoon oil, ¼ teaspoon pepper, and ¼ teaspoon salt in separate bowl. Arrange green beans crosswise down center of rimmed baking sheet, leaving room on both sides for potatoes. Toss potatoes with ¼ teaspoon pepper, remaining ¼ teaspoon salt, and remaining 2 tablespoons oil in now-empty bowl, then arrange cut side down on either side of green beans on sheet.

3 Pat pork dry with paper towels, sprinkle with remaining ¼ teaspoon pepper, then brush thoroughly with hoisin sauce. Lay tenderloins lengthwise on top of green beans, leaving some space between tenderloins. Roast until pork registers 135 degrees, 20 to 25 minutes.

4 Remove sheet from oven and transfer tenderloins to cutting board. Dot each tenderloin with 1 tablespoon chive butter, tent with aluminum foil, and let rest while vegetables finish cooking. Gently stir vegetables on sheet to combine; redistribute into even layer over sheet; and continue to roast until tender and golden, 5 to 10 minutes longer.

5 Remove sheet from oven, add remaining 2 tablespoons chive butter to vegetables, and toss to coat. Slice tenderloins ¾ inch thick and serve with vegetables.

Pork Tenderloins and Panzanella Salad

Serves 4 | **Total Time** 1 hour

- 3 tablespoons balsamic vinegar, divided
- 2 tablespoons whole-grain mustard, divided
- 1 tablespoon packed brown sugar
- 1 teaspoon cornstarch
- 2 (12- to 16-ounce) pork tenderloins, trimmed
- 1 teaspoon plus ⅛ teaspoon table salt, divided
- ¾ teaspoon plus ⅛ teaspoon pepper, divided
- 1 (12-inch) baguette, cut into 1-inch pieces
- 1 red onion, cut into 1-inch pieces
- 1 red bell pepper, stemmed, seeded, and cut into ½-inch-wide strips
- 1 yellow summer squash, quartered lengthwise and cut into 1-inch pieces
- ½ cup extra-virgin olive oil, divided
- 1 tablespoon capers, rinsed, plus 1 tablespoon brine
- 1 garlic clove, minced
- ½ English cucumber, quartered lengthwise and sliced crosswise ½ inch thick
- 6 ounces cherry tomatoes, halved
- ½ cup coarsely chopped fresh basil, divided

Why This Recipe Works Just imagine a platter with two perfectly roasted and glazed pork tenderloins surrounded by a striking panzanella salad with a colorful mix of fresh and roasted vegetables and a dressing that stands up to the bread (and the pork). First, we place two pork tenderloins on a rimmed baking sheet and brush them with a mixture of balsamic vinegar, brown sugar, and whole-grain mustard that complements the sweet nuances of the pork. We add a bit of cornstarch to the mixture to ensure that the vinegar mix adheres to the pork. The sheet pan provides ample space for us to surround the tenderloins with pieces of summer squash, red onion, bell pepper, and baguette and roast everything together until the pork is rosy in the center, the vegetables are tender, and the bread toasted and crunchy. While the pork rests, we toss the bread and roasted vegetables with fresh cucumber, cherry tomatoes, basil, and a bright balsamic vinaigrette with whole-grain mustard, garlic, capers, and caper brine. To ensure that the tenderloins don't curl during cooking, be sure to remove the silverskin from the meat. Sourdough bread can be used in place of the baguette.

1 Adjust oven rack to middle position and heat oven to 450 degrees. Whisk 1 tablespoon vinegar, 1 tablespoon mustard, sugar, and cornstarch in bowl until no lumps of cornstarch remain.

2 Pat tenderloins dry with paper towels and sprinkle with ½ teaspoon salt and ¼ teaspoon pepper. Place tenderloins in center of rimmed baking sheet (it's OK if they are touching) and brush tops and sides with all of vinegar mixture.

3 Toss baguette, onion, bell pepper, squash, ¼ cup oil, ½ teaspoon salt, and ½ teaspoon pepper in large bowl until baguette and vegetables are well coated with oil. Distribute vegetable mixture around tenderloins on sheet. Roast until pork registers 135 degrees, 20 to 25 minutes, stirring vegetable mixture halfway through roasting.

4 Whisk capers and brine, garlic, remaining 2 tablespoons vinegar, remaining 1 tablespoon mustard, remaining ⅛ teaspoon salt, remaining ⅛ teaspoon pepper, and remaining ¼ cup oil together in now-empty bowl.

5 Transfer tenderloins to cutting board, tent with aluminum foil, and let rest for 10 minutes. Meanwhile, add cucumber, tomatoes, 6 tablespoons basil, and vegetable mixture to bowl with caper dressing and toss to combine; transfer to serving platter. Slice tenderloins ½ inch thick and arrange over salad. Sprinkle with remaining 2 tablespoons basil and serve.

Weeknight Porchetta with Lemony Broccolini

Serves 4 | **Total Time** 50 minutes

- 1 teaspoon fennel seeds
- 1 teaspoon table salt, divided
- 1 teaspoon garlic powder, divided
- ¾ teaspoon pepper, divided
- ½ teaspoon minced fresh rosemary
- ½ teaspoon minced fresh thyme
- 2 (12- to 16-ounce) pork tenderloins, trimmed
- 8 thin slices prosciutto
- 1 pound broccolini, trimmed
- 1 tablespoon extra-virgin olive oil
- 2 teaspoons grated lemon zest, plus lemon wedges for serving
- ⅛ teaspoon red pepper flakes

Why This Recipe Works Craving the deep, aromatic flavors of porchetta? This weeknight-friendly recipe delivers all that slow-roasted goodness—no fuss, no mess. Two pork tenderloins get the full porchetta treatment: We rub them with fennel seeds, fresh herbs, and garlic powder before wrapping them snugly in prosciutto. Then we do all the cooking on a single sheet pan. The tenderloins land in the center, while broccolini, tossed with lemon, garlic powder, and red pepper flakes, nestles around it. As the oven works its magic, the prosciutto crisps into a crackly, golden shell, sealing in the tenderloins' juices. The broccolini softens and chars at the edges, soaking up the savory drippings for even more flavor. The sheet pan does all the heavy lifting here—roasting, crisping, caramelizing—delivering a meal that feels like a dinner-party centerpiece but comes together with weeknight ease.

1 Adjust oven rack to middle position and heat oven to 450 degrees. Spray rimmed baking sheet with vegetable oil spray. Combine fennel seeds, ¾ teaspoon salt, ½ teaspoon garlic powder, ½ teaspoon pepper, rosemary, and thyme in bowl. Pat pork dry with paper towels then sprinkle evenly with spice mixture. Wrap each tenderloin crosswise with 4 overlapping slices of prosciutto. Transfer pork to center of prepared sheet, prosciutto seam side down.

2 Cut broccolini stalks measuring more than ½ inch in diameter at base in half lengthwise. Cut stalks measuring ¼ to ½ inch in diameter at base in half lengthwise, starting below where florets begin and keeping florets intact. Leave stalks measuring less than ¼ inch in diameter at base whole. Toss broccolini with oil, lemon zest, red pepper flakes, remaining ¼ teaspoon salt, remaining ½ teaspoon garlic powder, and remaining ¼ teaspoon pepper together in bowl, then arrange broccolini around pork on sheet. Roast until pork registers 135 degrees, 20 to 25 minutes.

3 Transfer pork to cutting board, tent with aluminum foil, and let rest for 10 minutes. Slice tenderloins ½ inch thick and transfer to sheet pan with broccolini. Serve with lemon wedges.

Sweet Potato Vermicelli with Vegetables and Pork

Serves 4 to 6 | **Total Time** 1¼ hours

- 8 ounces dangmyeon
- 1 pound boneless pork butt roast, trimmed and sliced ¼ inch thick
- 3 tablespoons honey
- 3 tablespoons soy sauce
- 1–1½ tablespoons gochujang
- 2 teaspoons toasted sesame oil
- 6 ounces shiitake mushrooms, stemmed and sliced ¼ inch thick
- 2 carrots, peeled and cut into 2-inch-long matchsticks
- 1 red bell pepper, stemmed, seeded, and sliced thin
- 1 onion, halved and sliced thin
- 4 scallions, white parts cut into 2-inch pieces, green parts sliced thin
- 1 tablespoon vegetable oil
- ¼ teaspoon table salt
- ¼ teaspoon pepper
- 6 ounces (6 cups) baby spinach
- 1 tablespoon toasted sesame seeds

Why This Recipe Works Inspired by Korea's famous party dish, called japchae (meaning "mixed vegetables"), this recipe features springy transparent noodles. Tossed with a deeply umami sauce and a rainbow of vegetables, these noodles take center stage. This is classically a labor-intensive dish, but the sheet-pan version makes it easier while preserving all its elements, including the sauce, which is used multiple times. Instead of stir-frying the noodles, we spread them out over the pan on top of the vegetables and pork; we cover the pan with foil so the noodles become even more tender. Better yet, they soak up the flavorful juices from the pork, and take on a slight amber hue. Dangmyeon, Korean sweet potato starch noodles, are sometimes labeled as japchae noodles or sweet potato starch vermicelli. If you buy noodles longer than 8 inches, cut them down after soaking. Pork butt roast is often labeled Boston butt in the supermarket.

1 Adjust 1 oven rack to middle position and second rack 4 inches from broiler element. Heat broiler. Spray rimmed baking sheet with vegetable oil spray. Soak noodles in boiling water for 20 minutes. Drain well and set aside.

2 Meanwhile, pat pork dry with paper towels. Whisk honey, soy sauce, gochujang, and sesame oil together in medium bowl. Measure out 3 tablespoons honey mixture and transfer to separate medium bowl. Measure out 2 tablespoons honey mixture and set aside for serving. Add pork to remaining honey mixture and toss to coat.

3 Arrange pork in even layer over prepared sheet and broil until beginning to char in some spots, 3 to 5 minutes. Remove sheet from oven and heat oven to 425 degrees.

4 Toss mushrooms, carrots, bell pepper, onion, scallion whites, oil, salt, and pepper together in bowl. Scatter vegetables evenly over sheet, covering pork. Roast on lower rack until vegetables are tender and beginning to brown, 15 to 20 minutes.

5 Add drained noodles to bowl with reserved 3 tablespoons honey mixture and toss to coat. Remove sheet from oven, then pour noodles over vegetables, spreading into even layer. Scrape any sauce remaining in bowl over top, then sprinkle spinach over noodles. Cover sheet tightly with aluminum foil and cook on lower rack until noodles are tender and spinach is beginning to wilt, about 5 minutes.

6 Discard foil and, using tongs, toss noodles and vegetables gently to combine. Drizzle with reserved 2 tablespoons honey mixture and sprinkle with scallion greens and sesame seeds. Serve.

Lamb and Bulgur-Stuffed Eggplant

Serves 4 | **Total Time** 1½ hours

- 4 (10-ounce) Italian eggplants, halved lengthwise
- 2 tablespoons plus 1¼ teaspoons extra-virgin olive oil, divided
- 3 garlic cloves, peeled and lightly smashed
- 1 onion, peeled, halved, and sliced ½ inch thick
- ½ cup medium-grind bulgur, rinsed
- ⅓ cup water
- 1½ teaspoons Baharat (page 24)
- 1¾ teaspoons table salt, divided
- 8 ounces ground lamb
- 3 tablespoons pine nuts, toasted, divided
- ½ cup pomegranate seeds
- ¼ cup chopped fresh parsley
- Plain yogurt

Why This Recipe Works This simple lamb and bulgur stuffing pairs with creamy roasted eggplant for a delicious Moroccan-inspired meal. The key to rich, melt-in-your-mouth eggplant is roasting it cut side down on a preheated sheet pan. That direct contact jump-starts caramelization while keeping the flesh silky, not watery. Onions and garlic join the eggplant in the pan, picking up deep, roasted sweetness to build layers of flavor in the filling. That filling? It's a hearty mix of nutty bulgur and spiced ground lamb, bolstered by toasted pine nuts and warm, aromatic baharat. Instead of toasting the baharat on the stovetop, we bloom it in the microwave with a little oil to unlock its full depth. Breaking the lamb into small pieces ensures the perfect mix of crispy, browned bits and juicy, tender bites. And there is real magic in the toppings: A final flourish of pine nuts, sweet-tart pomegranate seeds, fresh parsley, and a drizzle of creamy yogurt takes this from simple to showstopping. You can sometimes find 10-ounce eggplants labeled "baby eggplant." When shopping, do not confuse bulgur with cracked wheat, which has a much longer cooking time and will not work in this recipe. We prefer our recipe for baharat but you can use store-bought.

1 Adjust oven racks to upper-middle and lowest positions, place parchment paper–lined rimmed baking sheet on lower rack, and heat oven to 400 degrees.

2 Score flesh of each eggplant half in 1-inch diamond pattern, about 1 inch deep. Brush scored sides of eggplants with 1 tablespoon oil. Drizzle garlic cloves with ¼ teaspoon oil and wrap in aluminum foil. Lay eggplants cut side down on hot sheet, followed by onion slices. Brush onion slices with 1 teaspoon oil. Roast until eggplant flesh is tender and onion is softened and slightly browned, 30 to 35 minutes, flipping onion slices halfway through. After 10 minutes roasting, add foil-wrapped garlic to sheet.

3 Transfer eggplants cut side down to paper towel–lined sheet and let drain for 5 minutes. Transfer onion and garlic to cutting board and let cool slightly. Chop onion fine and mash garlic into paste.

4 While eggplants roast, toss bulgur with water in bowl and let sit until grains are softened and liquid is fully absorbed, 20 to 40 minutes.

5 Combine baharat, 1 teaspoon salt, and remaining 1 tablespoon oil in large bowl and microwave until fragrant and bubbling, about 1 minute. Break ground lamb into small pieces and add to bowl with spice mixture along with softened bulgur, onion, garlic, and 1½ tablespoons pine nuts; mix until well combined.

6 Return eggplants cut side up to parchment-lined sheet. Using 2 forks, gently push eggplant flesh to sides to make room for filling and sprinkle cavities with remaining ¾ teaspoon salt. Break lamb mixture into small pieces and divide evenly among eggplant halves (do not pack tightly). Bake on upper rack until filling is firm and lightly browned, 15 to 20 minutes.

7 Sprinkle with pomegranate seeds, parsley, and remaining 1½ tablespoons pine nuts. Drizzle with yogurt and sprinkle with flake sea salt; serve warm or at room temperature.

Coriander-Cumin Butterflied Leg of Lamb with Radicchio Salad and Herb-Shallot Relish

Serves 6 | **Total Time** 1¾ hours, plus 1½ hours salting and resting

Lamb and Salad

- 1 (3- to 4-pound) boneless butterflied leg of lamb
- 1 tablespoon plus ½ teaspoon kosher salt, divided
- ⅓ cup plus 1½ tablespoons vegetable oil, divided
- 3 shallots, sliced thin
- 4 garlic cloves, peeled and smashed
- 1 (1-inch) piece ginger, sliced into ½-inch-thick rounds and smashed
- 1 tablespoon coriander seeds
- 1 tablespoon cumin seeds
- 1 tablespoon mustard seeds
- 3 bay leaves
- 2 (2-inch) strips lemon zest
- 3 heads radicchio (10 ounces each), quartered
- 1½ tablespoons honey
- 3 oranges
- ¾ cup pitted dates, chopped

Relish

- ⅓ cup chopped fresh mint
- ⅓ cup chopped fresh cilantro
- 1 shallot, minced
- 2 tablespoons lemon juice

Why This Recipe Works A boneless butterflied leg of lamb makes an impressive centerpiece for a celebratory meal but it takes a bit of time to get it ready for the oven; that said, it offers a beautifully balanced ratio of crust to juicy meat, and a cooking method that guarantees perfect results every time. We start by roasting the lamb low and slow in a 250-degree oven to lock in moisture. Then, for the grand finale, a quick blast under the broiler crisps up the exterior to golden perfection. Instead of giving the lamb a spice rub (which would scorch under the broiler), we make a rich spice-infused oil that does double duty, seasoning the lamb as it cooks and serving as part of a relish that we later serve with the lamb. To round out the meal we create a bold broiled radicchio salad. Tossed with juicy orange pieces, sweet dates, and some of the relish, this salad is bright, balanced, and utterly satisfying. The 1 tablespoon of salt in step 1 is for a 3-pound leg. If using a larger leg, add an additional teaspoon of salt for every pound. The coarse texture of kosher salt makes it easier to sprinkle evenly over a large roast; if you don't have kosher salt, you can substitute table salt, but reduce the amount to 1½ teaspoons for the lamb and ¼ teaspoon for the radicchio.

1 Place roast on cutting board with fat cap facing down. Using sharp knife, trim any pockets of fat and connective tissue from underside of roast. Flip roast over and trim fat cap to between ⅛ and ¼ inch thick. Cover roast with plastic wrap and pound to even 1-inch thickness. Using sharp knife, cut slits ½ inch apart in crosshatch pattern in fat cap of roast, being careful not to cut into meat. Rub 1 tablespoon salt over entire surface of roast and into slits. Let sit, uncovered, at room temperature for 1 hour or refrigerate, uncovered, up to 24 hours. (If refrigerating, let lamb sit at room temperature for 1 hour while roasting spices.)

2 Meanwhile, adjust 1 oven rack to lower-middle position and second rack 6 inches from broiler element. Heat oven to 250 degrees. Combine ⅓ cup oil, shallots, garlic, ginger, coriander seeds, cumin seeds, mustard seeds, bay leaves, and lemon zest on rimmed baking sheet. Transfer sheet to lower rack and bake until spices are softened and fragrant and shallots and garlic turn golden, about 1 hour. Remove sheet from oven and discard bay leaves and lemon zest.

3 Thoroughly pat roast dry with paper towels and transfer, fat side up, to sheet (directly on top of spices). Return sheet to oven and roast on lower rack until lamb registers 120 degrees, 25 to 35 minutes. Remove sheet from oven and heat broiler. Broil roast on upper rack until surface is well browned and charred in spots and lamb registers 125 degrees (for medium-rare), 3 to 5 minutes. Remove sheet from oven and transfer roast to carving board (some spices will cling to roast); let rest for 20 minutes. Carefully pour pan juices from sheet through fine-mesh strainer into medium bowl, pressing on solids to extract as much liquid as possible; discard solids. Reserve 3 tablespoons juices and discard remainder.

4 While lamb rests, clean sheet then, spray clean, dry sheet with vegetable oil spray. Place radicchio, cut side down, evenly spaced on sheet. Whisk honey, remaining ½ teaspoon salt, and remaining 1½ tablespoons oil together in bowl, then brush over cut sides of radicchio. Broil on upper rack until tender and charred 8 to 9 minutes, turning radicchio halfway through.

5 **For the relish** Stir mint, cilantro, shallot, and lemon juice into 3 tablespoons reserved juices. Add any accumulated lamb juices from carving board to relish and season with salt and pepper to taste.

6 Cut out and discard core from radicchio, then cut leaves into bite-size pieces and transfer to bowl. Cut away peel and pith from oranges. Cut each orange in half from pole to pole, then slice crosswise into ¼-inch-thick pieces. Transfer orange pieces to bowl with radicchio. Stir in dates and half of relish and toss to coat.

7 With long side facing you, slice roast with grain into 3 equal pieces. Turn each piece and slice against grain ¼ inch thick. Serve with radicchio salad and remaining relish.

VARIATION

Coriander-Fennel Butterflied Leg of Lamb with Radicchio Salad

Substitute 1 tablespoon fennel seeds for cumin seeds and 1 tablespoon black peppercorns for mustard seeds in step 2. Substitute parsley for mint in relish.

CHAPTER FOUR

Seafood

Miso Salmon with Kabocha and Cabbage

Serves 4 | **Total Time** 55 minutes, plus 6 hours marinating

- ½ cup white miso paste
- ¼ cup sugar
- 3 tablespoons sake
- 3 tablespoons mirin
- 4 (6- to 8-ounce) skin-on salmon fillets, 1 inch thick
- 1 kabocha squash (2 pounds), halved pole to pole and seeded
- 5 tablespoons vegetable oil, divided
- ¾ teaspoon plus ⅛ teaspoon table salt, divided
- ¼ teaspoon pepper
- 3 cups shredded red or green cabbage
- 2 tablespoons unseasoned rice vinegar, divided
- 3 scallions, white and green parts separated and sliced thin on bias
- 2 tablespoons soy sauce
- 2 teaspoons toasted sesame oil
- 2 teaspoons grated fresh ginger
- 1 garlic clove, minced
- ¾ teaspoon red pepper flakes
- ½ cup edamame, thawed
- ¼ English cucumber, cut into ½-inch pieces (½ cup)

Why This Recipe Works Miso is a surefire way to add flavor to a meaty fish like salmon. We use it in a marinade for the fish along with sugar, sake, and mirin, so the fish is flavored through and through. Because of all the sugar in the marinade, the fish, when broiled, develops a beautiful sweet char. We pair the salmon with roasted squash and serve it atop shredded cabbage with a crisp cucumber and edamame salad, for a meal that sings with a harmony of flavors and textures. Yellow, red, or brown miso paste can be used instead of white. For evenly cooked salmon, buy a 1½- to 2-pound center-cut salmon fillet and cut it up yourself. If using wild salmon, check for doneness earlier and cook it until it registers 120 degrees.

1 Whisk miso, sugar, sake, and mirin in medium bowl until sugar and miso are dissolved (mixture will be thick). Place fish skin side down on large platter and pour miso mixture evenly over fillets, spreading to coat all flesh sides. Cover with plastic wrap and refrigerate for at least 6 hours or up to 24 hours.

2 Adjust oven rack 8 inches from broiler element and heat oven to 475 degrees. Cut squash into 1-inch-thick wedges, then halve wedges crosswise. Toss squash, 3 tablespoons vegetable oil, ¾ teaspoon salt, and pepper together on rimmed baking sheet, then redistribute into even layer over sheet. Roast until squash is well browned and tender, 20 to 25 minutes, rotating sheet halfway through roasting. Transfer squash to bowl and set aside.

3 Heat broiler. Place wire rack in now-empty sheet and cover rack with aluminum foil. Using your fingers, scrape miso mixture from fillets (do not rinse) and place fish skin side down on foil, leaving 1 inch between fillets. Broil until salmon is deeply browned and center of salmon is still translucent when checked with tip of paring knife and registers 125 degrees (for medium-rare), 8 to 12 minutes, rotating sheet halfway through cooking and shielding edges of fillets with foil if beginning to scorch.

4 While salmon broils, combine cabbage, 1 tablespoon rice vinegar, and remaining ⅛ teaspoon salt in bowl. Squeeze and massage with your hands until cabbage is slightly wilted, about 1 minute; divide among individual serving bowls. Combine scallion whites, soy sauce, sesame oil, ginger, garlic, pepper flakes, remaining 2 tablespoons vegetable oil, and remaining 1 tablespoon rice vinegar in small bowl. Toss reserved squash with 2 tablespoons dressing, then add to serving bowls. Toss edamame and cucumbers with 2 tablespoons dressing, then add to serving bowls.

5 Divide salmon fillets among serving bowls, drizzle with remaining dressing, sprinkle with scallion greens, and serve.

Lime-Glazed Salmon and Crispy Rice Salad

Serves 4 | **Total Time** 45 minutes

- ¾ cup lime juice (6 limes), divided, plus lime wedges for serving
- 6 tablespoons sugar, divided
- 3 tablespoons fish sauce, divided
- 2 teaspoons grated fresh ginger
- 1 garlic clove, minced
- 1–2 Thai chiles, stemmed and sliced thin
- 1 teaspoon cornstarch
- 4 cups cooked medium-grain or short-grain rice
- 3 tablespoons vegetable oil, divided
- 4 (6- to 8-ounce) skin-on salmon fillets, 1 inch thick
- ¾ teaspoon table salt, divided
- 6 ounces shiitake mushrooms, stemmed and sliced ¼ inch thick
- 6 ounces sugar snap peas, strings removed and halved lengthwise
- 1½ cups fresh Thai basil, mint, and/or cilantro leaves and stems
- 3 scallions, sliced thin on bias
- 1 recipe Crispy Shallots (page 26)
- ¼ cup salted dry-roasted peanuts (optional)

Why This Recipe Works If you've tried to glaze salmon only to have the glaze slide right off and burn, this recipe will show you how to do it right. Inspired by the crispy rice salads of Thailand and Laos, this recipe features a delightful interplay of flavors and textures. A fragrant chile-lime dressing is used as both a drizzling sauce and, when thickened with cornstarch, a glaze for the salmon. Starting with cooked rice and giving it a spin under the broiler ensures that it has a satisfyingly crispy texture. For evenly cooked salmon, buy a 1½- to 2-pound center-cut salmon fillet and cut it up yourself. For salmon less than 1 inch thick at its thickest point, check for doneness after 8 minutes of broiling. If using wild salmon, check for doneness earlier and cook it until it registers 120 degrees.

1 Adjust oven rack 8 inches from broiler element and heat broiler. Whisk ½ cup lime juice, ¼ cup sugar, 2 tablespoons fish sauce, ginger, garlic, and Thai chiles together in bowl; set dressing aside. Whisk remaining ¼ cup lime juice, remaining 2 tablespoons sugar, remaining 1 tablespoon fish sauce, and cornstarch together in small bowl. Microwave, stirring every 30 seconds, until bubbling, thickened, and translucent, 2 to 3 minutes. Measure out and reserve 2 tablespoons thickened glaze in separate small bowl.

2 Spray rimmed baking sheet with vegetable oil spray. With short edge of sheet parallel to counter, spread rice in even layer over bottom third of sheet, then brush top of rice with 2 tablespoons oil. Fold sheet of aluminum foil so it is 12 inches long by 6 inches wide. Spray foil with vegetable oil spray. Place foil in empty space on sheet, then lay salmon fillets across foil leaving ¼ inch space between fillets. Pat salmon dry, sprinkle with ½ teaspoon salt, and brush with reserved 2 tablespoons glaze.

3 Toss mushrooms with remaining 1 tablespoon oil and remaining ¼ teaspoon salt in bowl, then scatter directly on sheet around foil sling, rearranging placement of foil sling as needed and making sure ends of foil are not obscuring rice or salmon (crimp foil as needed).

4 Broil until salmon is deeply browned and center of salmon is still translucent when checked with tip of paring knife and registers 125 degrees (for medium-rare), 10 to 15 minutes, rotating sheet halfway through broiling.

5 Using foil as sling, transfer fish to plate; discard foil. Brush salmon with remaining glaze. If rice is not deep golden brown, return sheet to oven and broil until deep golden brown, 2 to 7 minutes longer. Break up rice into rough 2-inch pieces using spatula and gently stir in mushrooms. Sprinkle with snap peas, Thai basil, and scallions and drizzle with half of dressing. Top with crispy shallots and peanuts, if using. Serve salmon and rice with lime wedges, passing remaining dressing separately.

Salmon with Crispy Potatoes, Broccoli, and Mustard Sauce

Serves 4 | **Total Time** 50 minutes

- 5 tablespoons plus 2 teaspoons extra-virgin olive oil, divided
- 1 pound small red potatoes, unpeeled, halved
- 1¼ teaspoons plus pinch table salt, divided
- 1 teaspoon plus pinch pepper, divided
- 1 pound broccoli florets, cut into 2-inch pieces
- ¼ cup minced fresh chives
- 2 tablespoons whole-grain mustard
- 2 teaspoons lemon juice, plus lemon wedges for serving
- 1 teaspoon honey
- 4 (6- to 8-ounce) skinless salmon fillets, 1 inch thick

Why This Recipe Works We think meaty salmon and pungent mustard make an excellent combo. This recipe is easy to pull together and relies on the simplest ingredients, making it a great weeknight option. The dilemma is how to cook the salmon, broccoli, and potatoes all on one sheet pan without anything being overcooked. Our first step was to look at the roasting time for each. Since the potatoes require the most time in the oven and the salmon the least, we start by roasting the potatoes and broccoli together on a sheet pan at high heat (for some browning), and then we lower the heat (so the salmon won't overcook) and swap in the salmon for the broccoli. Cooking in stages prevents overcrowding the pan and ensures even cooking. A vibrant sauce of chopped chives, whole-grain mustard, lemon juice, olive oil, and honey completes this one-pan meal. Use small red potatoes measuring 1 to 2 inches in diameter. If using wild salmon, check for doneness earlier and cook it until it registers 120 degrees.

1 Adjust oven rack to lowest position and heat oven to 500 degrees. Brush rimmed baking sheet with 1 tablespoon oil. Toss potatoes with 1 tablespoon oil, ½ teaspoon salt, and ½ teaspoon pepper in bowl, then place cut side down on half of sheet. In now-empty bowl, toss broccoli with 1 tablespoon oil, ¼ teaspoon salt, and ¼ teaspoon pepper, then place on empty side of sheet. Roast until potatoes are light golden brown and broccoli is well browned and tender, 22 to 24 minutes, rotating sheet halfway through roasting.

2 Meanwhile, combine chives, mustard, lemon juice, honey, 2 tablespoons oil, pinch salt, and pinch pepper in bowl; set aside for serving. Pat salmon dry with paper towels, rub thoroughly with remaining 2 teaspoons oil, and sprinkle with remaining ½ teaspoon salt and remaining ¼ teaspoon pepper; refrigerate until needed.

3 Remove sheet from oven and reduce oven temperature to 275 degrees. Transfer broccoli, browned side up, to plate and cover with aluminum foil to keep warm. Place salmon, skinned side down on now-empty side of sheet and roast until center of salmon is still translucent when checked with tip of paring knife and registers 125 degrees (for medium-rare), 11 to 15 minutes, rotating sheet halfway through roasting.

4 Transfer broccoli to sheet pan with salmon and sweet potatoes. Serve with lemon wedges and reserved mustard sauce.

Roasted Salmon with White Beans, Fennel, and Tomatoes

Serves 4 | **Total Time** 50 minutes

- 2 fennel bulbs, stalks discarded, bulbs halved, cored, and sliced ¼ inch thick
- 2 tablespoons extra-virgin olive oil, divided
- 1¼ teaspoons table salt, divided
- ¾ teaspoon pepper, divided
- 2 (15-ounce) cans cannellini beans, rinsed
- 10 ounces cherry tomatoes, halved (2 cups)
- ¼ cup dry white wine
- 3 garlic cloves (2 sliced thin, 1 minced)
- 6 tablespoons unsalted butter, softened
- 1 teaspoon minced fresh thyme
- 1 teaspoon grated lemon zest plus 1 tablespoon juice
- 4 (6- to 8-ounce) skinless salmon fillets, 1 inch thick
- 2 tablespoons chopped fresh parsley

Why This Recipe Works This ingenious, easy recipe puts fennel in a starring role that will have you looking at this often underappreciated vegetable with new eyes. When roasted, fennel transforms into a slightly sweet, subtly caramelized treat with a faint hint of licorice aroma. What could pair better with meaty salmon? Add roasted white beans and jammy cherry tomatoes, and you have a combo that is both unusual and delicious. For this recipe, we make everything on a sheet pan in two quick stages. First, since fennel is a rather fibrous vegetable, it needs some solo time in the oven. We slice two fennel bulbs thin; toss the slices with oil, salt, and pepper; and get them started in a hot oven. When the fennel is well on its way to perfection, we stir in the cherry tomatoes, white beans, and garlic (plus a little wine), and place the salmon fillets—which we coat with a tasty compound butter—right on top before roasting it all together. By the time the salmon is perfectly cooked through, the vegetables are tender. The cherry tomatoes give off flavorful juices, which, with the addition of extra compound butter and some lemon juice, make a luscious sauce that ties the whole dish together. If using wild salmon, check for doneness earlier and cook it until it registers 120 degrees.

1 Adjust oven rack to middle position and heat oven to 450 degrees. Toss fennel, 1 tablespoon oil, ¼ teaspoon salt, and ¼ teaspoon pepper together on rimmed baking sheet. Spread fennel into even layer and roast until beginning to brown around edges, about 15 minutes.

2 Meanwhile, toss beans, tomatoes, wine, sliced garlic, ½ teaspoon salt, ¼ teaspoon pepper, and remaining 1 tablespoon oil together in bowl. Combine butter, thyme, lemon zest, and minced garlic in small bowl. Pat salmon dry with paper towels and sprinkle with remaining ½ teaspoon salt and remaining ¼ teaspoon pepper. Spread 1 tablespoon butter mixture on top of each fillet; refrigerate until needed.

3 Remove sheet from oven. Add bean mixture to sheet with fennel, stir to combine, then redistribute into even layer over sheet. Place salmon on top of bean mixture, butter side up, evenly spaced across sheet. Roast until center of salmon is still translucent when checked with tip of paring knife and registers 125 degrees (for medium-rare), 17 to 20 minutes.

4 Transfer salmon to serving platter. Stir lemon juice and remaining 2 tablespoons butter mixture into bean mixture, transfer to serving platter with salmon, and sprinkle with parsley. Serve.

Pomegranate-Glazed Salmon with Black-Eyed Peas and Walnuts

Serves 4 | **Total Time** 25 minutes

- 4 (6- to 8-ounce) skin-on salmon fillets, 1 inch thick
- ¼ cup pomegranate molasses, divided
- ¾ teaspoon table salt, divided
- ¼ teaspoon plus ⅛ teaspoon pepper, divided
- 3 tablespoons extra-virgin olive oil
- 2 tablespoons lemon juice
- 2 (15-ounce) cans black-eyed peas, rinsed
- ½ cup pomegranate seeds
- ½ cup walnuts, toasted and chopped
- ½ cup chopped fresh parsley
- 4 scallions, sliced thin

Why This Recipe Works Pomegranate molasses is a good cook's secret weapon, which is why it's always in our pantry. Its concentrated sweet-tart flavor adds brightness to so many things, from vinaigrettes and grain dishes to meat, fish, and desserts. Here it serves as a short-cut glaze (just brush it on) that pairs perfectly with the bold taste of salmon. And we use it to add vibrancy to the vinaigrette for our no-cook black-eyed pea salad. As a first step, we preheat our pan in an oven set to 500 degrees. After placing the salmon on the hot pan, we quickly lower the oven temp to 275 degrees and return the pan to the oven. This crisps up the salmon skin and gives the fish a jump start on cooking; as the heat in the oven lowers, it allows the salmon to cook to moist perfection. Before serving, we brush the salmon with another tablespoon of pomegranate molasses, which adds a hit of fresh flavor and unmistakable color. We serve it with the black-eyed pea salad, to which we add tart pomegranate seeds that complement the glaze and provide pops of vivid scarlet. For evenly cooked salmon, buy a 1½- to 2-pound center-cut salmon fillet and cut it up yourself. If using wild salmon, check for doneness earlier and cook it until it registers 120 degrees.

1 Adjust oven rack to lowest position, place rimmed baking sheet on rack, and heat oven to 500 degrees. Pat salmon dry with paper towels, brush with 1 tablespoon pomegranate molasses, and sprinkle with ½ teaspoon salt and ¼ teaspoon pepper; refrigerate until needed.

2 Once oven reaches 500 degrees, reduce oven temperature to 275 degrees. Remove sheet from oven and carefully place salmon skin side down on hot sheet. Roast salmon until center is still translucent when checked with tip of paring knife and registers 125 degrees (for medium-rare), 9 to 13 minutes.

3 While salmon roasts, whisk oil, lemon juice, 2 tablespoons pomegranate molasses, remaining ¼ teaspoon salt, and remaining ⅛ teaspoon pepper in large bowl until combined. Add black-eyed peas, pomegranate seeds, walnuts, parsley, and scallions and toss to combine. Season with salt and pepper to taste.

4 Remove sheet from oven and brush salmon with remaining 1 tablespoon pomegranate molasses. Slide fish spatula along underside of salmon fillets and transfer to serving platter, leaving skin behind; discard skin. Serve salmon with black-eyed pea salad.

Roasted Salmon and Broccoli Rabe with Pistachio Gremolata

Serves 4 | **Total Time** 25 minutes

- ¼ cup shelled pistachios, toasted and chopped fine
- 2 tablespoons minced fresh parsley
- 2 garlic cloves, minced, divided
- 1 teaspoon grated lemon zest
- 1 pound broccoli rabe, trimmed and cut into 1½-inch pieces
- 2 tablespoons plus 2 teaspoons extra-virgin olive oil, divided
- ¾ teaspoon table salt, divided
- ½ teaspoon pepper, divided
- Pinch red pepper flakes
- 4 (6- to 8-ounce) skinless salmon fillets, 1 inch thick

Why This Recipe Works Quick-cooking, low-prep fish is an appealing dinner choice for the busy cook who needs a healthful, satisfying dinner. Streamlining things further by combining fish with a quick-cooking side in a one-pan dinner is the ultimate in convenience—and appeal. Salmon pairs well with many quick-cooking vegetables because it doesn't emit a lot of juices during cooking. We like it with broccoli rabe; the pleasant bitterness of this deeply green vegetable counterbalances the rich salmon. We reinforce the broccoli rabe's bite with some red pepper flakes and minced garlic and then relegate it to one half of the sheet pan, resting the salmon on the other half. Roasted in a hot oven, the fillets cook through to a silky medium-rare right as the broccoli rabe turns tender. To bring the dish together, we sprinkle a fresh, nutty pistachio gremolata over the top before serving. Broccoli rabe is sometimes called rapini. If using wild salmon, check for doneness earlier and cook the fillets to 120 degrees and start checking for doneness after 4 minutes.

1 Adjust oven rack to middle position and heat oven to 450 degrees. Combine pistachios, parsley, half of garlic, and lemon zest in small bowl; set gremolata aside until ready to serve.

2 Toss broccoli rabe, 2 tablespoons oil, ¼ teaspoon salt, ¼ teaspoon pepper, pepper flakes, and remaining garlic together in bowl. Arrange on half of rimmed baking sheet. Pat salmon dry with paper towels, rub with remaining 2 teaspoons oil, and sprinkle with remaining ½ teaspoon salt and remaining ¼ teaspoon pepper. Arrange salmon skinned side down on other half of sheet.

3 Roast until center of salmon is still translucent when checked with tip of paring knife and registers 125 degrees (for medium-rare) and broccoli rabe is tender, 8 to 12 minutes. Sprinkle salmon with gremolata and serve.

Sweet Chili Salmon with Cauliflower and Lime

Serves 4 | **Total Time** 35 minutes

---

2 teaspoons chili powder

2 teaspoons kosher salt

1 teaspoon pepper

1 large head cauliflower (3 pounds), cored and cut into 2-inch florets

1 tablespoon extra-virgin olive oil

4 (6- to 8-ounce) skin-on salmon fillets, 1 inch thick

2 tablespoons honey

2 tablespoons minced fresh cilantro

Lime wedges

Why This Recipe Works Combining sweet, sour, and savory flavors, this recipe is on your table in just about 30 minutes with the endgame being a platter of beautifully caramelized cauliflower florets and salmon fillets with a flavorful crust. It takes two sheet pans—one for roasting the cauliflower and another for the salmon—so you can get deep browning on the cauliflower and also cook the salmon perfectly. We think salmon always pairs well with a sprinkling of a sharp spice; here, chili powder plus salt and pepper are all you need. Brushing a bit of honey on each fillet first glues the spice mix to the salmon. The cauliflower gets the same spice treatment and just needs a toss with olive oil before we add it to the sheet pan. We arrange the cauliflower cut side down on the pan, place it on the lower rack, and give it a 10-minute jump start on the salmon. After 10 minutes, we place the sheet pan with our salmon on the upper rack. In about 12 minutes, both are perfectly cooked. What could be easier? For evenly cooked salmon, buy a 1½- to 2-pound center-cut salmon fillet and cut it up yourself. If using wild salmon, check for doneness earlier and cook it until it registers 120 degrees.

1 Adjust oven racks to upper-middle and lower-middle positions and heat oven to 450 degrees. Combine chili powder, salt, and pepper in small bowl. Toss cauliflower with oil and 2 teaspoons spice mixture on rimmed baking sheet, then spread into even layer over sheet. Line second rimmed baking sheet with aluminum foil. Place salmon, skin side down, on foil-lined sheet and brush tops of fillets with honey. Sprinkle remaining 1 tablespoon spice mixture evenly over salmon.

2 Place cauliflower on lower rack and roast for 10 minutes. After 10 minutes, place sheet with salmon on upper rack and roast until cauliflower is well browned and tender and center of salmon is still translucent when checked with tip of paring knife and registers 125 degrees (for medium-rare), 12 to 15 minutes. Transfer cauliflower to serving platter and sprinkle with cilantro. Serve cauliflower with salmon and lime wedges.

Curry Salmon with Sweet Potato Wedges and Asparagus

Serves 4 | **Total Time** 50 minutes

- 1½ pounds sweet potatoes, unpeeled, cut into 1-inch wedges
- 2 tablespoons extra-virgin olive oil, divided
- 1 teaspoon table salt, divided
- ¾ teaspoon pepper, divided
- 1 pound asparagus, trimmed
- 2 teaspoons curry powder
- ½ teaspoon cayenne pepper
- 4 (6- to 8-ounce) skinless salmon fillets, 1 inch thick
- ½ cup torn fresh mint leaves
- ½ cup plain whole-milk yogurt

Why This Recipe Works This weeknight wonder of a salmon meal highlights the benefits of smart ingredient arrangement on your sheet pan, and is quick to prepare, boldly flavored, and a snap to clean up. While the dense sweet potatoes are in the oven, we turn to the microwave to bloom the spices for the salmon rub, where the mix of curry powder, cayenne, and oil turns bubbly and fragrant. We brush it on the salmon fillets and then sprinkle them with salt and a good amount of pepper. After the potatoes have cooked for 25 minutes, we move them to the center of the sheet pan, place the spice-rubbed salmon on one side, and place the asparagus on the other. After a mere 10 minutes (or less) in the hot oven, the salmon and asparagus are perfectly cooked thanks to their placement on the perimeter of the pan, which exposes them to the most heat. A scattering of fragrant torn mint leaves complements the salmon, asparagus, and sweet potatoes alike, and a dollop of cooling yogurt makes an easy one-ingredient sauce. Do not use pencil-thin asparagus spears here; they will overcook. If using wild salmon, check for doneness earlier and cook it until it registers 120 degrees.

1 Adjust oven rack to lower-middle position and heat oven to 450 degrees. Toss potatoes, 1 tablespoon oil, ¼ teaspoon salt, and ¼ teaspoon pepper together on rimmed baking sheet, then spread into even layer, skin side down, over half of sheet. Roast until potatoes begin to soften, about 25 minutes.

2 Meanwhile, toss asparagus with 1 teaspoon oil and ¼ teaspoon salt in bowl; set aside. Combine curry powder, cayenne, and remaining 2 teaspoons oil in small bowl. Microwave until bubbling and fragrant, about 1 minute. Pat salmon dry with paper towels, then brush with spice mixture and sprinkle with remaining ½ teaspoon salt and remaining ½ teaspoon pepper; refrigerate until needed.

3 Remove sheet from oven. Push sweet potato wedges to center of sheet and arrange salmon fillets skinned side down on 1 side of potatoes, spaced evenly apart. Arrange asparagus on other side of potatoes, spreading into even layer. Roast until center of salmon is still translucent when checked with tip of paring knife and registers 125 degrees (for medium-rare), 8 to 10 minutes.

4 Sprinkle salmon, sweet potatoes, and asparagus with mint and serve with yogurt.

How to Build the Sheet Pan

Toss the potatoes with oil, salt, and pepper on the sheet, then roast on half of the sheet. Shift the sweet potatoes to the center, then arrange the salmon fillets on one side of the sweet potatoes and place the asparagus on the other side; return the sheet to the oven.

Pistachio-Crusted Cod Fillets with Broccoli Rabe

Serves 4 | **Total Time** 55 minutes

- ¼ cup shelled pistachios
- ¼ cup panko bread crumbs
- 1 shallot, minced
- ¼ cup extra-virgin olive oil, divided
- 2 garlic cloves, minced, divided
- 1 teaspoon minced fresh thyme or ¼ teaspoon dried
- ⅛ teaspoon plus 1¼ teaspoons table salt, divided
- Pinch plus ¼ teaspoon pepper, divided
- 1 tablespoon minced fresh parsley
- 1 large egg yolk
- 1 teaspoon Dijon mustard
- ½ teaspoon grated lemon zest, plus lemon wedges for serving
- 4 (6- to 8-ounce) skinless cod fillets, 1 to 1½ inches thick
- 1 pound broccoli rabe
- ¼ teaspoon red pepper flakes

Why This Recipe Works Whether roasting or sautéing it, we like to dress up cod more often than not because it takes well to just about any flavoring. And since cod is plentiful in our neck of the woods (Boston) we eat it quite often. Here we coat it with pistachios and pair it with a side. We use two clever cooking methods (and two sheet pans) to get everything just right. First up, the cod gets a low-and-slow roast on a wire rack, which keeps it tender and flaky. Then, once that's done, we crank up the heat to broil the broccoli rabe tossed on the sheet pan with oil, garlic, and red pepper flakes; the broiler caramelizes it and renders it irresistibly crispy in minutes. The star of the show? That nutty, golden crust. Ground pistachios bring crunch, color, and a hint of sweetness, while panko, herbs, shallot, and garlic add depth. A quick zap in the microwave pretoasts the mix, giving it a head start before it even hits the fish. To make sure it sticks, we brush the fillets with a zippy combo of egg yolk, mustard, and lemon zest and then press on the crumbs—just on top, where they belong. A gentle roast locks in moisture while crisping up the crust to perfection. With the cod resting, it's time to turn up the heat! The broccoli rabe goes straight onto the sheet pan and under the broiler, where it takes on a beautiful char without turning mushy. Since slicing the florets can unleash bitterness, we keep the leafy tops whole and only trim the stems for even cooking. The result? A punchy, flavor-packed sheet-pan dinner with crispy, nut-crusted cod and charred, smoky greens—all without breaking a sweat. You can substitute haddock or halibut for the cod. Any nut will work for the topping; see the variations for some ideas.

1 Adjust 1 oven rack to middle position and second oven rack 4 inches from broiler element. Heat oven to 300 degrees. Set wire rack in rimmed baking sheet and spray with vegetable oil spray. Process pistachios in food processor until finely chopped, 20 to 30 seconds. Toss pistachios, panko, shallot, 1 tablespoon oil, half of garlic, thyme, ⅛ teaspoon salt, and pinch pepper together in bowl. Microwave, stirring frequently, until panko is light golden brown, 2 to 4 minutes. Let cool for 10 minutes, then stir in parsley.

2 Whisk egg yolk, mustard, and lemon zest together in bowl. Pat cod dry with paper towels and sprinkle with ½ teaspoon salt and remaining ¼ teaspoon pepper. Brush tops of fillets evenly with yolk mixture. Working with 1 fillet at a time, dredge coated side in nut mixture, pressing gently to adhere. Transfer cod, crumb side up, to prepared rack and bake on lower rack until fish flakes apart when gently prodded with paring knife and registers 135 degrees, 20 to 30 minutes, rotating sheet halfway through baking.

3 While cod roasts, trim and discard bottom 1 inch of broccoli rabe stems. Wash broccoli rabe with cold water, then dry with clean dish towel. Cut tops (leaves and florets) from stems, then cut stems into 1-inch pieces (keep tops whole). Drizzle 1 tablespoon oil over second clean sheet, then arrange broccoli rabe in even layer over sheet. Combine remaining 2 tablespoons oil, remaining garlic, remaining ¾ teaspoon salt, and pepper flakes in bowl, then drizzle evenly over broccoli rabe on sheet and toss to combine; set aside.

4 Remove cod from oven and set aside. Heat broiler. Broil broccoli rabe on upper rack until exposed half of leaves are well browned, 2 to 2½ minutes. Using tongs, toss to expose unbrowned leaves. Return sheet to oven and continue to broil until most leaves are lightly charred and stalks are crisp-tender, 2 to 2½ minutes. Serve cod and broccoli rabe with lemon wedges.

VARIATIONS

Almond-Crusted Cod Fillets

Substitute almonds for pistachios, ¼ teaspoon chipotle chile powder for thyme, and lime zest for lemon zest. Add ⅛ teaspoon ground cumin, ⅛ teaspoon ground coriander, and pinch cayenne to panko mixture in step 1.

Hazelnut-Crusted Cod Fillets

Substitute hazelnuts for pistachios, ¼ teaspoon dried oregano for thyme, and orange zest for lemon zest. Add pinch cayenne to panko mixture in step 1.

Lemon-Herb Cod Fillets with Crispy Garlic Potatoes

Serves 4 | **Total Time** 1 hour

- 1½ pounds russet potatoes, unpeeled, sliced into ¼-inch-thick rounds
- 2 tablespoons unsalted butter, melted, plus 3 tablespoons cut into ¼-inch pieces
- 3 garlic cloves, minced
- 1 teaspoon minced fresh thyme, plus 4 sprigs
- 1 teaspoon table salt, divided
- ½ teaspoon pepper, divided
- 4 (6- to 8-ounce) skinless cod fillets, 1 to 1½ inches thick
- 1 lemon, sliced thin

Why This Recipe Works Looking for a fish dinner that hits all the high marks and is perfect for entertaining? Your search is over. This clever sheet-pan cod and potatoes is no ordinary dinner: This is restaurant-quality fare, in both taste and looks. Just picture individually arranged beds of thinly sliced and crispy, herby, garlicky potatoes topped with tender cod enhanced by butter, thyme, and lemon. The potatoes are sliced very thin; a mandoline makes this task easy, but it can certainly be accomplished with a sharp knife. You want these potatoes to get deliciously crispy all around, including the slivers of skin surrounding each piece. The potatoes need a head start on the fish, so after tossing the slices with melted butter, garlic, and fresh thyme, we shingle them on the sheet pan into 4 separate rectangles. When the potatoes have roasted for 30 minutes, we place a cod fillet on top of each pile. To highlight the fish's clean flavor and keep things easy, we top each fillet with a small pat of butter, a sprig of fresh thyme, and a thin slice of lemon (which really adds to the appealing look of the dish). The pan goes back in the oven at this point, where the dry heat melts the butter, basting the fish and drawing the herbal and citrus flavors through the fillets and down over the potatoes. After another 15 minutes, this simple yet striking dish is ready to serve. You can substitute haddock or halibut for the cod. Thin tail-end fillets can be folded under to achieve proper thickness.

1 Adjust oven rack to lower-middle position and heat oven to 425 degrees. Toss potatoes with melted butter, garlic, minced thyme, ½ teaspoon salt, and ¼ teaspoon pepper in bowl. Shingle potatoes into four 6 by 4-inch rectangular piles on rimmed baking sheet. Roast until spotty brown and just tender, 30 to 35 minutes, rotating sheet halfway through roasting.

2 Pat cod dry with paper towels and sprinkle with remaining ½ teaspoon salt and remaining ¼ teaspoon pepper. Lay 1 cod fillet skinned side down on top of each potato pile and top fillets with butter pieces, thyme sprigs, and lemon slices, in that order. Bake until cod flakes apart when gently prodded with paring knife and registers 135 degrees, about 15 minutes.

3 Remove sheet from oven. Slide spatula underneath potatoes and cod and gently transfer to individual plates. Serve.

Roasted Trout with White Bean and Tomato Salad

Serves 4 | **Total Time** 25 minutes

- 4 (8- to 10-ounce) boneless, butterflied whole trout
- ½ teaspoon table salt
- ¼ teaspoon pepper
- ½ cup extra-virgin olive oil, divided
- 2 shallots, minced
- ¼ cup lemon juice, plus lemon wedges for serving (2 lemons)
- 2 tablespoons capers, rinsed and chopped
- 2 garlic cloves, minced
- 4 teaspoons minced fresh rosemary
- 2 (15-ounce) cans cannellini beans, rinsed
- 12 ounces cherry tomatoes, halved
- ¼ cup chopped fresh parsley

Why This Recipe Works If your fishmonger stocks butterflied trout, roast it, don't pan-sear it. Why? First, it's far easier, and by using a sheet pan, you can cook four trout to flaky perfection in under 10 minutes. One trick is to preheat the sheet pan by placing it in the oven as it preheats (to the high temperature of 450 degrees). We then remove the hot sheet pan from the oven and add oil to coat the pan, and return our pan to the oven for another 4 minutes to heat further. You might ask why we take this additional step to heat the pan a second time, but it makes sense when you consider how quickly thin fish cook. A thin and delicate fish like this can overcook in an instant, so timing is everything. While the oven preheats we whisk together an aromatic dressing with shallots, lemon juice, capers, garlic, and rosemary. For a colorful side salad to pair with the trout, we toss canned beans, parsley, and cherry tomatoes with the dressing. Note that whole trout is usually available already boned and butterflied. We like cannellini beans for this salad but any small white beans will work.

1 Adjust oven rack to middle position, place rimmed baking sheet on rack, and heat oven to 450 degrees.

2 Pat trout dry with paper towels and sprinkle with salt and pepper. Add ¼ cup oil to preheated sheet, tilting to coat evenly, and return to oven for 4 minutes. Carefully place trout skin side down on hot sheet; return to oven and cook until trout flakes apart when gently prodded with paring knife, 7 to 9 minutes.

3 While trout roasts, whisk remaining ¼ cup oil, shallots, lemon juice, capers, garlic, and rosemary together in large bowl. Add beans, tomatoes, and parsley and toss to coat. Season with salt and pepper to taste.

4 Serve trout with bean salad and lemon wedges.

WUSTHOF

Lemon-Poached Halibut with Roasted Fingerling Potatoes

Serves 4 | **Total Time** 50 minutes

- 1½ pounds fingerling potatoes, halved lengthwise
- 2 tablespoons extra-virgin olive oil, divided
- 1 teaspoon table salt, divided
- ¾ teaspoon pepper, divided
- 8 ounces grape tomatoes, halved
- 4 (6- to 8-ounce) skinless halibut fillets, 1 inch thick
- ½ teaspoon dried oregano
- 8 thin slices lemon
- 2 tablespoons minced fresh parsley

Why This Recipe Works Do the words "poaching" and "fish" together scare you? Then this method is for you, trust us. Simply set four rectangles of foil on your counter, add a pile of grape tomatoes and then a halibut fillet to each, and then dust the fish with bold oregano and top with thin slices of lemon. Fold the foil into packets and bake. What emerges is perfectly steamed and flavorful fish and a bounty of jammy tomatoes, with a rich broth beneath it all: no court bouillon required. Using foil packets means we can steam the fish and tomatoes while roasting elegant fingerling potatoes all on the same pan. We start the potatoes first to give them some initial browning. We then add our folded packets, which rest right on top of the potatoes for the final stint in the oven. We slide the moist poached fish, infused with lemon and oregano, and the colorful tomatoes on top of the beautifully browned and crusted fingerlings before serving. To take this dish over the top, we drizzle the flavorful broth from the packets over everything. Use potatoes of a similar size to ensure consistent cooking. To test for doneness without opening the foil packets, use a permanent marker to mark an "X" on the outside of the foil where the fish fillet is the thickest; then, insert an instant-read thermometer through the "X" into the fish to measure its internal temperature. You can substitute mahi-mahi, red snapper, striped bass, or swordfish for the halibut in this recipe.

1 Adjust oven rack to lower-middle position and heat oven to 450 degrees. Toss potatoes with 2 teaspoons oil, ½ teaspoon salt, and ½ teaspoon pepper on rimmed baking sheet, then spread into single layer, cut side down, over sheet. Roast until cut sides begin to brown, about 10 minutes.

2 Meanwhile, lay four 16 by 12-inch rectangles of foil on counter with short sides parallel to counter edge. Divide tomatoes evenly among foil rectangles, arranging in center of lower half of each sheet of foil, then place 1 fillet on each tomato pile. Sprinkle halibut with oregano, remaining ½ teaspoon salt, and remaining ¼ teaspoon pepper, then top each with 2 lemon slices and 1 teaspoon oil. Fold top half of foil over halibut and tomatoes, then tightly crimp edges into rough 9 by 6-inch packets.

3 Place packets on top of potatoes on sheet and bake until fish registers 130 degrees, about 15 minutes. Divide potatoes among 4 individual serving bowls. Carefully open packets, allowing steam to escape away from you, and using thin metal spatula, gently slide halibut and tomatoes onto potatoes, then pour accumulated juices over top. Sprinkle with parsley and serve.

Old Bay Halibut with Red Potatoes, Corn, and Andouille

Serves 4 | **Total Time** 55 minutes

- ¼ cup vegetable oil, divided
- 1½ pounds small red potatoes, unpeeled, halved
- 1 teaspoon table salt, divided
- ½ plus ⅛ teaspoon pepper, divided
- 4 ears corn, husks and silk removed, cut into thirds
- 12 ounces andouille sausage, sliced 1 inch thick
- 4 tablespoons unsalted butter, softened
- 2 teaspoons Old Bay seasoning
- 1 teaspoon lemon juice
- 4 (6- to 8-ounce) skinless halibut fillets, 1 inch thick
- 1 tablespoon minced fresh parsley

Why This Recipe Works This recipe puts an unmistakable Lowcountry spin on a halibut dinner. We pair the halibut with smoky andouille sausage, sweet corn, and tender red potatoes. And we do it all on our handy sheet pan. The best thing about roasting halibut this way is that it concentrates the mild fish's sweetness in mere minutes, and we can incorporate multiple sides by staggering the cook times. We give the corn and halibut a rich, authentic finish by slathering them with a citrusy Old Bay compound butter. To ensure that your fish cooks evenly, purchase fillets that are similarly shaped and uniformly thick. If andouille is not available, Portuguese linguiça or Polish kielbasa can be substituted. You can substitute mahi-mahi, red snapper, striped bass, or swordfish for the halibut. Use small red potatoes 1 to 2 inches in diameter.

1 Adjust oven rack to lowest position and heat oven to 500 degrees. Brush rimmed baking sheet with 1 tablespoon oil. Toss potatoes with 2 tablespoons oil, ¼ teaspoon salt, and ¼ teaspoon pepper in bowl, then place cut side down on half of sheet. Toss corn in now-empty bowl with remaining 1 tablespoon oil, ¼ teaspoon salt, and ⅛ teaspoon pepper, then place on empty side of sheet. Nestle andouille onto sheet around corn. Roast until potatoes and andouille are lightly browned and corn kernels are plump, 20 to 25 minutes, rotating sheet halfway through roasting.

2 Meanwhile, mash butter, Old Bay, and lemon juice together in bowl; set aside for serving. Pat halibut dry with paper towels and sprinkle with remaining ½ teaspoon salt and remaining ¼ teaspoon pepper; refrigerate until needed.

3 Remove sheet from oven and reduce oven temperature to 425 degrees. Transfer corn to clean bowl, leaving andouille and potatoes on sheet. Add 2 tablespoons Old Bay butter to corn, toss to coat, and cover bowl tightly with aluminum foil; set aside for serving. Slide andouille to side of sheet with potatoes, then place halibut on now-empty side of sheet. Continue to roast potatoes, andouille, and halibut until fish is just opaque when checked with tip of paring knife and registers 130 degrees, 8 to 10 minutes, rotating sheet halfway through roasting.

4 Remove sheet from oven. Transfer potatoes, andouille, and halibut, browned side up, to platter. Dot remaining Old Bay butter over halibut, cover platter with aluminum foil, and let rest for 5 minutes. Add corn to platter, sprinkle with parsley, and serve.

How to Build the Sheet Pan

Season the potatoes and corn with oil, salt, and pepper and then place the potatoes cut side down on one half of the sheet and the corn on the other half. Nestle the andouille around the corn and roast. Remove the corn, slide the andouille to the side of the sheet with the potatoes, add the seasoned fish to the empty side, and transfer to the oven.

Swordfish with Bulgur and Tomato-Eggplant Caponata

Serves 4 to 6 | **Total Time** 1 hour

- 1½ cups boiling water
- 1 cup fine-grind bulgur
- 2¼ teaspoons table salt, divided
- ¼ cup minced fresh parsley, divided
- 1 small eggplant (12 ounces), sliced into ¼-inch-thick rounds
- 12 ounces cherry tomatoes
- ¼ cup extra-virgin olive oil, divided
- 5 teaspoons ground coriander, divided
- ½ teaspoon pepper, divided
- 4 (6- to 8-ounce) skinless swordfish steaks, 1 to 1½ inches thick
- 6 scallions, trimmed
- 1 tablespoon grated lemon zest, plus 1 lemon halved crosswise
- 1½ tablespoons honey
- 2 garlic cloves, minced
- 1 teaspoon ground cumin
- ¼ teaspoon ground cinnamon
- ⅛ teaspoon ground nutmeg
- ¼ cup pitted kalamata olives, chopped

Why This Recipe Works Swordfish is a bold, brash, meaty fish—so bring on the assertive ingredients! In this case it's a Sicilian-style caponata. The sheet pan is a multitasker here, making it all possible in just an hour. Broiling the eggplant and cherry tomatoes renders them soft and caramelized. Next, swordfish, lemon, and scallions take a turn under the broiler for that perfect char. Ground coriander, which we sprinkle on the swordfish, heightens the aroma and flavors overall of this fancy-seeming, but easy, dinner. If swordfish isn't available, you can substitute halibut or striped bass. For an accurate measurement of boiling water, bring a kettle of water to a boil and then measure out the desired amount.

1 Adjust oven rack 4 inches from broiler element and heat broiler. Line rimmed baking sheet with aluminum foil and spray with vegetable oil spray. Whisk boiling water, bulgur, and ½ teaspoon salt together in large bowl. Cover and let sit until bulgur is tender and all liquid has been absorbed, about 20 minutes. Fluff bulgur with fork, stir in 3 tablespoons parsley, and cover with aluminum foil to keep warm; set aside until ready to serve. Meanwhile, spread eggplant on paper towel–lined plate, sprinkle all over with ¼ teaspoon salt, and let sit for 15 minutes.

2 Thoroughly pat eggplant dry with paper towels. Arrange tomatoes and eggplant on prepared sheet, brush with 1 tablespoon oil, and broil for 8 minutes, flipping eggplant and rotating sheet halfway through broiling. Remove sheet from oven and transfer eggplant to cutting board and tomatoes to second bowl; set aside.

3 Combine 1 tablespoon coriander, ¼ teaspoon pepper, and ¾ teaspoon salt together in small bowl. Pat swordfish dry with paper towels and sprinkle with coriander mixture, then place swordfish steaks, scallions, and lemon halves, cut side up, on now-empty sheet and brush evenly with 1 tablespoon oil. Broil until swordfish flakes apart when gently prodded with paring knife and registers 130 degrees and scallions and lemon halves are softened and lightly charred, 4 to 8 minutes. (You may need to remove scallions before lemon and swordfish are done cooking.) Transfer swordfish to serving platter and scallions and lemon halves to cutting board.

4 Whisk lemon zest, honey, garlic, cumin, cinnamon, nutmeg, remaining ¾ teaspoon salt, remaining 2 tablespoons oil, remaining 2 teaspoons coriander, and remaining ¼ teaspoon pepper together in large bowl. Microwave, stirring occasionally, until fragrant, about 1 minute. Once lemon is cool enough to handle, squeeze into fine-mesh strainer set over small bowl. Measure out 1 tablespoon juice, add to bowl with oil-honey mixture, and whisk to combine. Stir in olives and reserved tomatoes.

5 Coarsely chop reserved eggplant and scallions then transfer to bowl with dressing and gently toss to combine and season with salt and pepper to taste. Sprinkle swordfish with remaining 1 tablespoon parsley, and serve with caponata and bulgur.

Mexican Rice with Spiced Tilapia

Serves 4 to 6 | **Total Time** 1¼ hours

- 1 large onion, chopped
- 3 poblano peppers, stemmed, seeded, and chopped, divided
- ¼ cup vegetable oil, divided
- 1¾ teaspoons table salt, divided
- 1 cup fresh or frozen corn
- 1½ cups long-grain white rice, rinsed
- 3 tablespoons tomato paste
- 1½ teaspoons garlic powder, divided
- 4 (5- to 7-ounce) skinless tilapia fillets
- ¾ teaspoon ground cumin
- ½ teaspoon chipotle chili powder
- ⅓ cup chopped fresh cilantro leaves and tender stems, plus extra for serving
- 1 cup thinly sliced red cabbage
- 1 recipe Lime Crema (page 26)
- Lime wedges, for serving

Why This Recipe Works Do you love fish taco bowls—the type served up at many restaurants that leave you wanting more? We decided to simplify this craveable dish and make it on a sheet pan, Mexican rice included. For the fish, we use widely available tilapia, an often overlooked fish that has a wonderful flaky texture and mild, sweet taste. To create the layers of flavor that this sort of recipe demands, we give our sheet pan a workout. First, we roast two groups of distinct vegetables and aromatics on opposite ends of the sheet: onion and some chopped poblanos (which will later be combined with the rice) on one end, and corn and more chopped poblanos (which will ultimately be scattered over the rice) on the other end. For the rice, we get bold flavor by combining the roasted onion-poblano mixture with uncooked rice, tomato paste, and garlic powder in a large bowl. We add boiling water to the bowl and then carefully transfer everything to our now-empty sheet pan. Wrapping the pan in a double layer of foil makes it easier to transfer to the oven and allows the rice to steam-cook. Once the rice is tender, we top it with the roasted corn-poblano mixture, nestle spice-rubbed fish pieces into the rice, and return the sheet pan to the oven. After just 5 or so minutes, the fish is perfectly cooked and everything is hot. To finish, we platter it up, scatter sliced cabbage over the top, and drizzle everything with the lime crema. We like the color of purple cabbage in this recipe, but you can use green if you prefer.

1 Adjust oven rack to middle position and heat to 400 degrees. Combine onion, 1 cup chopped poblano, 1 tablespoon oil, and ¾ teaspoon salt in bowl, then transfer to rimmed baking sheet, spreading into even layer over half of sheet. Combine corn, remaining 2 cups chopped poblano, 1 tablespoon oil, and ¼ teaspoon salt in now-empty bowl, then spread into even layer on other half of sheet, leaving some space between vegetables. Roast until vegetables are nearly tender, about 20 minutes.

2 Transfer roasted corn-poblano mixture to again-empty bowl; set aside. Transfer roasted onion-poblano mixture to large bowl; add rice, tomato paste, 1 tablespoon oil, and 1 teaspoon garlic powder; and stir until rice is well coated. Stir in 2½ cups boiling water, then carefully pour rice mixture onto now-empty sheet. Using spatula, carefully spread rice into even layer over sheet. Cover sheet with aluminum foil, crimping edges tightly (using 2 sheets and overlapping in center if necessary) and bake until rice is tender, about 25 minutes. Wipe bowl dry.

3 While rice cooks, pat tilapia dry with paper towels. Create small pieces of similar size by cutting each fillet along seam running down middle to create 1 thick half and 1 thin half. Cut each thick piece in half crosswise, then in half again lengthwise. Cut each thin piece in half crosswise. Toss tilapia pieces with cumin, chili powder, remaining 1 tablespoon oil, remaining ¾ teaspoon salt, and remaining ½ teaspoon garlic powder in now-empty, dry bowl.

4 Once rice is tender (uncover 1 corner of sheet to test rice doneness), transfer sheet to wire rack and let rest, covered, for 5 minutes. Increase oven temperature to 450 degrees. Remove foil from sheet, sprinkle cilantro on top of rice, and fluff rice with fork. Spoon reserved corn-poblano mixture over rice, then nestle fish into rice, spaced evenly around sheet. Return sheet to oven and roast until fish is opaque and thickest pieces register 135 degrees, 5 to 7 minutes.

5 Scatter cabbage over top and drizzle with lime crema. Serve with extra cilantro and lime wedges.

Mediterranean Shrimp with Potatoes, Fennel, and Feta

Serves 4 to 6 | **Total Time** 45 minutes

- 1½ pounds Yukon Gold potatoes, peeled and sliced ½ inch thick
- 2 fennel bulbs, stalks discarded, bulbs halved and cut into 1-inch-thick wedges
- 3 tablespoons extra-virgin olive oil, divided, plus extra for drizzling
- 1½ teaspoons table salt, divided
- ½ teaspoon pepper, divided
- 2 pounds jumbo shrimp (16 to 20 per pound), peeled, deveined, and tails removed
- 2 teaspoons dried oregano
- 1 teaspoon grated lemon zest, plus lemon wedges for serving
- 4 ounces feta cheese, crumbled (1 cup)
- ½ cup pitted kalamata olives, halved
- 2 tablespoons chopped fresh parsley

Why This Recipe Works Shrimp is our ace in the hole. Keep it in your freezer and you have the basis for many an interesting and quick meal that feels luxe. So often the default for using shrimp is pasta, but here we take a different route inspired by the Mediterranean diet, combining the shrimp with fennel, potatoes, briny olives, and feta. While shrimp are often sautéed, roasting our shrimp on a sheet pan is simple and allows us to cook our vegetables on the pan as well. We start with the vegetables: After tossing sliced potatoes and wedges of fennel with oil, we spread them over the length of the sheet pan and transfer them to a hot oven. We give them a flip after 25 minutes so every side has contact with the hot sheet for beautiful browning, and scatter the shrimp and the feta across the top. It takes mere minutes for the shrimp to cook through and the feta to soften. As a final flavor boost, we scatter halved briny kalamata olives over everything. Don't core the fennel before cutting it into wedges; the core helps hold the wedges together during cooking. We prefer untreated shrimp, but if your shrimp are treated with salt or additives such as sodium tripolyphosphate (STPP), do not add the salt in step 2.

1 Adjust oven rack to lower-middle position and heat oven to 450 degrees. Toss potatoes and fennel with 2 tablespoons oil, 1 teaspoon salt, and ¼ teaspoon pepper on rimmed baking sheet then spread into even layer over sheet. Roast until just tender, about 25 minutes.

2 Meanwhile, pat shrimp dry with paper towels. Toss shrimp with oregano, lemon zest, remaining 1 tablespoon oil, remaining ½ teaspoon salt, and remaining ¼ teaspoon pepper in bowl; refrigerate until needed.

3 Using spatula, flip potatoes and fennel so browned sides are facing up. Scatter shrimp and feta over top. Return to oven and roast until shrimp are cooked through, 6 to 8 minutes. Sprinkle olives and parsley over top and drizzle with extra oil. Serve with lemon wedges.

Crab Cakes with Roasted Corn and Seasoned Fries

Serves 4 | **Total Time** 1½ hours

Crab Cakes

- 1 pound lump crabmeat, picked over for shells
- ¼ cup panko bread crumbs
- 3 scallions, minced
- 1 large egg
- 2 tablespoons mayonnaise
- 1 tablespoon Dijon mustard
- ⅛ teaspoon cayenne pepper
- 1 tablespoon unsalted butter

Corn and Potatoes

- 4 ears corn, kernels cut from cobs
- 1 onion, chopped
- 1 red bell pepper, stemmed, seeded, and cut into ½-inch pieces
- ¼ cup extra-virgin olive oil, divided
- 2 garlic cloves, sliced thin
- ½ teaspoon table salt
- ¼ teaspoon pepper
- 2 russet potatoes, unpeeled, each cut lengthwise into 8 equal wedges
- 1½ teaspoons Old Bay seasoning
- 2 tablespoons chopped fresh basil
- 2 teaspoons lemon juice

Why This Recipe Works Looking for a way to make Maryland-style crab cakes with just a little binder and a lot of tender crabmeat, we use a sheet pan to cook the delicate cakes, which also allows us to roast a couple of side dishes as well. Before putting the delicate crab cakes on the sheet pan, we kick-start the roasting of potato wedges seasoned with Old Bay and a mixture of fresh corn kernels, bell pepper, and onion. We then push the softened vegetables to the sides, add a pat of butter to the empty middle of the pan, and place the crab cakes there to cook. Buy crabmeat (either fresh or pasteurized) packed in plastic containers in the refrigerated section of your grocer's fish department. We do not recommend canned crabmeat.

1 For the crab cakes Line plate with triple layer of paper towels. Transfer crabmeat to prepared plate and pat dry with additional paper towels. Combine panko, scallions, egg, mayonnaise, mustard, and cayenne in bowl. Using rubber spatula, gently stir in crabmeat until combined. Discard paper towels. Divide crab mixture into 4 equal portions (about ½ cup each). Shape portions into tight balls, then shape balls into cakes measuring about 1 inch thick and 3 inches wide (cakes will be delicate). Transfer cakes to now-empty plate and refrigerate until ready to use.

2 For the corn and potatoes Adjust oven rack to lower-middle position and heat oven to 475 degrees. Toss corn, onion, bell pepper, 2 tablespoons oil, garlic, salt, and pepper together in bowl. Transfer corn mixture to one half of rimmed baking sheet.

3 In now-empty bowl, toss potatoes, Old Bay, and remaining 2 tablespoons oil together. Arrange potatoes cut side down in single layer on empty half of sheet. Bake until corn mixture is just softened and potatoes are lightly browned on bottom, about 15 minutes.

4 Remove sheet from oven. Using metal spatula, clear section in middle of sheet by pushing potatoes into pile at 1 end of sheet and corn mixture into another pile at opposite end of sheet. Place butter on now-empty middle section of sheet and use metal spatula to evenly distribute. Using spatula, gently place crab cakes on middle section of sheet. Return sheet to oven and bake until crab cakes are golden on bottom and potatoes are tender, about 20 minutes.

5 Transfer sheet to wire rack. Stir basil and lemon juice into corn mixture and season with salt and pepper to taste. Flip crab cakes browned side up. Serve.

CHAPTER FIVE

Vegetable Mains

Roasted Gnocchi with Blistered Cherry Tomato Sauce

Serves 4 | **Total Time** 40 minutes

- 2 tablespoons extra-virgin olive oil, divided
- 4 garlic cloves, peeled and sliced thin
- 1½ teaspoons tomato paste
- 1 teaspoon table salt
- ¾ teaspoon sugar
- ⅛ teaspoon pepper
- ⅛ teaspoon red pepper flakes
- 24 ounces cherry tomatoes
- 1 pound shelf-stable potato gnocchi
- ¼ cup grated Parmesan cheese
- 2 tablespoons torn fresh basil

Why This Recipe Works Cherry tomatoes are a kitchen miracle. You can use them raw in so many dishes, but when you roast them, they become something altogether different. Here we place them whole in the center of a sheet pan with gnocchi (which is a canvas just waiting for more color and flavoring) around the perimeter. This exposes the starchy gnocchi to more heat while the tomatoes soften gently and release their jammy juices. Tossing them with a bit of tomato paste adds umami undertones, and garlic slivers, red pepper flakes, salt, pepper, and sugar ensure they are anything but dull. Roasting potato gnocchi in the oven—rather than boiling them—makes them golden and crispy on the outside and tender and creamy on the inside. Be sure to use shelf-stable (not refrigerated or frozen) gnocchi in this recipe. Separate any stuck-together gnocchi before tossing with the oil in step 2.

1 Adjust oven rack to middle position and heat oven to 500 degrees. Whisk 1 tablespoon oil, garlic, tomato paste, salt, sugar, pepper, and pepper flakes together in large bowl. Add tomatoes and toss until well coated.

2 Transfer tomato mixture to rimmed baking sheet, pushing tomatoes toward center of sheet. Scrape any remaining garlic mixture from bowl into center of tomatoes on sheet. Toss gnocchi with remaining 1 tablespoon oil in now-empty bowl to coat. Transfer gnocchi to edges of sheet, leaving about 1 inch of space between tomatoes and gnocchi.

3 Roast until gnocchi are golden brown and tomatoes are blistered and browned, about 20 minutes. Remove sheet from oven, add Parmesan and basil to sheet, and stir gently to combine gnocchi and sauce. Season with salt and pepper to taste. Serve.

Eggplant Parmesan with Burrata and Basil

Serves 4 | **Total Time** 1¾ hours

- ½ cup plus 1 tablespoon extra-virgin olive oil, divided
- 3 (14- to 16-ounce) eggplants
- ¾ teaspoon plus ⅛ teaspoon table salt, divided
- 1 (25-ounce) jar marinara sauce (2½ cups)
- ½ cup chopped fresh basil, divided
- ½ teaspoon pepper
- ½ teaspoon red pepper flakes (optional)
- ¾ cup panko bread crumbs
- 1 garlic clove, minced
- 1 teaspoon minced fresh thyme
- 1 teaspoon grated lemon zest
- 3 ounces Parmesan cheese, grated (1½ cups)
- 8 ounces burrata cheese

Why This Recipe Works Nonnas everywhere would no doubt roll their eyes at this recipe. Eggplant stacks on a sheet pan? No large casserole dish gloriously topped with cheese and basil for everyone to dig into? Here's a different, easier, and just as delicious path forward that will satisfy your longing for eggplant Parmesan. Instead of laboriously breading eggplant rounds and frying them in multiple skillets (a messy job for sure), cut the eggplants into thin planks and roast them. While they're roasting, you can jazz up store-bought marinara with basil, pepper, and red pepper flakes and toast the panko in the microwave. As for making those tidy stacks, start by putting a smear of tomato sauce onto each quadrant of your pan; now, let the layering begin. When they're done baking, use a spatula and transfer each stack to a serving plate. For a luxe finishing touch, tear burrata into pieces over each serving; it softens when it hits the hot eggplant. A little extra toasted panko and fresh basil scattered over the stacks give them traditional crunch and flavor.

1 Adjust oven racks to upper-middle and lower-middle positions and heat oven to 475 degrees. Brush 2 rimmed baking sheets with ¼ cup oil (2 tablespoons per sheet). Cut stem end off eggplants and discard. Cut ¼-inch-thick slice from 1 long side of each eggplant and discard. Starting on cut side, slice eggplants lengthwise ⅜ inch thick until you have 20 slices total. Discard final rounded skin-on slices.

2 Arrange eggplant slices in single layer over prepared sheets (eggplant slices may overlap slightly). Brush evenly with ¼ cup oil and sprinkle with ¾ teaspoon salt. Roast until deeply browned on bottom, 35 to 40 minutes, switching and rotating sheets every 10 minutes.

3 Meanwhile, combine marinara; ¼ cup basil; pepper; and pepper flakes, if using. In second bowl combine panko, garlic, remaining 1 tablespoon oil, and remaining ⅛ teaspoon salt. Microwave until panko is golden brown, 2 to 4 minutes, stirring occasionally. Stir in thyme and lemon zest and set aside.

4 Remove sheets from oven and decrease oven temperature to 375 degrees. Transfer eggplant to cutting board (slices can overlap at this point). Dollop one 2-tablespoon-size portion of marinara sauce in each quadrant of 1 now-empty sheet, then spread into ovals roughly the same size as largest eggplant slices. Place 4 largest eggplant slices on top of each sauce oval, one in each quadrant of sheet. Divide ½ cup marinara sauce among eggplant slices, spreading to cover slices, then divide ⅓ cup Parmesan over all 4 slices.

5 Repeat layering 3 more times to make 4 stacks of 4 slices, trying to match up size and shape of eggplant slices to make neat, sturdy stacks. Place remaining eggplant slices on top, spread remaining sauce over top layer of eggplant, and sprinkle with remaining Parmesan. Bake on upper rack until warmed through and liquid on sheet has mostly evaporated, 20 to 25 minutes.

6 Use sturdy spatula to transfer eggplant stacks to individual serving plates. Holding burrata over eggplant, tear burrata into rough 1-inch pieces and scatter over each serving. Sprinkle with reserved panko mixture and remaining ¼ cup basil and serve.

Crispy-Creamy Macaroni and Cheese

Serves 4 to 6 | **Total Time** 40 minutes

- 1 pound elbow macaroni
- 8 ounces sharp cheddar cheese, shredded (2 cups), divided
- 8 ounces American cheese, shredded (2 cups)
- 1 (12-ounce) can evaporated milk
- ½ cup sour cream
- 1¼ teaspoons table salt
- ½ teaspoon dry mustard
- 4 tablespoons unsalted butter, melted, divided
- ¾ cup panko bread crumbs

Why This Recipe Works Who doesn't love macaroni and cheese? And tailoring it to work on a sheet pan eliminates the need for multiple pots and lots of stirring. Our ingredient list was the same as our latest version, which relies on deli American cheese because it contains a lot of emulsifiers and makes a béchamel unnecessary. Here's the basic technique and where the sheet pan comes in: After soaking the macaroni in boiling water and draining it, we toss it with the cheese and some reserved starchy water and stir vigorously. Then we add sour cream, evaporated milk, and mustard powder, all standard stuff. And yes, we spread this mixture on a sheet pan that we've brushed with butter. After about 15 minutes in the oven, what we see is a sheet pan full of creamy macaroni and cheese. Oh, did we mention the lovely frico we made on the sheet pan earlier? We break it into pieces and sprinkle it and some toasted bread crumbs over the top. Mission accomplished. Buy an 8-ounce block of American cheese from the deli rather than presliced cheese.

1 Adjust oven racks to upper-middle and lower-middle positions and heat oven to 400 degrees. Combine macaroni with 4 cups boiling water in large bowl. Cover and let sit for 12 minutes, stirring occasionally.

2 Meanwhile, line rimmed baking sheet with parchment paper and sprinkle 1 cup cheddar in center of sheet, spreading into rough 10 by 8-inch rectangle. Bake on upper rack until cheese is browned and lacy, 8 to 12 minutes. Transfer sheet to wire rack and let cool slightly, then use spatula to slide crispy cheddar onto double layer of paper towels. Discard parchment, reserving sheet. Once cool enough to handle, break crispy cheddar into ½- to 1-inch pieces; set aside.

3 Reserve ½ cup soaking water, then drain pasta and return it to bowl. Add American cheese, remaining 1 cup cheddar, and reserved soaking water and stir vigorously until most of cheese is melted (some small clumps of cheese will remain; that is OK) and water has been absorbed. Stir in evaporated milk, sour cream, salt, and mustard until well combined.

4 Brush bottom and sides of now-empty sheet with 3 tablespoons melted butter. Transfer pasta mixture to sheet, being sure to scrape out any remaining cheese mixture in bowl, spreading into even layer if needed. Bake on lower rack until sauce is bubbling, 13 to 15 minutes.

5 Meanwhile, toss panko with remaining 1 tablespoon butter in bowl until evenly coated. Microwave, stirring frequently, until light golden brown, 2 to 4 minutes.

6 Remove sheet from oven and sprinkle crispy cheddar pieces and toasted panko evenly over top. Serve immediately.

VARIATIONS

Crispy-Creamy Macaroni and Cheese with Asparagus and Peas

Add 1 cup frozen peas and 8 ounces trimmed asparagus, cut into 1-inch pieces, to pasta mixture with evaporated milk in step 3. Add ¼ teaspoon grated lemon zest to panko after microwaving in step 5.

French Onion Macaroni and Cheese

You can use store-bought crispy shallots or use our recipe for Crispy Shallots (page 26). Substitute Gruyère for cheddar. Stir full 8 ounces Gruyère into pasta with American cheese in step 3; skip step 2. Add 1½ teaspoons minced fresh thyme to pasta with evaporated milk mixture in step 3. Reduce butter to 3 tablespoons and omit panko; skip step 5. Sprinkle 1 cup crispy shallots over macaroni and cheese just before serving.

How to Build the Sheet Pan

Place a 4-inch square of foil in the center of the wire rack. Toss tomatoes, garlic, and onions with tomato paste, oil, thyme, pepper flakes, salt and pepper, then arrange the onions and garlic on the foil and the tomatoes, cut side down, on the wire rack around the foil.

Roasted Tomato Sauce

Makes 3 cups; enough to sauce 1 pound of pasta | **Total Time** 1¼ hours

- 2 tablespoons tomato paste
- 2 tablespoons extra-virgin olive oil, divided
- 2 teaspoons minced fresh thyme
- ⅛ teaspoon red pepper flakes
- ¾ teaspoon table salt
- ¼ teaspoon pepper
- 3 pounds vine-ripe tomatoes, cored and halved pole to pole
- 6 garlic cloves, crushed and peeled
- 1 small onion, sliced into ½-inch-thick rounds
- 1 teaspoon red wine vinegar
- Sugar
- 2 tablespoons chopped fresh basil

Why This Recipe Works We love tomato sauce made with height-of-the-season tomatoes, but it does take some work; namely, scoring and blanching the tomatoes and removing the skin while they are still hot—a tedious task if there ever was one. For a great fresh tomato sauce recipe with out-of-season fresh tomatoes, we turn to roasting, which caramelizes the natural sugars in the tomatoes, intensifying their flavors, while adding a light touch of smokiness to the sauce. Keeping the seeds in the roasted tomatoes contributes moisture to our sauce, and tossing them with tomato paste gives the sauce a deep red color and more flavor. Save some pasta cooking water to adjust the sauce's consistency before serving.

1 Adjust oven rack to middle position and heat oven to 475 degrees. Place 4-inch square of foil in center of wire rack set in rimmed baking sheet. Combine tomato paste, 1 tablespoon oil, thyme, pepper flakes, salt, and pepper in large bowl. Add tomatoes, garlic, and onion and toss until well coated. Arrange garlic cloves and onion rounds on foil and arrange tomatoes, cut side down, around garlic and onion directly on rack.

2 Roast until vegetables are soft and tomato skins are well charred, 45 to 55 minutes. Remove sheet from oven and let cool for 5 minutes.

3 Transfer garlic and onion to food processor and pulse until finely chopped, about 5 pulses. Add tomatoes, vinegar, and remaining 1 tablespoon oil to food processor and pulse until tomatoes are broken down but still chunky, about 5 pulses. Scrape down sides of processor bowl; season with salt, pepper, and sugar to taste; and pulse until only slightly chunky, about 5 pulses. Stir in basil and serve. (Sauce can be refrigerated in airtight container for up to 3 days or frozen for up to 2 months; add basil just before serving.)

Roasted Paneer Tikka Masala

Serves 4 | **Total Time** 1¼ hours

- 3 pounds vine-ripe tomatoes, cored and quartered
- ¼ cup vegetable oil, divided
- 1 tablespoon garam masala, divided
- 1 teaspoon table salt, divided
- 1 tablespoon sugar
- 1 tablespoon tomato paste
- 1 tablespoon white wine vinegar
- 1 large onion, coarsely chopped
- 1 serrano chile, seeded and chopped
- 4 garlic cloves, smashed and peeled
- 1 (1-inch) piece ginger, peeled and chopped
- 12 ounces paneer cheese, cut into ¾-inch pieces
- 1 teaspoon ground coriander
- 1 teaspoon ground cumin
- ½ teaspoon ground turmeric
- ¼ teaspoon cayenne pepper
- ½ cup heavy cream
- 1 cup cilantro leaves, divided
- Plain whole-milk yogurt

Why This Recipe Works Tikka masala made with chicken, shrimp, or paneer is one of the most-ordered dishes at Indian restaurants. Roasting the aromatic vegetables for the creamy, spicy sauce deepens their flavor and there's plenty of room to roast the paneer on the same sheet pan. First, we toss tomatoes with oil and garam masala and broil them, which gives them a slight char and concentrates their flavor. Next we toss onion pieces and a chile with tomato paste and a mix of spices (turmeric, coriander, cumin and cayenne) along with smashed garlic and chopped ginger and add them to the sheet to mingle with the tomatoes. After 15 minutes, we simply push the tomato mixture to one side of the sheet and now the paneer gets its turn on the other side. If you can only find 8-ounce blocks of paneer, go ahead and use 1 pound total in this recipe. Serve with rice.

1 Adjust oven rack 6 inches from broiler element and heat broiler. Toss tomatoes with 2 tablespoons oil, 2 teaspoons garam masala, and ¾ teaspoon salt on aluminum foil–lined rimmed baking sheet, then spread into single layer over sheet. Broil on upper rack until tomatoes have released their liquid and skins are lightly charred, 15 to 25 minutes.

2 Meanwhile, whisk sugar, tomato paste, vinegar, 1 tablespoon oil, remaining 1 teaspoon garam masala, and remaining ¼ teaspoon salt together in large bowl. Add onion, serrano, garlic, and ginger and toss to coat. In separate bowl, toss paneer with remaining 1 tablespoon oil, coriander, cumin, turmeric, and cayenne until evenly coated.

3 Remove tomatoes from oven and heat oven to 450 degrees. Add onion mixture to tomatoes on sheet, drizzling any oil left in bowl over top, stir to combine, then redistribute into even layer over sheet. Roast on upper-middle rack for 15 minutes. Move vegetables to 1 side of sheet, then add paneer to empty side of sheet. Return sheet to oven and roast until onion is softened and juices have thickened slightly, 25 to 30 minutes.

4 Transfer paneer to serving bowl. Carefully transfer vegetable mixture and juices left in sheet to blender. Add cream and half of cilantro and blend until slightly chunky, about 20 seconds. Add to bowl with paneer, stirring to combine. Serve, garnishing individual bowls with yogurt and remaining cilantro.

How to Build the Sheet Pan

Bake prosciutto on parchment-lined sheet until dry and crisp; set aside. Toss zucchini, leek, oil, garlic, salt, and pepper together on sheet then spread into even layer cut side up. Roast until tender and slightly browned.

Zucchini, Leek, and Pea Soup with Crispy Prosciutto

Serves 4 to 6 | **Total Time** 55 minutes

- 4 thin slices prosciutto (2 ounces)
- 3 zucchini (8 to 10 ounces each), trimmed and halved lengthwise
- 1 leek (8 ounces), white and light-green part only, halved lengthwise and washed thoroughly
- 3 tablespoons extra-virgin olive oil
- 3 garlic cloves, peeled
- ¾ teaspoon table salt, divided
- ¼ teaspoon pepper
- 1½ cups frozen peas, thawed, divided
- ½ cup fresh basil leaves plus 2 tablespoons chopped fresh basil
- 1 teaspoon grated lemon zest, plus lemon wedges for serving
- 4 cups chicken broth, warmed, divided

Why This Recipe Works Soup? In a sheet pan? Yes, you heard that right. Forget the chopping and simmering and let the oven and blender do all the work for this simple yet full-bodied soup. First, use the sheet pan to transform sliced prosciutto into a crispy garnish. (Watch closely because it burns easily.) Then, roast halved zucchini and leeks with a few cloves of garlic, and blend with hot broth and thawed frozen peas. The addition of basil and lemon zest rounds out the flavors and makes this pretty green puree sing. Use a microwave to quickly heat up the broth without dirtying a pot. When choosing zucchini, opt for those of medium size—anything larger than 10 ounces will have too many seeds and result in a watery soup. Be sure to wash the halved leek thoroughly to remove dirt and sand that's often trapped between the layers.

1 Adjust oven rack to middle position and heat oven to 400 degrees. Line rimmed baking sheet with parchment paper. Arrange prosciutto slices in single layer on sheet and bake until dry and crisp, 8 to 12 minutes. Transfer prosciutto to paper towel–lined plate and set aside to cool. Discard parchment. Once cool, crumble prosciutto into bite-size pieces.

2 Line now-empty sheet with aluminum foil. Toss zucchini, leek, oil, garlic, ¼ teaspoon salt, and pepper together on sheet, then arrange vegetables into even layer, cut sides up. Roast until vegetables are tender and slightly browned, about 25 minutes.

3 Transfer roasted vegetables and garlic to blender. Add remaining ½ teaspoon salt, 1 cup peas, basil leaves, lemon zest, and 1 cup warm broth and blend until smooth, about 2 minutes. Transfer soup to saucepan and stir in remaining 3 cups warm broth. Season with salt and pepper to taste. Transfer to serving bowls and garnish with remaining ½ cup peas, chopped basil, and crumbled crispy prosciutto. Serve.

Roasted Aloo Gobi

Serves 4 | **Total Time** 45 minutes

- 6 tablespoons vegetable oil
- 1 onion, chopped fine
- 5 garlic cloves, minced (5 teaspoons)
- 5 teaspoons minced fresh ginger
- 2 teaspoons cumin seeds
- 1¾ teaspoons table salt
- 1½ teaspoons ground coriander
- 1½ teaspoons amchoor
- ¾ teaspoon ground turmeric
- ¾ teaspoon Kashmiri chile powder
- ½ teaspoon ground asafetida
- 1½ pounds Yukon Gold potatoes, unpeeled, cut into ½-inch pieces
- 1½ pounds cauliflower florets, cut into 1-inch pieces
- 1½ tablespoons chopped fresh cilantro
- Plain whole-milk yogurt

Why This Recipe Works Aloo gobi (Hindi for "potato cauliflower") is one of the pillars of Indian home cooking; it's a dish of softened, spiced potatoes and cauliflower. It coaxes a lively complexity out of quotidian vegetables in record time, requiring little more than the vegetables and a well-stocked spice cabinet. It is normally made in a large pot on the stovetop, but here we turn to the sheet pan. Now, here's the fun part: Toss those veggies with oil, spices, and aromatics, spread them on a foil-lined sheet pan, and let the oven do all the work. No need to prebloom the spices—they'll get all the flavor magic they need from the high heat and generous splash of oil. The result? A golden, crispy aloo gobi with zero cleanup drama and all the flavor you crave. Leaving the skin on the potatoes provides extra texture and keeps the potatoes from falling apart. Asafetida (also known as hing), is a powerful flavor enhancer in Indian cooking. When cooked with other aromatics, its bitterness softens and it adds deep umami flavor. If unavailable, you can omit it. Amchoor, made from green mangos, is a citrusy seasoning that adds tart flavor. If unavailable, stir 1½ teaspoons lemon juice into the dish at the end of cooking. If Kashmiri chile powder is unavailable, substitute ½ teaspoon paprika plus a pinch of cayenne. Note that all the spices used in this recipe are readily available online or at South Asian markets. Serve with roti or basmati rice and drizzle with yogurt.

1 Adjust oven rack to middle position and heat oven to 425 degrees. Line rimmed baking sheet with aluminum foil. Whisk oil, onion, garlic, ginger, cumin seeds, salt, coriander, amchoor, turmeric, chile powder, and asafetida together in large bowl. Add potatoes and cauliflower and toss to coat then spread into even layer over prepared sheet.

2 Roast until potatoes are tender and cauliflower is spotty brown, 25 to 35 minutes. Sprinkle with cilantro, drizzle with yogurt, and serve.

Charred Cauliflower and Crispy Chickpeas with Romesco

Serves 4 | **Total Time** 40 minutes

- 1 head cauliflower (2 pounds), cored and cut into 2-inch florets
- 1 (15-ounce) can chickpeas, rinsed
- 7 tablespoons extra-virgin olive oil, divided
- 1¼ teaspoons table salt, divided
- ⅔ cup jarred roasted red peppers, patted dry
- ¼ cup slivered almonds, toasted
- 6 tablespoons fresh parsley leaves, divided
- 1 tablespoons sherry vinegar
- 1 garlic clove, minced
- 2 heads Belgian endive (4 ounces each), leaves separated
- ½ cup Sumac Onion (page 27)

Why This Recipe Works You cannot have too many recipes for cauliflower, especially ones that involve roasting, which brings out its nutty essence; char it, as we do here, and it's even more inviting. This inventive dish is a study in contrasts, with soft cauliflower paired with crispy chickpeas; a bright and nutty romesco sauce; and tart, crunchy sumac-pickled red onion. It's also easy to put together since you can roast the cauliflower and chickpeas on a sheet pan in about 30 minutes. While they're roasting you can make the romesco in a food processor. With everything arranged on elegant endive leaves, this dish is a feast for the eyes. The sumac onions need an hour for pickling, but they last a week so you can certainly make them in advance. We love the flavor they bring to this dish but you can skip them and serve the dish with lemon wedges.

1 Adjust oven rack to middle position and heat oven to 475 degrees. Toss cauliflower, chickpeas, ¼ cup oil, and 1 teaspoon salt together on rimmed baking sheet, then spread into even layer over sheet. Roast until cauliflower is golden in spots, about 20 minutes.

2 Meanwhile, process red peppers, almonds, ¼ cup parsley, vinegar, garlic, remaining 3 tablespoons oil, and remaining ¼ teaspoon salt in food processor until smooth, about 1 minute, scraping down sides of bowl as needed. Season with salt and pepper to taste, and set aside until ready to serve. (Romesco sauce can be refrigerated in airtight container for up to 3 days; bring to room temperature and thin with hot water if needed before serving.)

3 Remove sheet from oven, stir cauliflower and chickpeas, and redistribute evenly over sheet. Return to oven and roast until lightly charred throughout, 8 to 10 minutes. Arrange endive leaves in even layer over platter, then top with roasted cauliflower and chickpeas. Dollop with reserved romesco and sprinkle with sumac onions and remaining 2 tablespoons parsley. Serve.

Roasted Cauliflower and Grape Salad with Chermoula

Serves 4 | **Total Time** 50 minutes

Salad

- 1 head cauliflower (2 pounds), core chopped coarse, florets cut into 1-inch pieces (6 cups)
- 1 cup seedless red grapes
- ½ small red onion, sliced thin
- 2 tablespoons extra-virgin olive oil
- ½ teaspoon table salt
- ¼ teaspoon pepper
- 2 tablespoons fresh cilantro or parsley leaves
- 2 tablespoons coarsely chopped toasted walnuts or sliced almonds

Chermoula

- 1 cup fresh cilantro or parsley leaves
- 5 tablespoons extra-virgin olive oil
- 2 tablespoons lemon juice
- 4 garlic cloves, minced
- ½ teaspoon ground cumin
- ½ teaspoon paprika
- ¼ teaspoon table salt
- ⅛ teaspoon cayenne pepper

Why This Recipe Works Cauliflower's delicate flavor makes it an ideal canvas on which to paint other flavors. Here those "paints" come from grapes, cilantro, and red onion. We start by roasting cauliflower florets on a sheet pan until they're caramelized. Instead of discarding the core, we blitz it in the food processor and add it to the salad for a contrasting rice-like texture. Then we make the chermoula, a North African sauce made with hefty amounts of cilantro, lemon, and garlic. To balance the chermoula, we add sliced red onion and whole red grapes to the same baking sheet as the cauliflower roasts. Roasting the grapes and onion creates complex flavors as they caramelize and sweeten. Fresh cilantro leaves and crunchy walnuts are the finishing touches to this substantial roasted vegetable salad. This salad is satisfying enough to be a meal but also lovely doled out as a side to accompany hearty grains or rich meat.

1 For the salad Adjust oven rack to lowest position and heat oven to 475 degrees. Toss cauliflower florets, grapes, onion, oil, salt, and pepper together on rimmed baking sheet, then spread into even layer over sheet. Roast until vegetables are tender, florets are deep golden, and onion slices are charred at edges, 12 to 15 minutes, stirring halfway through roasting. Let cool slightly, about 15 minutes.

2 Meanwhile, pulse cauliflower core in food processor until finely ground into ⅛-inch pieces, 6 to 8 pulses, scraping down sides of bowl as needed; transfer to large bowl.

3 For the chermoula Process all ingredients in now-empty processor until smooth, about 1 minute, scraping down sides of bowl as needed. (Chermoula can be refrigerated in airtight container for up to 2 days.) Transfer to bowl with cauliflower core.

4 Add roasted cauliflower mixture to chermoula mixture in bowl and toss to combine. Season with salt and pepper to taste. Sprinkle with cilantro and walnuts. Serve.

Overstuffed Sweet Potatoes with Tofu and Red Curry Vinaigrette

Serves 4 | **Total Time** 1¼ hours

- ½ cup plus 1 teaspoon vegetable oil, divided
- 14 ounces firm tofu, cut into ¾-inch pieces
- 1 teaspoon table salt, divided
- ½ teaspoon pepper, divided
- 6 tablespoons cornstarch
- 2 sweet potatoes (12 ounces each), unpeeled, halved lengthwise
- 8 ounces broccoli florets, cut into ½-inch pieces
- 8 ounces white or cremini mushrooms, trimmed and quartered
- 1 red bell pepper, stemmed, seeded, and cut into ¼-inch-wide strips
- 1 teaspoon grated lime zest plus 2 tablespoons juice
- 2 teaspoons Thai green or red curry paste
- ¼ cup shredded fresh Thai basil

Why This Recipe Works This fresh, modern take on stuffed potatoes takes its cue from the tangy and sweet flavors of Thai-style curries. All of the elements—rich, earthy sweet potato halves along with morsels of tofu, broccoli, mushrooms, and bell peppers—are roasted to perfection on a single baking sheet. To create extra-crispy tofu, we dust pieces of tofu with cornstarch and then we arrange them on one side of an oiled baking sheet and place the sweet potato halves on the other side. (Halving the sweet potatoes reduces the roasting time from an hour for whole potatoes to a mere 20 minutes.) Once the potatoes are done, we add the other vegetables to the space left on the baking sheet and roast them until tender in the time it takes to finish the crispy tofu. After stuffing the potatoes with the tofu and vegetables, we drizzle them with a curry vinaigrette packed with the bold flavors of lime and curry paste. All this hearty meal needs is a simple green salad. Do not substitute soft tofu here. If you can't find Thai basil, you can substitute Italian basil. Green and red curry paste work equally well here.

1 Spread tofu over paper towel–lined plate and let drain for 20 minutes. Adjust oven rack to lower-middle position and heat oven to 450 degrees. Brush rimmed baking sheet with 3 tablespoons oil.

2 Gently pat tofu dry with paper towels, sprinkle with ½ teaspoon salt and ¼ teaspoon pepper, then toss with cornstarch in bowl. Arrange tofu in even layer on half of sheet. Arrange potato halves cut side down on other half of sheet and brush skins with 1 teaspoon oil. Roast until potato halves yield to gentle pressure and centers register 200 degrees, 20 to 25 minutes, flipping tofu with spatula halfway through roasting.

3 Toss broccoli, mushrooms, and bell pepper with 1 tablespoon oil, ¼ teaspoon salt, and ⅛ teaspoon pepper in bowl. Remove sheet from oven, transfer potato halves to plate, and cover with aluminum foil to keep warm. Arrange broccoli mixture in even layer on now-empty side of sheet and roast until vegetables are tender and beginning to brown and tofu is crisp and lightly browned, 10 to 15 minutes, tossing vegetables and flipping tofu halfway through roasting.

4 Whisk lime zest and juice, curry paste, remaining ¼ cup oil, remaining ¼ teaspoon salt, and remaining ⅛ teaspoon pepper together in bowl. Arrange potato halves cut side up on individual serving plates, top with tofu and vegetable mixture, drizzle with vinaigrette, and sprinkle with basil. Serve.

Roasted Tofu and Sweet Potato Bowls with Snap Pea Salad

Serves 4 | **Total Time** 1¼ hours, plus 20 minutes draining

- 28 ounces firm tofu, cut into 1-inch-wide by 1½-inch-long pieces
- 2 pounds sweet potatoes, peeled and cut into 1-inch rounds
- 1 tablespoon vegetable oil
- 2 teaspoons table salt, divided
- 3 tablespoons soy sauce
- 2 tablespoons honey
- 2 tablespoons toasted sesame oil
- 1 tablespoon sambal oelek, plus extra for serving
- 1 tablespoon lime juice plus lime wedges for serving
- 1 tablespoon fish sauce
- 1 teaspoon grated fresh ginger
- 12 ounces sugar snap peas, strings removed, halved on bias
- 1 large red bell pepper, stemmed, seeded, and cut into ¼-inch-wide strips
- 1 cup cilantro leaves and tender stems, chopped coarse, divided
- ⅓ cup dry-roasted peanuts, chopped coarse
- 1 serrano chile, sliced into thin rounds (optional)

Why This Recipe Works If you are reluctant to make a tofu-centric recipe, this one will change your mind. It packs an abundance of flavors, textures, and colorful ingredients into each bowl and it's easy to make, thanks to a rimmed baking sheet. Roasting the tofu makes all the difference, as it gives us the opportunity to flavor the tofu at several points along the way. First, before roasting, we toss it with a heady mix of soy sauce, honey, sesame oil, and sambal, which acts as a powerful glaze; the sugars encourage quick browning on the outside, allowing the tofu to stay tender inside. As for the potatoes, we give them a head start on the tofu in a very hot oven because honestly, what is better than sweet potato rounds that are deeply caramelized? Partway through roasting we add more glaze to both the tofu and sweet potatoes, and we use the remaining glaze to make an aromatic drizzling sauce, ensuring that this dish delivers harmonious flavors through and through.

1 Adjust oven rack to middle position and heat oven to 475 degrees. Spread tofu over paper towel–lined plate and let drain for 20 minutes. Toss potatoes with vegetable oil and ¾ teaspoon salt on rimmed baking sheet, then arrange cut side down in single layer over sheet. Roast until deeply browned on bottom, 12 to 16 minutes.

2 Whisk soy sauce, honey, sesame oil, and sambal together in bowl. Gently pat tofu dry with paper towels, then toss with 3 tablespoons soy-honey mixture and 1 teaspoon salt. Remove sheet from oven and immediately reduce oven temperature to 375 degrees. Flip potato rounds, shifting to 1 half of sheet, then spread tofu on empty side. Roast for 15 minutes.

3 Remove sheet from oven and gently stir tofu pieces. Brush potatoes and tofu with 3 tablespoons soy-honey mixture, then return to oven and roast until tofu is golden brown around edges, 14 to 18 minutes.

4 Whisk lime juice, fish sauce, ginger, remaining ¼ teaspoon salt, and remaining soy-honey mixture together in large bowl. Set aside half of dressing for serving, then add snap peas, bell pepper, and half of cilantro to remaining dressing in bowl, tossing to coat. Divide potatoes, tofu, and snap pea salad among individual serving bowls and drizzle with reserved dressing. Top with peanuts; serrano, if using; and remaining cilantro and serve with lime wedges and extra sambal.

Fattoush with Butternut Squash and Apple

Serves 4 to 6 | **Total Time** 45 minutes

- 2 pounds butternut squash, peeled, seeded, and cut into ½-inch pieces
- 5 tablespoons extra-virgin olive oil, divided
- ¾ teaspoon table salt, divided
- 3 tablespoons lemon juice
- 4 teaspoons ground sumac, plus extra for serving
- 1 garlic clove, minced
- 3 cups pita chips, crumbled into ½-inch pieces
- 1 apple, cored and cut into ½-inch pieces
- ¼ head radicchio, cored and chopped (1 cup)
- ½ cup chopped fresh parsley
- 4 scallions, sliced thin

Why This Recipe Works Flatbreads are a mainstay of tables across the Mediterranean, but the thin breads stale quickly, so creative dishes designed to use them up abound. Such recipes are called fatteh, derived from the Arabic word "fatta," meaning "to crumble." Pita bread salad, or fattoush, is a common example—and its appeal goes far beyond leftovers. The vibrant mix is simple but a textural marvel that combines crumbled toasted, fried, or day-old bread with summertime produce (tomatoes and cucumbers), fresh herbs, and greens, all simply dressed with lemon juice and olive oil and lavished with sumac. We thought about how to carry the experience into the colder months, when tomatoes and cucumbers aren't at their peak. We conjured a combination with distinctly fall flavors that still boasts fantastic contrasts in texture. Crisp sweet apples and slightly bitter radicchio provide fresh crunch, while roasted butternut squash gives the salad complexity. To keep things simple we used pita chips instead of cutting up pita breads and toasting them in the oven. We prefer a sweeter crisp apple like Pink Lady or Fuji to complement the bright lemony dressing.

1 Adjust oven rack to lowest position and heat oven to 450 degrees. Toss squash with 1 tablespoon oil and ½ teaspoon salt on rimmed baking sheet and spread into even layer. Roast on lower rack until browned and tender, 20 to 25 minutes, stirring halfway through. Set aside to cool slightly, about 10 minutes.

2 Meanwhile, whisk lemon juice, sumac, garlic, and remaining ¼ teaspoon salt together in large bowl and let sit for 10 minutes. Whisking constantly, slowly drizzle in remaining ¼ cup oil.

3 Add roasted squash, pita chips, apple, radicchio, parsley, and scallions to bowl with dressing and toss gently to coat. Season with salt and pepper to taste. Serve, sprinkling individual portions with extra sumac.

Charred Cabbage Salad with Torn Tofu and Plantain Chips

Serves 4 | **Total Time** 1¼ hours

- 14 ounces firm tofu, torn into bite-size pieces
- 3 tablespoons seasoned rice vinegar, divided
- 2 tablespoons lime juice
- 4 teaspoons grated fresh ginger, divided
- 1 tablespoon honey
- 1 tablespoon fish sauce
- 1 head red cabbage (2 pounds)
- 7 tablespoons vegetable oil, divided
- 4 teaspoons Thai red or green curry paste, divided
- 1 tablespoon ground turmeric, divided
- ½ teaspoon table salt
- 1 tablespoon water
- 2 scallions, sliced thin on bias
- ¼ cup plantain or banana chips, crushed

Why This Recipe Works Cooked cabbage suffers from a bad reputation. This recipe will change that. Roasting transforms cabbage into a treat; the charred edges and smoky, savory flavor will have everyone asking you how to make it. Plus, the layers hidden beneath the side that hits the hot pan take on a sweetness that is hard to describe. Brushing the wedges with a heady turmeric-and-garlic-infused oil adds yet another distinct layer—one that we mimic with the marinade for the raw tofu and the vinaigrette that finally ties everything together. Tearing the tofu into pieces by hand creates a craggy surface area ideal for soaking up flavor—in this case, a sweet-sour marinade of lime juice, honey, and fish sauce. And finally, for the vinaigrette that takes this salad from good to great, we bloom more curry paste, turmeric, and ginger in the microwave, bringing their flavors to life, before adding a hit of seasoned rice vinegar, which jolts the warm dressing with an edginess so that the finished salad really shines.

1 Adjust oven rack to lowest position and heat oven to 500 degrees. Gently press tofu dry with paper towels. Whisk 1 tablespoon vinegar, lime juice, 2 teaspoons ginger, honey, and fish sauce together in medium bowl. Add tofu and toss gently to coat; set aside for 20 minutes. (Tofu can be refrigerated in airtight container for up to 24 hours.)

2 Halve cabbage through core and cut each half into 4 approximately 2-inch-wide wedges, leaving core intact (you will have 8 wedges). Whisk ¼ cup oil, 1 teaspoon curry paste, 2 teaspoons turmeric, and salt together in bowl. Arrange cabbage wedges in single layer on aluminum foil–lined rimmed baking sheet, then brush cabbage all over with oil mixture. Cover tightly with foil and roast for 10 minutes. Remove foil and drizzle 2 tablespoons oil evenly over wedges. Return sheet to oven and roast, uncovered, until cabbage is tender and sides touching sheet are well browned, 10 to 15 minutes. Let cool slightly, about 15 minutes.

3 Whisk remaining 2 teaspoons ginger, remaining 1 tablespoon oil, remaining 1 tablespoon curry paste, and remaining 1 teaspoon turmeric together in bowl. Microwave until fragrant, about 30 seconds. Whisk water and remaining 2 tablespoons vinegar into ginger mixture.

4 Chop cabbage coarse and divide among individual plates. Top individual portions with scallions, if using, and tofu. Drizzle with vinaigrette and sprinkle with plantain chips. Serve.

Roasted Vegetable and Chickpea Salad

Serves 4 to 6 | **Total Time** 1¼ hours

- 1 pound golden beets, trimmed
- 1 delicata squash (12 to 16 ounces), ends trimmed, halved lengthwise, seeded, and sliced crosswise ½ inch thick
- 3 tablespoons extra-virgin olive oil, divided, plus extra for drizzling
- ½ teaspoon table salt, divided
- 1 cup plain Greek yogurt
- ¼ cup chopped fresh cilantro, divided
- ¾ teaspoon grated lemon zest, divided, plus 1½ tablespoons juice
- 2 (15-ounce) cans chickpeas, rinsed
- ¼ cup Harissa (page 24)
- ½ cup pomegranate seeds
- ¼ cup shelled pistachios, toasted and chopped

Why This Recipe Works The name of this recipe belies its true genius. So exactly how does a combo of earthy vegetables and ordinary chickpeas become a special-occasion dish? Through the magic of roasting. And on a sheet pan it's dead simple to make. Both beets and squash take on another persona when roasted. Delicata squash and golden beets offer a nice visual contrast while their natural sweetness tempers the earthiness of the chickpeas. A bed of herbed yogurt anchors the components of this dish and makes the salad feel cohesive and special. A lemony dressing pulls it all together and a few final finishes seal the deal. A drizzle of harissa ensures that the flavors don't lean too sweet and it looks beautiful. Showers of cilantro, pomegranate seeds, and pistachios are the final touch. We prefer golden beets because they don't discolor the rest of the salad. We prefer to use our recipe for harissa, but you can use store-bought. If you're looking to elevate this salad, heirloom dried black chickpeas make a stunning replacement for the canned chickpeas. (Simply boil 8 ounces in ample amount of lightly salted water.)

1 Adjust oven rack to middle position and heat oven to 425 degrees. Wrap beets individually in aluminum foil and place on aluminum foil–lined rimmed baking sheet. Roast for 30 minutes.

2 Toss squash with 1 tablespoon oil and ¼ teaspoon salt in bowl. Remove sheet with beets from oven and push beets to half of sheet. Spread squash in even layer on other half of sheet, then return to oven and roast until beets and squash are tender (you will need to unwrap beets to test for doneness), about 15 minutes.

3 Remove beets and squash from oven and carefully open beet foil packets. Once beets are cool enough to handle, carefully rub off skins using paper towels. Slice beets into ½-inch-thick wedges, and, if large, cut in half crosswise.

4 Whisk yogurt, 1 tablespoon cilantro, ¼ teaspoon lemon zest, 1 tablespoon oil, and ⅛ teaspoon salt together in bowl; set aside. Whisk lemon juice, remaining 1 tablespoon oil, remaining ⅛ teaspoon salt , and remaining ½ teaspoon lemon zest together in large bowl. Add chickpeas, beets, and squash and toss to combine. Season with salt and pepper to taste.

5 Spread yogurt mixture over wide serving platter. Arrange bean-vegetable mixture over top, then drizzle with harissa and sprinkle with pomegranate seeds, pistachios, and remaining 3 tablespoons cilantro. Drizzle with extra oil and serve.

Spinach and Herb-Stuffed Mushrooms with Blistered Cherry Tomatoes and Onions

Serves 4 | **Total Time** 50 minutes

- 1 pound cherry tomatoes
- 1 red onion, cut through root end into ½-inch-thick wedges
- 4 large portobello mushrooms (5 inches in diameter), gills removed, stems removed, quartered, and reserved
- 6 tablespoons extra-virgin olive oil, divided
- 1¼ teaspoons table salt, divided
- 1 teaspoon pepper, divided
- 10 ounces frozen chopped spinach, thawed and squeezed dry
- 5 ounces feta, crumbled (1¼ cups)
- 4 ounces (½ cup) whole-milk ricotta cheese
- ½ cup panko bread crumbs
- ½ cup toasted walnuts, coarsely chopped
- 1½ ounces Parmesan cheese, grated (¾ cup), divided
- 3 scallions, sliced thin
- ⅓ cup plus 1 tablespoon chopped fresh dill, divided
- ⅓ cup plus 1 tablespoon chopped fresh parsley, divided
- 1 large egg, lightly beaten

Why This Recipe Works Hearty portobello mushrooms, stuffed with a savory spanakopita-like mixture of spinach, feta, and herbs, will satisfy vegetarians and carnivores alike. By roasting juicy cherry tomatoes and wedges of red onion on the same pan as the mushrooms, you get a meaty main and a saucy side all in one. We prefer multicolored cherry tomatoes because they are consistently juicy and sweet all year round, but red cherry tomatoes are fine too. You will have enough stuffing to generously fill four 5-inch-wide mushroom caps or eight 3-inch caps.

1 Adjust oven rack to upper-middle position and heat oven to 400 degrees. Toss cherry tomatoes, onion wedges, mushroom stems, ¼ cup oil, ¾ teaspoon salt, and ¼ teaspoon pepper together on rimmed baking sheet, then spread into even layer. Brush mushroom caps all over with remaining 2 tablespoons oil, then sprinkle them with ¼ teaspoon salt and ¼ teaspoon pepper. Nestle mushroom caps into tomato mixture on sheet, arranging 1 mushroom cap in each quadrant of sheet.

2 Combine spinach, feta, ricotta, panko, walnuts, ½ cup Parmesan, scallions, ⅓ cup dill, ⅓ cup parsley, egg, remaining ¼ teaspoon salt, and remaining ½ teaspoon pepper in bowl, stirring until well combined. Divide spinach mixture evenly among mushroom caps, filling cavity to each edge. Transfer sheet to oven and roast for 15 minutes.

3 Remove sheet from oven and increase oven temperature to 475 degrees. Sprinkle mushroom caps evenly with remaining ¼ cup Parmesan. Return sheet to oven and roast until cheese is golden and cherry tomatoes are blistered and lightly charred, 10 to 15 minutes.

4 Using large spoon, gently smash about half of cherry tomatoes on sheet to release juices, then stir to combine with roasted onions and any pan juices. Sprinkle with remaining 1 tablespoon dill and remaining 1 tablespoon parsley. Serve.

Garlic-Roasted Mushrooms and Escarole with Couscous and Lemon Vinaigrette

Serves 4 | **Total Time** 40 minutes

- 2½ pounds wild mushrooms, trimmed and torn into 2-inch pieces
- 1 onion, chopped fine
- ¼ cup plus 5 teaspoons extra-virgin olive oil, divided
- 3 garlic cloves, sliced thin
- 1 tablespoon plus ⅛ teaspoon plus pinch kosher salt, divided
- 1 head escarole (1 pound), cut into 2-inch wedges through core
- 1 cup boiling water
- 1 cup couscous
- 3 tablespoons minced fresh parsley, divided
- 1 tablespoon lemon juice plus lemon wedges for serving
- ¾ teaspoon Dijon mustard
- ¼ cup dry white wine

Why This Recipe Works For a vegetarian sheet pan meal bursting with flavor, we turn to mushrooms and escarole. The mushrooms bring a savory, meaty depth, while the escarole offers a bright, slightly bitter crunch. Roasting them on a sheet pan takes it to the next level, turning the escarole's natural sweetness up a notch and intensifying the mushrooms' umami richness. We start by roasting the mushrooms until they're golden brown and full of savory goodness, creating a tasty fond on the pan. Once they're perfectly roasted, we deglaze the pan with a splash of wine, lifting those caramelized bits and folding them back into the mushrooms for extra flavor. At the same time, we put escarole wedges on another sheet pan, where the high heat renders them crispy, with charred edges and sweet, tender centers. For an accurate measurement of boiling water, bring a full kettle of water to a boil and then measure out the desired amount. We prefer to use a combination of wild mushrooms for this recipe. If using shiitakes, be sure to remove the stems.

1 Adjust oven racks to upper-middle and lower-middle positions and heat oven to 450 degrees. Toss mushrooms, onion, 2 tablespoons oil, garlic, and 2 teaspoons salt together on rimmed baking sheet, then spread into even layer over sheet. Place escarole wedges on second rimmed baking sheet, then brush all over with 2 tablespoons oil and sprinkle with 1 teaspoon salt. Roast mushrooms on lower rack for 5 minutes, then place sheet with escarole on upper rack and roast until mushrooms are browned and escarole is tender and slightly browned, 10 to 15 minutes.

2 Meanwhile, combine boiling water, couscous, and ⅛ teaspoon salt in bowl. Cover and let sit until couscous is tender and all liquid has been absorbed, about 7 minutes. Fluff couscous with fork and stir in 2 tablespoons parsley; cover and set aside until ready to serve. Whisk lemon juice, mustard, remaining pinch salt, and remaining 1 tablespoon parsley together in bowl. Whisking constantly, slowly drizzle in remaining 5 teaspoons oil until emulsified; set aside until ready to serve, whisking to recombine if needed.

3 Transfer escarole to serving platter and sheet with mushrooms to wire rack. Immediately drizzle wine evenly over mushrooms on sheet and toss until most of liquid is evaporated, about 1 minute, scraping up any browned bits on sheet. Add mushrooms and couscous to platter with escarole and drizzle with reserved vinaigrette. Serve with lemon wedges.

Roasted Vegetables and Lentils with Feta and Herb Oil

Serves 4 | **Total Time** 55 minutes

Herb Oil

½ cup fresh parsley leaves

¼ cup fresh dill

¼ cup fresh mint leaves

¼ cup extra-virgin olive oil

2 tablespoons lemon juice

1 garlic clove, minced

Roasted Vegetables

8 ounces small Yukon gold or red potatoes, quartered

1 large fennel bulb, stalks discarded, bulb halved, core left intact, and cut through core into ½-inch-thick wedges

2 tablespoons extra-virgin olive oil, divided

¾ teaspoon ground cumin

¾ teaspoon table salt, divided

½ teaspoon pepper, divided

2 zucchini, cut ½ inch thick on bias

8 ounces cherry tomatoes

2 shallots, sliced thin

1 (15-ounce) can lentils, rinsed

4 ounces feta cheese, crumbled (1 cup)

Why This Recipe Works We've all experienced a vegetarian dish that just seems like a plate of vegetables with barely a punch of flavor. This recipe, bursting with roasted vegetables, not to mention a drizzling oil that has a full cup of fresh herbs, is the antithesis of that. Canned lentils soak up every bit of herby goodness and vegetable juices while making the dish feel substantial. As for the vegetables, we roast them in two stages. First, we give hearty potatoes and fennel a bold cumin rub and arrange them cut side down on the pan. Covering the pan with foil allows for some browning and virtually steam-cooks the vegetables to perfect tenderness. When the foil comes off after 15 minutes, we add faster-cooking zucchini and cherry tomatoes, along with lentils, and sprinkle a full cup of salty, briny feta on top. Once everything is browned and tender, it just needs a drizzle of that colorful oil and it's ready to serve. Make this recipe when the farmers' markets are in full swing packed with huge bunches of herbs, just-dug potatoes, fennel, piles of zucchini, tomatoes, and more. Leaving the core in the fennel (it softens nicely) ensures that the pretty wedges stay intact and are easy to flip. Use small potatoes measuring 1 to 2 inches in diameter.

1 For the herb oil Pulse all ingredients in food processor until coarsely chopped, about 10 pulses, scraping down sides of bowl as needed. Transfer to bowl and season with salt to taste; set aside until ready to serve.

2 For the roasted vegetables Adjust oven rack to upper-middle position and heat oven to 475 degrees. Toss potatoes, fennel, 1 tablespoon oil, cumin, ½ teaspoon salt, and ¼ teaspoon pepper together in bowl. Arrange vegetables cut side down on rimmed baking sheet and cover tightly with aluminum foil. Roast until vegetables are beginning to brown and are nearly tender, 15 to 20 minutes.

3 Remove foil and flip fennel wedges. Toss zucchini, tomatoes, shallots, lentils, remaining 1 tablespoon oil, remaining ¼ teaspoon salt, and remaining ¼ teaspoon pepper together in bowl. Scatter evenly over top of vegetables on sheet, then sprinkle with feta. Roast until tomatoes blister, feta starts to soften and brown slightly, and vegetables are fully tender, about 15 minutes. Drizzle with herb oil and serve.

Asparagus and Goat Cheese Tart

Serves 4 (makes one 9-inch tart) | **Total Time** 1 hour

- 6 ounces thin asparagus, trimmed and sliced thin on bias ¼ inch thick (1 cup)
- 2 scallions, sliced thin
- 3 tablespoons extra-virgin olive oil, divided
- 2 tablespoons chopped pitted kalamata olives
- 1 garlic clove, minced
- ¼ teaspoon grated lemon zest
- ¼ teaspoon table salt
- ¼ teaspoon pepper
- 4 ounces (1 cup) goat cheese, softened, divided
- 1 (9½ by 9-inch) sheet puff pastry, thawed

Why This Recipe Works Fresh, grassy asparagus really shines as the main attraction of this impressive tart, which takes just minutes to assemble. Store-bought puff pastry—buttery, flaky, and easy to prep—is the baker's best friend here. The plentiful but light filling is predominantly flavored by the asparagus; cutting the spears into thin pieces ensures that the asparagus doesn't need any precooking and also makes the tart easier to eat. Toss the pieces with olive oil, garlic, lemon zest, scallions, and kalamata olives, and then scatter the mixture over the creamy base of goat cheese. Blending some olive oil in with the goat cheese makes it easier to spread evenly over the puff pastry. Dollop some more cheese on top and then bake the tart to golden perfection. Look for asparagus spears no thicker than ½ inch. If your puff pastry is longer than what we call for, you may need to trim (rather than roll) the sheet to achieve the dimensions in step 2. To thaw frozen puff pastry, let it sit in the refrigerator for 24 hours or on the counter for 30 minutes to 1 hour.

1 Adjust oven rack to upper-middle position and heat oven to 425 degrees. Line rimmed baking sheet with parchment paper. Combine asparagus, scallions, 1 tablespoon oil, olives, garlic, lemon zest, salt, and pepper in bowl. In separate bowl, mix ¾ cup goat cheese and 1 tablespoon oil until smooth; set aside.

2 Dust counter lightly with flour. Unfold puff pastry and roll into 10-inch square; transfer to prepared sheet. Lightly brush outer ½ inch of pastry square with water to create border, then fold border toward center, pressing gently to seal.

3 Spread goat cheese mixture in even layer over center of pastry, avoiding folded border. Scatter asparagus mixture over goat cheese, then crumble remaining ¼ cup goat cheese over top of asparagus mixture.

4 Bake until pastry is puffed and golden and asparagus is crisp-tender, 15 to 20 minutes. Transfer tart to wire rack and let cool for 15 minutes. Drizzle with remaining 1 tablespoon oil, slide onto cutting board or serving platter, cut into 4 equal pieces, and serve warm or at room temperature.

Fresh Tomato Galette

Serves 4 to 6 (makes one 8-inch galette) | **Total Time** 1 hour, plus 50 minutes salting and cooling

- 1½ pounds mixed tomatoes, cored and sliced ¼ inch thick
- 1½ teaspoons table salt, divided
- 1 (9-inch) store-bought pie dough round
- 1 shallot, sliced thin
- 2 tablespoons extra-virgin olive oil
- 1 teaspoon minced fresh thyme
- 1 garlic clove, minced
- ¼ teaspoon pepper
- 2 teaspoons Dijon mustard
- 3 ounces Gruyère cheese, shredded (¾ cup)
- 2 tablespoons grated Parmesan cheese
- 1 large egg, lightly beaten
- 1 tablespoon chopped fresh basil

Why This Recipe Works You just cannot have enough recipes where summer tomatoes are the star. And this one is a stunner. The challenging part about baking with such precious jewels, though, is their unpredictable levels of juice. To draw out not only the tomatoes' excess juice but also their best, most concentrated flavor, salt the slices and let them sit in a colander to drain before building the galette. Shaking the colander after the 30-minute rest helps ensure that no stray liquid sneaks into the crust. Lining the inside of the dough with a layer of mustard and shredded Gruyère cheese provides added protection to ensure a crisp crust. A no-fuss pleating technique is pretty and easy. You can use sharp cheddar cheese instead of the Gruyère, if desired. A baking stone helps to crisp the crust but is not essential; you can use a preheated rimless or overturned baking sheet instead.

1 Adjust oven rack to lower-middle position, place baking stone on rack, and heat oven to 375 degrees. Line rimmed baking sheet with parchment paper. Toss tomatoes and 1 teaspoon salt together in colander and set aside to drain for 30 minutes.

2 Roll dough into 12-inch circle on lightly floured counter, then transfer to prepared sheet (dough may run up lip of sheet slightly; this is OK). Shake colander to rid tomatoes of excess juice. Combine tomatoes, shallot, oil, thyme, garlic, pepper, and remaining ½ teaspoon salt in bowl. Spread mustard over dough, leaving 1½-inch border. Sprinkle Gruyère in even layer over mustard. Shingle tomatoes and shallot on top of Gruyère in concentric circles, maintaining 1½-inch border. Sprinkle Parmesan over tomato mixture.

3 Carefully grasp 1 edge of dough and fold up about 1 inch over filling. Repeat around circumference of tart, overlapping dough every 2 to 3 inches, gently pinching pleated dough to secure. Brush dough with egg. (You won't need it all.)

4 Set sheet on stone and bake until crust is golden brown and tomatoes are bubbling, 45 to 50 minutes. Transfer sheet to wire rack and let galette cool for 10 minutes. Using metal spatula, loosen galette from parchment and carefully slide onto wire rack; let cool until just warm, about 20 minutes. Sprinkle basil over filling, cut into wedges, and serve warm.

Eggplant and Tomato Phyllo Pie

Serves 4 to 6 (makes one 9-inch pie) | **Total Time** 1½ hours, plus 30 minutes salting

- 1 pound tomatoes, cored and sliced ¼ inch thick
- 1¼ teaspoons table salt, divided
- 1 pound eggplant, sliced into ¼-inch-thick rounds
- ½ cup extra-virgin olive oil, divided
- 12 sheets (14 by 9-inch) phyllo, thawed, room temperature
- 3 garlic cloves, minced
- 2 teaspoons minced fresh oregano
- ¼ teaspoon pepper
- 6 ounces block mozzarella cheese, shredded (1½ cups)
- 2 tablespoons grated Parmesan cheese
- 1 tablespoon chopped fresh basil

Why This Recipe Works Phyllo dough is another route to a visually alluring tart, with the paper-thin dough layers baking to a beautiful golden brown color and shatteringly crisp texture. Here phyllo is paired with eggplant and tomatoes layered between mild mozzarella and nutty Parmesan. Broiling the eggplant slices before assembling the tart gives them deeper flavor and a delightful char. Layering 12 sheets of phyllo dough creates a crust sturdy enough to stand up to the abundance of vegetables, and doing so in an offset pattern contributes to the beautiful presentation. The insulating layer of shredded mozzarella melts into the phyllo crust for a satisfyingly cheesy layer that also helps keep the crust from getting soggy. Fresh oregano and basil bring bold herbal flavor. Phyllo dough is also available in larger 18 by 14-inch sheets; if using, cut them in half to make 14 by 9-inch sheets. Don't thaw the phyllo in the microwave; let it sit in the refrigerator overnight or on the counter for 4 to 5 hours.

1 Adjust oven rack 6 inches from broiler element and heat broiler. Line rimmed baking sheet with aluminum foil. Toss tomatoes and ¾ teaspoon salt together in colander and set aside to drain for 30 minutes.

2 Meanwhile, arrange eggplant in single layer on prepared sheet and brush both sides with 2 tablespoons oil. Broil eggplant until softened and beginning to brown, 10 to 12 minutes, flipping eggplant halfway through broiling. Set aside to cool slightly, about 10 minutes.

3 Heat oven to 375 degrees. Line second rimmed baking sheet with parchment paper. Place ¼ cup oil in small bowl. Place 1 phyllo sheet on prepared sheet, then lightly brush phyllo with prepared oil. Turn baking sheet 30 degrees and place second phyllo sheet on first phyllo sheet, leaving any overhanging phyllo in place. Brush second phyllo sheet with oil. Repeat turning baking sheet and layering remaining 10 phyllo sheets in pinwheel pattern, brushing each with oil (you should have 12 total layers of phyllo).

4 Shake colander to rid tomatoes of excess juice. Combine tomatoes, garlic, oregano, pepper, 1 tablespoon oil, and remaining ½ teaspoon salt in bowl. Sprinkle mozzarella evenly in center of phyllo in 9-inch circle. Shingle tomatoes and eggplant on top of mozzarella in concentric circles, alternating tomatoes and eggplant as you go. Sprinkle Parmesan over top.

5 Gently fold edges of phyllo over vegetable mixture, pleating every 2 to 3 inches as needed, and lightly brush edges with remaining 1 tablespoon oil. Bake until phyllo is crisp and golden brown, 30 to 35 minutes. Let pie cool for 15 minutes, then sprinkle with basil. Slide onto cutting board or serving platter, cut into pieces, and serve.

Spinach Pie for a Crowd

Serves 10 to 12 (makes one 13 by 9-inch pie) | **Total Time** 1½ hours, plus 1 hour cooling

- 2 tablespoons unsalted butter
- 2 shallots, minced
- 4 garlic cloves, minced
- ¼ cup all-purpose flour
- 1½ cups whole milk
- 3 ounces Parmesan cheese, grated (1½ cups)
- 1¼ pounds frozen whole-leaf spinach, thawed and squeezed dry
- 1 teaspoon table salt
- ½ teaspoon pepper
- 2 (9½ by 9-inch) sheets puff pastry, thawed, divided
- 1 large egg beaten with 1 teaspoon water

Why This Recipe Works Creamy, buttery, savory, and thoroughly satisfying, this spinach pie has showstopping good looks. The filling starts with a simple béchamel sauce boosted with shallots and garlic and a generous dose of Parmesan cheese. Assembling the pie on a sheet pan lets you make a large enough pie to serve a crowd, and allows plenty of space and airflow in the oven to crisp up the puff pastry on all sides. Scoring the top sheet of pastry before baking makes it easy to cut the pie into individual portions later. To dry the spinach after you thaw it, place the leaves in the center of a clean dish towel, gather the ends of the towel, and twist firmly. Letting the filling cool completely before assembling the pie ensures a crisp crust. Some puff pastry comes in larger sheets than we call for here; they will still work in this recipe. To thaw frozen puff pastry, let it sit in the refrigerator for 24 hours or on the counter for 30 minutes to 1 hour.

1 Melt butter in medium saucepan over medium heat. Add shallots and garlic and cook until softened, about 2 minutes. Stir in flour and cook until golden, about 30 seconds. Slowly whisk in milk, scraping up any browned bits and smoothing out any lumps, and bring to simmer. Cook, stirring constantly, until thickened, about 3 minutes.

2 Off heat, stir in Parmesan until melted. Stir in spinach, salt, and pepper until combined. Transfer spinach mixture to bowl and let cool completely, about 30 minutes.

3 Adjust oven rack to lower-middle position and heat oven to 400 degrees. Grease rimmed baking sheet. Dust counter lightly with flour. Unfold 1 puff pastry sheet and roll into 14 by 10-inch rectangle. Loosely roll pastry around rolling pin and unroll onto prepared sheet. Spread spinach mixture evenly over pastry, leaving ½-inch border. Brush border with egg wash (reserve remaining egg wash).

4 Dust counter lightly with flour. Unfold remaining pastry sheet and roll into 14 by 10-inch rectangle. Loosely roll pastry around rolling pin and unroll it over filling. Press edges of top and bottom sheets together to seal. Roll edges inward and use your fingers to crimp edges. Using sharp knife, cut top pastry sheet into 24 squares. Brush top pastry sheet evenly with remaining egg wash.

5 Bake until crust is golden brown, 30 to 35 minutes. Transfer sheet to wire rack and let pie cool completely, about 30 minutes. Transfer pie to cutting board and cut along guidelines. Serve.

Potato and Parmesan Tart

Serves 6 to 8 (makes one 11 by 8-inch tart) | **Total Time** 1½ hours, plus 1 hour 20 minutes chilling and cooling

---

- 1½ cups (7½ ounces) all-purpose flour
- 1 teaspoon table salt, divided
- 10 tablespoons unsalted butter, cut into ½-inch pieces and chilled
- 6–7 tablespoons ice water
- 4 ounces cream cheese
- 2 ounces Parmesan or Pecorino Romano cheese, grated (1 cup), divided
- 2 tablespoons extra-virgin olive oil
- 2 teaspoons Dijon mustard
- 1½ teaspoons minced fresh rosemary or ½ teaspoon dried, divided
- ¼ teaspoon pepper
- 1 large egg, separated
- 1 pound russet or Yukon Gold potatoes, peeled and sliced ⅛ inch thick
- 1 shallot, sliced thin

Why This Recipe Works With little more than potatoes, Parmesan, and cream cheese, you have the makings of a buttery, crisp, free-form tart that's a major crowd-pleaser. Slicing the potatoes thin prevents any underdone spots. Folding the potatoes into a mixture of cream cheese, mustard, shallot, and Parmesan flavors them and also secures them in place. A bit of rosemary serves as a savory pairing for the Parmesan. A light brush of egg white on the pastry dough fosters a golden crust while acting as glue for anchoring a bit more sprinkled-on cheese, making the crust just as savory as the filling. A mandoline makes quick work of evenly slicing the potatoes.

1 Process flour and ½ teaspoon salt in food processor until combined, about 3 seconds. Scatter butter over top and pulse until mixture resembles coarse crumbs, about 10 pulses. Add 6 tablespoons ice water and process until almost no dry flour remains, about 10 seconds, scraping down sides of bowl after 5 seconds. Add up to 1 additional tablespoon ice water if dough doesn't come together.

2 Turn out dough onto lightly floured counter, form into 4-inch square, wrap tightly in plastic wrap, and refrigerate for 1 hour. (Wrapped dough can be refrigerated for up to 2 days or frozen for up to 1 month. If frozen, let dough thaw completely on counter before rolling.)

3 Adjust oven rack to lower-middle position and heat oven to 375 degrees. Line rimmed baking sheet with parchment paper. Let chilled dough sit on counter to soften slightly, about 10 minutes. Roll dough into 14 by 11-inch rectangle on lightly floured counter, then transfer to prepared sheet.

4 Microwave cream cheese in large bowl until softened, 20 to 30 seconds. Whisk in ½ cup Parmesan, oil, mustard, 1 teaspoon rosemary, pepper, and remaining ½ teaspoon salt until combined. Whisk in egg yolk. Add potatoes and shallot and stir to thoroughly coat potatoes.

5 Transfer filling to center of dough on sheet. Press filling into even layer, leaving 2-inch border on all sides. Sprinkle 6 tablespoons Parmesan and remaining ½ teaspoon rosemary over filling.

6 Grasp 1 long side of dough and fold about 1½ inches over filling. Repeat with opposing long side. Fold in short sides of dough, overlapping corners of dough to secure. Lightly beat egg white and brush over folded crust (you won't need it all). Sprinkle remaining 2 tablespoons Parmesan over crust.

7 Bake until crust and filling are golden brown and potatoes meet little resistance when poked with fork, about 45 minutes. Transfer sheet to wire rack and let tart cool for 10 minutes. Using metal spatula, loosen tart from parchment and carefully slide onto wire rack; let cool until just warm, about 20 minutes. Cut into slices and serve warm.

VARIATION

Potato Tart with Blue Cheese and Sun-Dried Tomatoes

Reduce Parmesan to ½ cup. Use ¼ cup in cream cheese mixture in step 4 and 2 tablespoons to sprinkle over filling in step 5. Add ¼ cup crumbled blue cheese and ¼ cup chopped sun-dried tomatoes to cream cheese mixture in step 4. Sprinkle additional ¼ cup crumbled blue cheese over filling in step 5.

CHAPTER SIX

Breakfast

Eggs in a Hole with Tomato, Avocado, and Herb Salad

Serves 4 | **Total Time** 45 minutes

- 3 tablespoons unsalted butter, softened, divided
- 1 tablespoon Dijon mustard
- 4 slices hearty white sandwich bread
- 8 ounces cherry tomatoes, halved
- 1 teaspoon extra-virgin olive oil, plus extra for drizzling
- ⅛ teaspoon plus ¼ teaspoon table salt, divided
- Pinch plus ¼ teaspoon pepper, divided
- 4 large eggs
- 2 avocados, halved, pitted, and cut into ½-inch pieces
- 1⅓ cups chopped fresh parsley
- 4 scallions, sliced thin
- 2 tablespoons plus 2 teaspoons lemon juice

Why This Recipe Works While this might be your first time making this breakfast of a runny fried egg nested in a piece of toast in the oven, it definitely won't be your last. A preheated, greased, and buttered sheet pan toasts the bread and cooks the eggs more evenly and easily from crust to crumb and yolk to white than a skillet can (and ensures absolutely no sticking). At the same time, we roast cherry tomatoes on the sheet in a foil boat, which contains the flavorful juices, and we then use them in a bright salad to complete the meal. A butter–Dijon mustard mixture spread on the bread before toasting creates a barrier that prevents the whites from leaking out. When the eggs are nearly done, we remove the sheet from the oven and let the carryover heat finish setting the whites without overcooking the yolks.

1 Adjust oven rack to middle position. Spray rimmed baking sheet with vegetable oil spray, then place sheet on rack and heat oven to 475 degrees. Thoroughly combine 2 tablespoons butter with mustard in bowl. Spread evenly over 1 side of each bread slice, then, using 2½-inch biscuit cutter or sturdy drinking glass of similar diameter, cut circle from center of each bread slice; reserve cut-out bread rounds.

2 Place cherry tomatoes in center of 12-inch piece of foil. Crinkle edges of foil up around cherry tomatoes to create foil boat, leaving center open and tomatoes fully exposed. Toss tomatoes with oil, ⅛ teaspoon salt, and pinch pepper in foil boat.

3 Remove sheet from oven and, being careful of hot pan, spread remaining 1 tablespoon butter evenly over two-thirds of sheet with spatula. Place bread slices and rounds, buttered side up, on buttered part of sheet (do not place cut-out bread rounds in holes), then place tomatoes in foil boat on open, unbuttered side of sheet. Bake until bread is lightly toasted on bottom, about 4 minutes.

4 Remove sheet from oven. Flip bread slices and rounds. Crack 1 egg into each bread hole and sprinkle eggs evenly with remaining ¼ teaspoon salt and remaining ¼ teaspoon pepper. Bake until yolks have clouded over but still give slightly when touched, 3 to 5 minutes. Transfer sheet to wire rack and let sit until whites are completely set, about 2 minutes.

5 Use foil boat to transfer tomatoes and their juices to large bowl. Let cool for 5 minutes. Add avocado, parsley, scallions, and lemon juice to bowl and toss to combine. Season with salt and pepper to taste. Using spatula, transfer 1 bread slice with egg and 1 bread round to each serving plate. Top with salad and drizzle with extra oil. Serve.

How to Build the Sheet Pan

Roast the potatoes, which take the longest to cook, until spotty brown. Place the sausages on top and roast until they're browned. Push everything to one side of the sheet pan to make room for the toast.

One-Pan Breakfast

Serves 4 | **Total Time** 1 hour

- 2 pounds Yukon Gold potatoes, unpeeled, cut into 1-inch pieces
- 1 tablespoon vegetable oil
- 1¼ teaspoons table salt, divided
- ½ teaspoon pepper, divided
- 4 slices hearty white sandwich bread
- 3 tablespoons unsalted butter, softened, divided
- 12 ounces breakfast sausage links
- 4 large eggs

Why This Recipe Works Serving the full diner special—runny eggs, buttery toast, crispy potatoes, and juicy sausage links—can be tough outside of a restaurant kitchen. Filling the stovetop with pans and monitoring all of the components with just two hands is nearly impossible for even the most seasoned short-order cook. The sheet pan turns out the works, hot, steamy, all at the same time—and without all those pans to clean. The sausages cook elevated on the potatoes, where they brown nicely. Then, when the sheet is hot enough to properly cook the eggs, we push the potatoes and sausages to the side to make room for an egg-in-hole setup. We prefer to use raw breakfast sausage links for this recipe, but fully cooked frozen links can also be used. The potatoes can be cut, submerged in water, and refrigerated for up to 24 hours. Dry them thoroughly with a dish towel before using.

1 Adjust oven rack to middle position and heat oven to 475 degrees. Spray rimmed baking sheet with vegetable oil spray. Toss potatoes with oil, 1 teaspoon salt, and ¼ teaspoon pepper on prepared sheet, then spread into even layer. Roast until potatoes are spotty brown on tops and sides, about 20 minutes.

2 Meanwhile, spread 1 side of each bread slice evenly with 2 tablespoons butter. Using 2½-inch biscuit cutter or sturdy drinking glass of similar diameter, cut circle from center of each bread slice; reserve cut-out bread rounds.

3 Remove sheet from oven. Distribute sausages over potatoes (it's OK if some fall onto sheet), return sheet to oven, and roast until sausages are lightly browned on top, about 12 minutes.

4 Remove sheet from oven. Using metal spatula, push potatoes and sausages into pile occupying about one-third of sheet, creating enough room for bread. Use spatula to spread remaining 1 tablespoon butter over now-empty part of sheet. Place all bread, buttered side up, on empty part of sheet (do not place cut-out bread rounds in holes). Bake until bread is lightly toasted on bottom, 4 to 5 minutes.

5 Remove sheet from oven. Flip bread. Crack 1 egg into each bread hole and sprinkle eggs evenly with remaining ¼ teaspoon salt and remaining ¼ teaspoon pepper. Bake until yolks have clouded over but still give slightly when touched, 3 to 5 minutes. Transfer sheet to wire rack and let sit until whites are completely set, about 2 minutes. Serve immediately.

Huevos Rancheros

Serves 4 | **Total Time** 1¼ hours

- 2 (28-ounce) cans diced tomatoes
- 1 tablespoon packed brown sugar
- 1 tablespoon lime juice
- 1 onion, chopped
- ½ cup canned chopped green chiles
- ¼ cup extra-virgin olive oil
- 3 tablespoons chili powder
- 4 garlic cloves, sliced thin
- 1 teaspoon table salt, divided
- 4 ounces pepper Jack cheese, shredded (1 cup)
- 8 large eggs
- ½ teaspoon pepper
- 1 avocado, halved, pitted, and diced
- 2 scallions, sliced thin
- ¼ cup minced fresh cilantro
- 8 (6-inch) corn tortillas, warmed

Why This Recipe Works This Tex-Mex breakfast opens morning eyes with a lively tomato-and-chile sauce, and satisfies with rich, runny eggs. Both are cooked right in the sheet pan to simplify the dish for the sleepiest of mornings while augmenting its flavor. Roasting the tomatoes, onion, chiles, and flavorings imparts deep char close to what is traditionally achieved from a comal griddle. To make sure there's freshness in the final dish, we reserve the drained tomato juice so we can thin out the concentrated tomato mixture after roasting. It's perfect for scooping into warm tortillas. We discovered that the key to perfect sauce-poached eggs in the oven is to add a second baking sheet for insulation. We like our eggs slightly runny; if you prefer well-done eggs, cook them to the end of the time range in step 4. Serve with hot sauce.

1 Adjust oven rack to middle position and heat oven to 500 degrees. Drain tomatoes in fine-mesh strainer set over bowl, pressing with rubber spatula to extract as much juice as possible. Combine 1¾ cups drained tomato juice, sugar, and lime juice in bowl and set aside; discard extra drained juice.

2 Combine tomatoes, onion, chiles, oil, chili powder, garlic, and ½ teaspoon salt in bowl, then spread mixture evenly over rimmed baking sheet. Roast until charred in spots, 35 to 40 minutes, stirring and redistributing into even layer halfway through roasting.

3 Remove sheet from oven and place inside second rimmed baking sheet. Carefully stir reserved tomato juice mixture into roasted vegetables on sheet, season with salt and pepper to taste, and redistribute into even layer. Sprinkle cheese over top and, using back of spoon, hollow out eight 3-inch-wide wells in mixture. Crack 1 egg into each hole and sprinkle eggs evenly with pepper and remaining ½ teaspoon salt.

4 Bake until whites are just beginning to set but still show some movement when sheet is shaken, 7 to 8 minutes for slightly runny yolks or 9 to 10 minutes for soft-cooked yolks, rotating sheet halfway through baking.

5 Remove sheet from oven and top with avocado, scallions, and cilantro. To serve, slide spatula underneath eggs and sauce and gently transfer to warm tortillas.

How to Build the Sheet Pan

Combine the sauce ingredients on the pan and roast. Stir in the tomato juice mixture and spread into an even layer. Sprinkle on the cheese and make wells to drop the eggs into.

Hash Browns with Smoked Salmon

Serves 4 | **Total Time** 1¼ hours

- 3 pounds Yukon Gold potatoes, unpeeled
- 6 tablespoons extra-virgin olive oil
- 1 teaspoon table salt
- ¼ teaspoon pepper
- 4 ounces smoked salmon
- 2 Persian cucumbers, shaved into thin ribbons
- 4 ounces cherry tomatoes, halved
- ¼ cup pitted Castelvetrano olives, sliced thin
- 2 radishes, trimmed, halved, and sliced thin
- ½ cup Quick Sweet and Spicy Pickled Red Onion (page 27)
- 1 recipe Crème Fraîche
- Lemon wedges

Why This Recipe Works If you're cooking hash browns for more than two people, put down the skillet and cook them all at once in the oven. It's easy to flip the potatoes and achieve lots of browned, crispy edges and a creamy interior in a sheet pan, so we make these hash browns the base of an elevated smoked salmon breakfast with lots of toppings. Starchy potatoes make tough, chewy hash browns, so we use only moderately starchy Yukon Golds, which we briefly soak to remove excess surface starch. We flip sections of the hash browns with a metal spatula partway through cooking and return the sheet to the oven for a crispy result. Then we top them fancifully: In addition to succulent slices of smoked salmon, we include all kinds of complementary garnishes, including cucumber ribbons, sliced olives and radishes, cherry tomatoes, and pickled red onions. The final flourish is a drizzle of herby, lemony crème fraîche. We prefer to use the shredding disk of a food processor to shred the potatoes, but you can also use the large holes of a box grater.

1 Adjust oven rack to middle position and heat oven to 450 degrees. Spray rimmed baking sheet with vegetable oil spray. Fit food processor with shredding disk. Halve or quarter potatoes as needed to fit through processor feed tube, then shred potatoes. Transfer potatoes to large bowl and cover with cold water. Let sit for 5 minutes.

2 One handful at a time, lift potatoes out of water and transfer to colander; discard water. Rinse and dry bowl.

3 Place one-quarter of shredded potatoes in center of clean dish towel. Gather ends of towel and twist tightly to wring out excess moisture from potatoes. Transfer dried potatoes to now-empty bowl. Repeat 3 more times with remaining potatoes.

4 Toss potatoes with oil, salt, and pepper. Distribute potatoes in even layer on prepared sheet, but do not pack down. Bake until top of potatoes is spotty brown, 34 to 38 minutes.

5 Remove sheet from oven. Flip hash browns in sections with metal spatula, then rearrange so that less-browned sections are closer to edge of sheet. Return sheet to oven and continue to bake until deep golden brown on top, 8 to 10 minutes longer.

6 Transfer hash browns to platter and sprinkle with flake sea salt to taste. Top with smoked salmon, cucumber ribbons, tomatoes, olives, radishes, and pickled onions. Drizzle with crème fraîche and serve with lemon wedges.

Crème Fraîche

Makes ½ cup
Total Time 5 minutes

- ½ cup crème fraîche
- 3 tablespoons minced fresh dill
- 1 tablespoon water
- ¾ teaspoon grated lemon zest
- ¼ teaspoon table salt
- ⅛ teaspoon pepper

Combine all ingredients in small bowl and refrigerate until serving. (Sauce can be refrigerated for up to 3 days.)

Egg Roulade with Spinach and Gruyère

Serves 4 to 6 | **Total Time** 30 minutes

- 12 large eggs
- 1 garlic clove, minced to a paste
- ¼ teaspoon table salt
- ⅛ teaspoon pepper
- ¼ cup half-and-half
- 2 tablespoons all-purpose flour
- 8 ounces frozen chopped spinach, thawed and squeezed dry
- 4 ounces Gruyère cheese, shredded (1 cup)

Why This Recipe Works Everyone loves an omelet. While they're the ideal egg breakfast to eat, omelets aren't particularly ideal to make for more than one person. Our answer is this egg roulade—a baked rolled omelet that's light and airy. We pour an egg mixture, held together with a little bit of flour, into a greased parchment-lined rimmed baking sheet. The parchment allows us to roll the baked omelet over itself into a tight cylinder. We top the eggs with chopped spinach, which doesn't weigh them down, before baking, and then sprinkle on cheese after baking; the melting cheese is delicious and also helps the roulade stay together once rolled. Then it's ready to cut into beautiful slices for up to six people: elegant omelets for all. You can substitute whole milk for the half-and-half in this recipe, but the eggs will be less rich and less tender.

1 Adjust oven rack to middle position and heat oven to 375 degrees. Spray rimmed baking sheet with vegetable oil spray. Fit 18 by 15-inch piece of parchment paper into sheet with about 1 inch overlapping long sides of sheet. Spray parchment with vegetable oil spray.

2 Whisk eggs, garlic, salt, and pepper together in large bowl. Whisk half-and-half and flour together in second bowl, then slowly whisk into egg mixture until uniform. Carefully pour egg mixture into prepared sheet and sprinkle spinach over top. Bake until eggs are just set, about 9 minutes, rotating sheet halfway through baking.

3 Remove sheet from oven and immediately sprinkle Gruyère over top. With long side of sheet parallel to counter edge, use parchment paper to roll egg away from you into tight cylinder, leaving parchment behind. Use parchment to transfer roulade to cutting board. Slice and serve.

VARIATION

Egg Roulade with Goat Cheese and Sun-Dried Tomatoes

Sprinkle 3 tablespoons chopped oil-packed sun-dried tomatoes over eggs with spinach. Substitute 1 cup crumbled goat cheese for Gruyère.

Sweet Potato and Poblano Frittata

Serves 6 | **Total Time** 1 hour 5 minutes

- 1 pound sweet potatoes, peeled and cut into 1-inch pieces
- 1 small red onion, sliced thin
- 1 poblano pepper, stemmed, seeded, and cut into 1-inch pieces
- 1 teaspoon plus 2 tablespoons extra-virgin olive oil, divided
- 1 teaspoon plus pinch table salt, divided
- 10 large eggs
- ¼ cup whole milk
- 2 garlic cloves, minced
- ½ teaspoon ground cumin
- ¼ teaspoon ground coriander
- ¼ teaspoon plus pinch pepper, divided
- ⅛–¼ teaspoon cayenne pepper
- 8 ounces pepper Jack cheese, shredded (2 cups)
- 1 tablespoon lime juice
- ½ teaspoon Dijon mustard
- ½ teaspoon honey
- 4 ounces (4 cups) baby arugula
- 1 cup cilantro leaves
- 3 radishes, trimmed and sliced thin

Why This Recipe Works We love that a frittata can be breakfast, lunch, or dinner, and this spiced sweet potato and poblano frittata is the most unique version we've tried. But for something so versatile, frittatas often require way too much stovetop monitoring. Not this one. We roast the vegetables on a quarter sheet pan and then simply pour our flavor-packed egg mixture right over them and bake in a hotter-than-usual oven to jump-start cooking and give the eggs lots of lift. The frittata deflates a bit in cooling but doesn't turn rubbery. A lime vinaigrette–dressed arugula salad provides texture and sharp flavor to accompany this anytime meal. You'll need a 13 by 9-inch quarter sheet pan for this recipe.

1 Adjust oven rack to middle position and heat oven to 450 degrees. Spray bottom and sides of small rimmed baking sheet with vegetable oil spray. Toss sweet potatoes, onion, poblano, 1 teaspoon oil, and ¼ teaspoon salt together on prepared sheet, then spread into even layer. Roast until sweet potatoes are tender, 20 to 25 minutes, stirring halfway through roasting.

2 Whisk eggs, milk, garlic, cumin, coriander, ¼ teaspoon pepper, cayenne, and ¾ teaspoon salt in bowl until thoroughly combined and mixture is pure yellow. Stir in pepper Jack, then pour over roasted vegetables on sheet. Bake until frittata has puffed and eggs are just set, about 15 minutes.

3 Meanwhile, whisk lime juice, mustard, honey, remaining pinch salt, and remaining pinch pepper together in large bowl. Whisking constantly, slowly drizzle in remaining 2 tablespoons oil until emulsified. Add arugula, cilantro, and radishes and toss to combine.

4 Let frittata cool for 10 minutes. Cut frittata into pieces and serve with arugula salad.

Breakfast Pizza

Serves 4 to 6 | **Total Time** 1¼ hours

- 6 slices bacon
- 8 ounces mozzarella cheese, shredded (2 cups)
- 1 ounce Parmesan cheese, grated (½ cup)
- 4 ounces (½ cup) small-curd cottage cheese
- ¼ teaspoon dried oregano
- ¼ plus ⅜ teaspoon pepper, divided
- Pinch cayenne pepper
- 1 pound store-bought pizza dough, room temperature
- 1 tablespoon extra-virgin olive oil
- 6 large eggs
- ⅜ teaspoon table salt
- 2 scallions, sliced thin

VARIATION

Smoked Salmon Breakfast Pizza

In step 5, after cooling, omit scallions and top pizza with ¼ cup sliced red onion and 3 ounces sliced smoked salmon (cut into thin strips). Drizzle with ¼ cup sour cream, sprinkle with chives and 1 tablespoon chopped fresh dill, and drizzle with extra oil.

Why This Recipe Works Combine bacon and perfectly cooked eggs with a crisp, golden-brown crust to make your pizza-for-breakfast dreams come true. This is a simple pie to put together in the morning. We parbake the crust to make sure it's crispy before adding the topping: a creamy herbed cottage cheese mixture, sprinkled with more cheese and bacon (which we crisp on the sheet before parbaking the crust). We press wells in the topping to hold six eggs. The pizza finishes cooking in 10 minutes, with cheese melted and eggs still runny. Small-curd cottage cheese is sometimes labeled "country style." Room-temperature dough is much easier than cold to shape, so pull the dough from the fridge about 1 hour before you start cooking.

1 Adjust oven racks to middle and lowest positions and heat oven to 400 degrees. Place bacon in single layer on rimmed baking sheet and cook on upper rack until crisp, about 15 minutes, rotating sheet halfway through baking. Transfer bacon to paper towel–lined plate, let cool slightly, then crumble. Transfer rendered fat to small bowl and set aside. Let sheet cool completely, about 10 minutes.

2 Increase oven temperature to 500 degrees. Combine mozzarella and Parmesan in bowl. Combine cottage cheese, oregano, ¼ teaspoon pepper, cayenne, and 1 tablespoon reserved fat in second bowl. Brush 1 tablespoon reserved bacon fat over cooled sheet.

3 Press and roll dough into 15 by 11-inch rectangle on lightly floured counter, then transfer to prepared sheet and push to edges of pan. (If dough resists stretching, let rest for 10 minutes before trying to stretch again.) Brush edges of dough with oil. Bake on lower rack until top of crust appears dry and bottom is just beginning to brown, about 5 minutes.

4 Remove sheet from oven and press on air bubbles with spatula to flatten, if needed. Spread cottage cheese mixture evenly over crust, leaving 1-inch border around edge, then sprinkle with crumbled bacon and cheese mixture. Using back of spoon, hollow out six 3-inch-wide holes in cheese. Crack 1 egg into each hole and sprinkle eggs evenly with salt and remaining pepper.

5 Bake until crust is light golden around edges and eggs are just set, 9 to 10 minutes for slightly runny yolks or 11 to 12 minutes for soft-cooked yolks, rotating sheet halfway through baking. Remove sheet from oven. Transfer pizza to cutting board and let cool for 5 minutes. Sprinkle with scallions, slice, and serve.

Everyday French Toast

Serves 4 | **Total Time** 30 minutes

- 3 large eggs
- 1 tablespoon vanilla extract
- 2 teaspoons packed brown sugar
- ½ teaspoon ground cinnamon
- ¼ teaspoon table salt
- 2 tablespoons unsalted butter, melted
- 1 cup milk
- 8 slices hearty white sandwich bread
- Salted butter (optional)
- Maple syrup
- Confectioners' sugar (optional)

Why This Recipe Works French toast is a simple comfort, but drippy soaking methods and tedious batch cooking can make it complicated. If you want better French toast and you want it in one batch, turn to the oven. A sheet pan perfectly contains the whole operation. We whisk together our custard and pour it into the sheet. We place all the bread slices in the sheet and then flip them; each side of the bread soaks up just enough egg mixture to give it a creamy, custardy center, but not so much that it cooks up flat and soggy. We bake the slices on the lowest oven rack to brown their bottoms and then turn on the broiler to brown and crisp their tops—no flipping needed. We developed this recipe to work with presliced supermarket bread that measures 4 by 6 inches and is ¾ inch thick; our favorite is Arnold Country Classics White Bread. Note that if you use a different brand you may need to adjust the number of bread slices to fit in the sheet.

1 Adjust 1 oven rack to lowest position and second rack 5 to 6 inches from broiler element. Heat oven to 425 degrees. Generously spray bottom and sides of rimmed baking sheet with vegetable oil spray. Whisk eggs, vanilla, sugar, cinnamon, and salt in large bowl until sugar is dissolved and no streaks of egg remain. Whisking constantly, drizzle in melted butter, then whisk in milk.

2 Pour egg mixture into prepared sheet. Arrange bread in single layer in egg mixture, leaving small gaps between slices. Working quickly, use your fingers to flip slices in same order you placed them in sheet. Let sit until slices absorb remaining custard, about 1 minute.

3 Bake on lower rack until bottoms of slices are golden brown, 10 to 15 minutes. Transfer sheet to upper rack and heat broiler. (Leave sheet in oven while broiler heats.) Broil until tops of slices are golden brown, watching carefully and rotating sheet if necessary to prevent burning, 1 to 4 minutes. Using thin metal spatula, carefully flip each slice. Serve with salted butter, if using; maple syrup; and confectioners' sugar, if using.

One Big Pancake

Serves 8 | **Total Time** 50 minutes

- 3 cups (15 ounces) all-purpose flour
- ¼ cup (1¾ ounces) sugar
- 4 teaspoons baking powder
- ¾ teaspoon baking soda
- 1½ teaspoons table salt
- 3 large eggs
- 6 tablespoons vegetable oil
- 2¼ cups milk
- ¾ teaspoon vanilla extract
- Salted butter
- Maple syrup

Why This Recipe Works Pancake batter is easy to mix up, but batch-cooking the cakes for more than one or two people can be cumbersome and often results in some pancakes being served hot and fluffy and others limp and rubbery. The solution: Make one big pancake! Here the pancake batter fills an entire half sheet pan and bakes in the oven. When it's done, you slice it for up to eight guests and serve it in squares with your preferred pancake toppings that melt and seep into the still-hot cake. Three eggs and plenty of baking powder ensure that this widescreen pancake achieves lift. If one big pancake proves a little too big for your table, leftover pancake freezes really well. After cutting the pancake into squares, you can put them in a zipper-lock bag and freeze them for up to one month; pull out individual slices as you like, and microwave them to thaw. Check out pages 264–265 for fun flavoring options for your pancake.

1 Adjust oven rack to middle position and heat oven to 375 degrees. Spray bottom and sides of rimmed baking sheet with vegetable oil spray.

2 Whisk flour, sugar, baking powder, baking soda, and salt together in large bowl. Whisk eggs and oil in second medium bowl until well combined, then whisk milk and vanilla into egg mixture. Add egg mixture to flour mixture and stir gently until just combined (batter should remain lumpy with few streaks of flour). Let batter sit for 10 minutes before cooking.

3 Using rubber spatula, transfer batter to prepared pan and spread into even layer, being sure to spread into corners as well. Bake until pancake is spotty brown and firm to touch, about 20 minutes, rotating sheet halfway through baking. Transfer to wire rack and let cool for 3 to 5 minutes. Serve with salted butter and maple syrup.

VARIATION

One Smaller Pancake (for 2 to 4 people)

You will need a 13 by 9-inch quarter sheet pan.

Reduce flour to 1 cup, sugar to 2 tablespoons, baking powder to 1¼ teaspoons, baking soda to ¼ teaspoon, salt to ¾ teaspoon, eggs to 2 large eggs, vegetable oil to ¼ cup, milk to 1½ cups, and vanilla to ½ teaspoon. Use small rimmed baking sheet and reduce baking time to 15 minutes.

Mix-and-Match Pancake Toppings

Maple syrup and butter melted over the hot cake are nice, but One Big Pancake (page 262) provides a few big opportunities to embellish breakfast. These creative toppings bake into the batter to give it pizzazz and are perfect for the kids (or kids at heart) at the breakfast table. Each recipe makes enough to cover a quarter of the pancake (or half of One Smaller Pancake [page 262]); use all four to create a pancake with four different flavors to satisfy different tastes, or scale up one recipe (it's easy) if you want enough to cover the whole pancake. Each recipe indicates when to add the topping to the pancake.

Apple Crisp Topping

Total Time 15 minutes

- 1 apple, peeled, cored, and cut into ¼-inch pieces
- ¼ teaspoon ground cinnamon
- 2 tablespoons all-purpose flour
- 2 tablespoons chopped pecans
- 1 tablespoon sugar
- 1 tablespoon old-fashioned rolled oats
- ⅛ teaspoon table salt
- 1 tablespoon unsalted butter, cut into 2 pieces
- Maple syrup

1 Toss apples and cinnamon together in bowl, then microwave until apples are soft, 2 to 3 minutes. After spreading pancake batter into even layer in prepared sheet in step 3, sprinkle apples evenly over top of one-quarter of sheet (or half of sheet if making One Smaller Pancake). Bake as directed.

2 While cooked pancake rests, mix flour, pecans, sugar, oats, and salt together in clean bowl. Using your fingers, rub butter into flour mixture until mixture has texture of coarse crumbs. Microwave until topping is golden, 3 to 4 minutes, stirring every 30 seconds. Sprinkle over apples on cooled pancake and serve with maple syrup.

Milk and Cereal Topping

Total Time 5 minutes

You can use a hand mixer or stand mixer to whip the cream.

- 1 cup Fruity Pebbles, Cocoa Pebbles, or Rice Krispies cereal, divided
- ½ cup heavy cream
- 2 tablespoons malted milk powder
- 2 teaspoons sugar

1 After spreading pancake batter into even layer in prepared sheet in step 3, sprinkle ¾ cup cereal evenly over top of one-quarter of sheet (or half of sheet if making One Smaller Pancake). Bake as directed.

2 While cooked pancake rests, using electric mixer, whip cream, malted milk powder, and sugar on medium-low speed until foamy, about 1 minute. Increase speed to medium-high and whip until stiff peaks form, 1 to 3 minutes. Dollop individual portions of pancakes with whipped cream and sprinkle with remaining ¼ cup cereal.

S'mores Topping

Total Time 5 minutes

- ½ cup mini chocolate chips
- ½ cup mini marshmallows
- 2 graham crackers, broken into ½-inch pieces
- Chocolate sauce

1 After spreading pancake batter into even layer in prepared sheet in step 3, sprinkle chocolate chips evenly over top of one-quarter of sheet (or half of sheet if making One Smaller Pancake). After baking for 10 minutes, sprinkle marshmallows over top, rotate sheet, and continue to bake until pancake is tender and marshmallows are softened and lightly browned, about 10 minutes.

2 Sprinkle individual portions of pancakes with cracker pieces and drizzle with chocolate sauce to taste.

Berries and Cream Topping

Total Time 15 minutes

You can use frozen strawberries and frozen blueberries in place of fresh if you prefer. There's no need to thaw the frozen fruit for the pancake or the compote; be sure to increase the microwave time to 6 minutes. You can use a hand mixer or stand mixer to whip the cream.

- 5 ounces (1 cup) strawberries, hulled (4 ounces halved, 1 ounce chopped), divided
- 5 ounces (1 cup) blueberries, divided
- ¼ cup sugar, divided
- 1½ teaspoons cornstarch
- 2 tablespoons water
- ¼ teaspoon lemon juice
- ½ cup heavy cream
- ¼ teaspoon vanilla extract

1 After spreading pancake batter into even layer in prepared sheet in step 3, sprinkle chopped strawberries and ¼ cup blueberries evenly over top of one-quarter of sheet (or half of sheet if making One Smaller Pancake).

2 While pancake cooks, combine halved strawberries, remaining ¾ cup blueberries, 2 tablespoons sugar, cornstarch, water, and lemon juice in bowl. Microwave until fruit is beginning to break down and juices are bubbling, about 4 minutes, stirring occasionally. Set aside until ready to serve.

3 While cooked pancake rests, using electric mixer, whip cream, vanilla, and remaining 2 tablespoons sugar on medium-low speed until foamy, about 1 minute. Increase speed to high and whip until soft peaks form, 1 to 3 minutes. Top individual portions with fruit compote and whipped cream.

Almond Granola with Dried Fruit

Makes about 9 cups | **Total Time** 55 minutes, plus 1 hour cooling

- ⅓ cup maple syrup
- ⅓ cup packed (2⅓ ounces) light brown sugar
- 4 teaspoons vanilla extract
- ½ teaspoon table salt
- ½ cup vegetable oil
- 5 cups old-fashioned rolled oats
- 2 cups (10 ounces) raw almonds, chopped coarse
- 2 cups raisins or other dried fruit, chopped

Why This Recipe Works Store-bought granola is often loose, sometimes stale, and always expensive. The secret to satisfying clusters and crisp texture is to firmly pack the granola mixture—oats, nuts, maple syrup, brown sugar, vanilla, salt, oil, and everything nice—into a rimmed baking sheet before baking. Once the mixture is baked, you get a granola "bark" that you break into perfectly crunchy clumps of any size. Chopping the almonds by hand is the first choice for superior texture and crunch. If you prefer not to hand chop, substitute an equal quantity of slivered or sliced almonds. (A food processor does a lousy job of chopping whole nuts evenly.) Use a single type of your favorite dried fruit or a combination. Do not use quick oats.

1 Adjust oven rack to upper-middle position and heat oven to 325 degrees. Line rimmed baking sheet with parchment paper.

2 Whisk maple syrup, brown sugar, vanilla, and salt in large bowl. Whisk in oil. Fold in oats and almonds until thoroughly coated.

3 Transfer oat mixture to prepared sheet and spread across sheet into thin, even layer (about ⅜ inch thick). Using stiff metal spatula, compress oat mixture until very compact. Bake until lightly browned, 40 to 45 minutes, rotating pan once halfway through baking. Remove granola from oven and let cool completely on wire rack, about 1 hour. Break cooled granola into pieces of desired size. Stir in dried fruit. (Granola can be stored in airtight container for up to 2 weeks.)

VARIATIONS

Pecan-Orange Granola with Dried Cranberries

Add 2 tablespoons finely grated orange zest and 2½ teaspoons ground cinnamon to maple syrup mixture in step 2. Substitute coarsely chopped pecans for almonds. After granola is broken into pieces, stir in 2 cups dried cranberries.

Spiced Walnut Granola with Dried Apple

Add 2 teaspoons ground cinnamon, 1½ teaspoons ground ginger, ¾ teaspoon ground allspice, ½ teaspoon freshly grated nutmeg, and ½ teaspoon pepper to maple syrup mixture in step 2. Substitute coarsely chopped walnuts for almonds. After granola is broken into pieces, stir in 2 cups chopped dried apples.

Nutella Bread Pudding

Serves 4 to 6 | **Total Time** 1 hour, plus 20 minutes soaking

- 1 (18- to 20-inch) baguette, torn into 1-inch pieces (8 cups)
- 1 cup heavy cream
- 1 cup plus 1 tablespoon whole milk, divided
- 4 large egg yolks
- 6 tablespoons Nutella spread, divided
- 1½ teaspoons vanilla extract
- ⅛ teaspoon table salt
- ¼ cup hazelnuts, toasted, skinned, and chopped
- 3 ounces blueberries, raspberries, and/or blackberries (blackberries halved, if using) (¾ cup)
- 2 ounces strawberries, hulled and quartered (½ cup)
- 2 teaspoons confectioners' sugar (optional)

Why This Recipe Works Bread and Nutella are breakfast icons. We turn them into a luxurious Nutella bread pudding that we bake in a sheet pan rather than a baking dish to achieve a large surface area of irresistibly crispy caramelized bread. We stir Nutella right into our custard so it coats every piece of toasted baguette. Because the sheet pan is so shallow, the pudding takes just 10 minutes to set and brown in a hot 425-degree oven. To reinforce the flavors and cap off this breakfast, we drizzle the finished pudding with warmed Nutella, a sprinkling of toasted hazelnuts, and some berries. If you want to share, serve this to guests at brunch; otherwise, bake a batch and then reheat squares each day for the sweetest week. You'll need an 18 by 13-inch half sheet pan to toast the bread and a 13 by 9-inch quarter sheet pan to assemble the bread pudding for this recipe.

1 Adjust oven rack to middle position and heat oven to 300 degrees. Spread baguette over large rimmed baking sheet in even layer and bake, stirring occasionally, until golden and crisp, about 25 minutes. Transfer bread to large bowl and let cool slightly.

2 Increase oven temperature to 425 degrees. Whisk cream, 1 cup milk, egg yolks, ¼ cup Nutella, vanilla, and salt in bowl until well combined. Add cooled bread and toss until evenly coated. Let mixture sit, tossing occasionally, until bread completely absorbs custard, about 20 minutes. Spray small rimmed baking sheet with vegetable oil spray, then transfer soaked bread mixture to prepared sheet.

3 Bake until bread pudding is just set and surface is slightly crisp, 10 to 15 minutes. Transfer sheet to wire rack and let cool for 10 minutes. Meanwhile, combine remaining 1 tablespoon milk and remaining 2 tablespoons Nutella in bowl, then microwave until pourable, about 30 seconds. Sprinkle bread pudding with hazelnuts, berries, and strawberries; drizzle with warmed Nutella mixture; and sprinkle with confectioners' sugar, if using. Serve.

Sausage and Cheddar Bread Pudding

Serves 4 to 6 | **Total Time** 1¼ hours, plus 20 minutes soaking

- 1 (18- to 20-inch) baguette, torn into 1-inch pieces (8 cups)
- 1¼ cups whole milk
- 1 cup heavy cream
- 4 large egg yolks
- 1 teaspoon minced fresh thyme or sage or ¼ teaspoon dried
- ¼ teaspoon pepper
- ⅛ teaspoon table salt
- 6 ounces breakfast sausage, casings removed
- 2 ounces cheddar cheese, shredded (½ cup)
- 2 tablespoons minced fresh chives
- 1 tablespoon maple syrup

Why This Recipe Works A savory bread pudding packages a complete breakfast—eggs, sausage, and toast—in a tasty casserole that is so much more comforting than a plate of those individual ingredients. Sprinkling cheese over the pudding before baking gives the warm bread pudding an irresistible melty top. A final sprinkling of chives and a drizzle of sweet maple syrup (for those who like to drizzle breakfast sausage with syrup) enhance the bread pudding and give this savory dish a breakfast-appropriate hit of sweet. You'll need an 18 by 13-inch half sheet pan to toast the bread and a 13 by 9-inch quarter sheet pan to assemble the bread pudding for this recipe.

1 Adjust oven rack to middle position and heat oven to 300 degrees. Spread baguette over large rimmed baking sheet in even layer and bake, stirring occasionally, until golden and crisp, about 25 minutes. Transfer bread to large bowl and let cool slightly.

2 Increase oven temperature to 425 degrees. Whisk milk, cream, egg yolks, thyme, pepper, and salt in bowl until well combined. Add cooled bread and toss until evenly coated. Let mixture sit, tossing occasionally, until bread completely absorbs custard, about 20 minutes. Spray small rimmed baking sheet with vegetable oil spray, then transfer soaked bread mixture to prepared sheet. Crumble sausage into rough ½-inch pieces over top, then sprinkle with cheddar.

3 Bake until bread pudding is just set and surface is slightly crisp, 15 to 20 minutes, rotating sheet halfway through baking. Transfer sheet to wire rack and let cool for 10 minutes. Sprinkle with chives, drizzle with maple syrup, and serve.

CHAPTER SEVEN

Sides + Snacks

Sides

Snacks

Roasted Asparagus with Mint-Orange Gremolata

Roasted Asparagus with Mint-Orange Gremolata

Serves 4 to 6 | **Total Time** 25 minutes

Why This Recipe Works Asparagus season is fleeting, so every serving should be spectacular. Roasting brings out the best in asparagus, and starting with a preheated sheet pan ensures a hard sear on the spears. We resist the urge to shake the sheet during roasting to really develop browning on one side of the spears and maintain the vibrant green color on the other. For a bright seasoning, we prepare an Italian gremolata, a garnish of citrus zest and minced fresh herbs. Thicker asparagus (½ to ¾ inch in diameter) holds up better to roasting. If using white asparagus, peel just the outermost layer of the bottom halves of the spears.

- 2 tablespoons minced fresh mint
- 2 tablespoons minced fresh parsley
- 2 teaspoons grated orange zest
- 1 garlic clove, minced
- Pinch cayenne pepper
- 2 pounds thick asparagus
- 2 tablespoons plus 2 teaspoons extra-virgin olive oil, divided
- ½ teaspoon table salt
- ¼ teaspoon pepper

1 Adjust oven rack to lowest position, place rimmed baking sheet on rack, and heat oven to 500 degrees. Combine mint, parsley, orange zest, garlic, and cayenne in bowl; set aside.

2 Trim bottom inch of asparagus spears and discard. Peel bottom halves of spears until white flesh is exposed. Toss asparagus with 2 tablespoons oil, salt, and pepper in dish.

3 Transfer asparagus to preheated sheet and spread into even layer. Roast, without moving asparagus, until undersides of spears are browned, tops are vibrant green, and tip of paring knife inserted at base of largest spear meets little resistance, 8 to 10 minutes. Drizzle asparagus with remaining 2 teaspoons oil, sprinkle with gremolata, and serve immediately.

VARIATIONS

Roasted Asparagus with Cilantro-Lime Gremolata

Omit mint and cayenne. Substitute ¼ cup minced fresh cilantro for parsley and lime zest for orange zest.

Roasted Asparagus with Tarragon-Lemon Gremolata

Omit cayenne. Substitute tarragon for mint and lemon zest for orange zest.

Roasted Broccoli

Serves 4 to 6 | **Total Time** 30 minutes

Why This Recipe Works To maximize contact with the sheet pan, we cut the broccoli crowns into wedges and the trimmed stalks into planks. We preheat the sheet on the lowest rack of a 500-degree oven so the broccoli sizzles and finishes with crisp-tipped florets and blistered and browned stalks.

- 1¾ pounds broccoli
- 3 tablespoons extra-virgin olive oil
- 3 garlic cloves, minced
- ½ teaspoon sugar
- ½ teaspoon table salt
- Pinch pepper
- Lemon wedges

1 Adjust oven rack to lowest position, place rimmed baking sheet on rack, and heat oven to 500 degrees. Cut broccoli horizontally at juncture of crowns and stalks. Cut crowns into 4 wedges if 3 to 4 inches in diameter or 6 wedges if 4 to 5 inches in diameter. Trim tough outer peel from stalks, then cut into ½-inch-thick planks about 2 to 3 inches long.

2 Combine oil, garlic, sugar, salt, and pepper in large bowl. Add broccoli and toss to coat. Working quickly, lay broccoli in single layer, flat sides down, on preheated sheet. Roast until stalks are well browned and tender and florets are lightly browned, 9 to 11 minutes. Serve with lemon wedges.

VARIATIONS

Roasted Broccoli with Parmesan and Black Pepper Topping

While broccoli roasts, mix ½ teaspoon pepper and ½ teaspoon lemon zest in small bowl with your fingers until evenly combined. Add ½ cup grated Parmesan and toss with your fingers or fork until lemon zest and pepper are evenly distributed. Sprinkle broccoli with topping.

Roasted Broccoli with Sesame-Orange Topping

While broccoli roasts, use spice grinder or mortar and pestle to grind 1 tablespoon toasted sesame seeds, ½ teaspoon grated orange zest, and ¼ teaspoon kosher salt to powder. Transfer to small bowl. Add 1 tablespoon more toasted sesame seeds and toss with your fingers until sesame seeds are evenly distributed. Sprinkle broccoli with topping.

Broiled Broccoli Rabe

Serves 4 | **Total Time** 20 minutes

Why This Recipe Works Broccoli rabe isn't too bitter; it's just misunderstood. Broiling it on a sheet pan takes minutes, it creates deep caramelization without overcooking, and it gives the rabe a sweetness that complements its pleasant bitterness. We also found a way to limit the bitterness from the start: Most of it comes from an enzymatic reaction triggered when the florets are cut or chewed, so we keep the leafy parts whole. The heat generated by a broiler varies; keep an eye on the broccoli rabe as it cooks. If the leaves are getting too dark or not browning in the time specified, adjust the distance of the oven rack from the broiler element. We developed this recipe with Diamond Crystal kosher salt. If using Morton kosher salt, which is denser, use only ½ teaspoon. The rabe is a great topping for pasta or polenta.

- 3 tablespoons extra-virgin olive oil, divided
- 1 pound broccoli rabe, trimmed
- 1 garlic clove, minced
- ¾ teaspoon kosher salt
- ¼ teaspoon red pepper flakes
- Lemon wedges

1 Adjust oven rack 4 inches from broiler element and heat broiler. Brush rimmed baking sheet with 1 tablespoon oil.

2 Cut tops (leaves and florets) of broccoli rabe from stalks, keeping tops whole, then cut stalks into 1-inch pieces. Transfer to prepared sheet.

3 Combine remaining 2 tablespoons oil, garlic, salt, and pepper flakes in small bowl. Pour oil mixture over broccoli rabe and toss to combine.

4 Broil until exposed half of leaves are well browned, 2 to 2½ minutes. Using tongs, toss to expose unbrowned leaves. Return sheet to oven and continue to broil until most leaves are lightly charred and stalks are crisp-tender, 2 to 2½ minutes. Serve with lemon wedges.

Roasted Brussels Sprouts with Mustard, Brown Sugar, and Pecans

Serves 4 to 6 | **Total Time** 45 minutes

Why This Recipe Works There are a few ways to achieve crispy, caramelized brussels sprouts that are tender on the inside—pan frying and deep frying among them—but the simplest and most foolproof method is roasting. We start out roasting them on a sheet pan, covered in foil, with some water to steam-cook them a bit. We then remove the foil and continue to roast, and the exteriors dry out and caramelize. If you can find only large sprouts (greater than 1½ inches in diameter), quarter them instead of halving them.

- 2 pounds brussels sprouts, trimmed and halved
- 3 tablespoons extra-virgin olive oil
- 1 tablespoon water
- ¾ teaspoon table salt
- ¼ teaspoon pepper
- 2 tablespoons Dijon mustard
- 2 tablespoons packed brown sugar
- 4 teaspoons white wine vinegar
- ⅛ teaspoon cayenne pepper
- ¼ cup pecans or walnuts, toasted and chopped

1 Adjust oven rack to upper-middle position and heat oven to 500 degrees. Toss brussels sprouts with oil, water, salt, and pepper in bowl. Arrange sprouts in single layer cut sides down on rimmed baking sheet.

2 Cover sheet tightly with aluminum foil and roast for 10 minutes. Remove foil and continue to roast until brussels sprouts are well browned and tender, 10 to 12 minutes.

3 Meanwhile, whisk mustard, sugar, vinegar, and cayenne together in bowl. Remove brussels sprouts from oven, drizzle with mustard mixture and gently toss to coat. Season with salt and pepper to taste. Transfer sprouts to large plate, sprinkle with pecans, and serve.

VARIATIONS

Roasted Brussels Sprouts with Chile, Mint, and Peanuts

Substitute 1 stemmed, seeded, and minced Fresno chile, 4 teaspoons lime juice, and 2 teaspoons fish sauce for mustard, sugar, and vinegar. Omit cayenne. Substitute ¼ cup finely chopped dry-roasted peanuts and 2 tablespoons chopped fresh mint for pecans.

Roasted Brussels Sprouts with Pomegranate, Cumin, and Pistachios

Substitute 2 tablespoons pomegranate molasses and ¾ teaspoon ground cumin for mustard, sugar, and vinegar. Omit cayenne. Substitute ¼ cup shelled pistachios, toasted and chopped, and 2 tablespoons pomegranate seeds for pecans.

Roasted Cabbage

Serves 4 to 6 | **Total Time** 50 minutes

Why This Recipe Works Cabbage becomes a stunningly caramelized, crisp-tender delight when roasted. We start by cutting the head straight through the core to create eight structurally sound wedges that lie flush against the sheet pan. We cover the pan with foil for the first 20 minutes of roasting to cook the wedges through until meltingly tender. Then we remove the foil to create a striking pattern of deep caramelization on the wedges. We developed this recipe with Diamond Crystal kosher salt. If using Morton kosher salt, which is denser, use only ¾ teaspoon.

Roasted Broccoli

Broiled Broccoli Rabe

1 head green cabbage (2 to 2½ pounds)

3 tablespoons vegetable oil, divided

1 teaspoon kosher salt, divided

¼ teaspoon pepper

1 Adjust oven rack to upper-middle position and heat oven to 500 degrees. Quarter cabbage through core and cut each quarter into 2 wedges, leaving core intact. Arrange wedges, 1 flat side down, on rimmed baking sheet. Brush 1½ tablespoons oil on exposed cut sides of wedges and sprinkle with ½ teaspoon salt. Flip wedges so oiled sides are flush with sheet. Brush second cut sides with remaining 1½ tablespoons oil and sprinkle with pepper and remaining ½ teaspoon salt. Cover sheet tightly with aluminum foil and roast for 20 minutes.

2 Remove foil (be careful of escaping steam) and continue to cook until cabbage wedges begin to brown on underside, 5 to 10 minutes. Using tongs and thin metal spatula, flip each wedge. Roast until edges are very well browned and some leaves have crisped, 5 to 10 minutes. Transfer cabbage to platter and serve.

VARIATION

Roasted Cabbage with Gochujang, Sesame, and Scallions

Stir 2 tablespoons gochujang paste, 1 tablespoon unseasoned rice vinegar, 2 teaspoons water, 1 teaspoon toasted sesame oil, and ½ teaspoon sugar together in small bowl. Drizzle half of gochujang mixture over serving platter. Transfer cabbage to platter. Drizzle with remaining gochujang mixture, sprinkle with 1 tablespoon toasted sesame seeds and 2 thinly sliced scallions (green parts only), and serve.

Parmesan Roasted Cauliflower

Serves 4 to 6 | **Total Time** 45 minutes

Why This Recipe Works A cheese crust is a fun addition to roasted vegetables (or sandwiches; see page 30), and mild, earthy cauliflower is a great candidate for a rich, salty boost. The sheet pan takes care of the browning and crisping, but we needed a way to make the grated Parmesan adhere to the florets. A little cornstarch was the right coating addition: It absorbs and traps a bit of the liquid released by the roasting cauliflower and prevents the Parmesan from sliding off. Quickly roasting the florets in a 450-degree oven ensures great browning without overcooking the cauliflower, and letting the florets rest for a few minutes helps the cheese stay put. You will need to purchase 3 pounds of whole cauliflower (one to two heads) to yield 2 pounds of florets. You can also use precut cauliflower florets. For the best results, we recommend using freshly grated Parmesan cheese; use a rasp-style grater to grate the Parmesan.

3 ounces Parmesan cheese, grated (1½ cups)

2 tablespoons cornstarch

1 teaspoon minced fresh thyme

¾ teaspoon table salt

½ teaspoon pepper

2 pounds cauliflower florets, cut into 2-inch pieces

3 tablespoons extra-virgin olive oil

1 Adjust oven rack to lowest position and heat oven to 450 degrees. Spray rimmed baking sheet with vegetable oil spray. Stir Parmesan, cornstarch, thyme, salt, and pepper in bowl until thoroughly combined; set aside.

2 Toss cauliflower and oil together in large bowl. Add Parmesan mixture to cauliflower mixture and toss until well coated. Pour contents of bowl onto prepared sheet, scraping out any remaining Parmesan from bowl with rubber spatula. Shake sheet to distribute cheese and cauliflower evenly. Where possible, flip florets cut side down.

3 Roast cauliflower until bottom edges of florets begin to brown, about 15 minutes. Remove sheet from oven and flip florets using thin metal spatula. Continue to roast until cauliflower is tender and spotty brown, about 5 minutes longer.

4 Transfer sheet to wire rack and let cool for 5 minutes. Using thin metal spatula, transfer cauliflower and any accompanying cheese to serving platter. Serve.

Parmesan Roasted Cauliflower

Roasted Green Beans with Goat Cheese and Hazelnuts

Roasted Green Beans with Goat Cheese and Hazelnuts

Serves 4 | **Total Time** 45 minutes

Why This Recipe Works Our steam-roasting technique gives mature supermarket green beans a flavor comparable to sweet fresh-picked beans. The quick-cooking green beans can handle only a short stay in the oven, so we cover them with aluminum foil and they gently steam and soften in the first 10 minutes of cooking. Uncovering the beans for the final 10 minutes turns them an appealing blistered, speckled brown that we augment with a touch of sugar sprinkled on the beans before cooking. They become a hearty, well-rounded side with a warm orange vinaigrette plus rich goat cheese and crunchy hazelnuts. We developed this recipe with Diamond Crystal kosher salt. If using Morton kosher salt, which is denser, use only ¾ teaspoon.

- 1½ pounds green beans, trimmed
- 5½ tablespoons extra-virgin olive oil, divided
- 1 teaspoon kosher salt, divided
- ¾ teaspoon pepper, divided
- ¾ teaspoon sugar
- 2 garlic cloves, minced
- 1 teaspoon grated orange zest plus 2 teaspoons juice
- 2 teaspoons lemon juice
- 1 teaspoon Dijon mustard
- 2 tablespoons minced fresh chives
- 2 ounces goat cheese, crumbled (½ cup)
- ¼ cup hazelnuts, toasted, skinned, and chopped

1 Adjust oven rack to lowest position and heat oven to 475 degrees. Combine green beans, 1½ tablespoons oil, ¾ teaspoon salt, ½ teaspoon pepper, and sugar on rimmed baking sheet and spread into even layer.

2 Cover sheet tightly with aluminum foil and roast for 10 minutes. Remove foil and continue to roast until green beans are spotty brown, about 10 minutes longer, stirring halfway through roasting.

3 Meanwhile, combine garlic, orange zest, and remaining ¼ cup oil in medium bowl and microwave until bubbling, about 1 minute; let steep for 1 minute. Whisk orange juice, lemon juice, mustard, remaining ¼ teaspoon salt, and remaining ¼ teaspoon pepper into garlic mixture.

4 Toss green beans with dressing and chives to combine. Sprinkle with goat cheese and hazelnuts. Serve.

VARIATIONS

Roasted Green Beans with Almonds and Mint

Substitute 1 teaspoon grated lime zest for orange zest and 4 teaspoons lime juice for orange juice. Substitute ¼ cup torn fresh mint leaves for chives; and ¼ cup whole blanched almonds, toasted and chopped, for hazelnuts. Omit goat cheese.

Roasted Green Beans with Pecorino and Pine Nuts

Omit orange juice, substitute grated lemon zest for orange zest, and increase lemon juice to 4 teaspoons. Substitute 2 tablespoons chopped fresh basil for chives; 1½ ounces Pecorino Romano cheese, shredded, for goat cheese; and ¼ cup pine nuts, toasted, for hazelnuts.

Elote

Elote

Serves 4 | **Total Time** 45 minutes

Why This Recipe Works In Mexico, this delightfully messy street-food snack is charred over fire and then coated in a creamy mixture of crema, spices, cilantro, and lime juice, along with a sprinkle of queso fresco. To enjoy this treat indoors, turn to your broiler, whose high, dry heat mimics the grill and creates good charring. Brushing the cobs with oil keeps them from drying out. To keep the crumbly queso fresco from sliding right off the corn and ending up on the plate, mix it with the mayo (or crema) just before slathering on the charred corn. You can substitute feta cheese for the queso fresco.

- 4 ears corn, husks and silk removed, stalks left intact
- 2 teaspoons extra-virgin olive oil
- 6 tablespoons mayonnaise or crema
- 2 tablespoons crumbled queso fresco
- 2 tablespoons minced fresh cilantro
- 2 teaspoons lime juice, plus lime wedges for serving
- 1 garlic clove, minced
- ½ teaspoon chili powder
- ⅛ teaspoon table salt

1 Adjust oven rack to middle position and heat broiler. Brush corn all over with oil and transfer to aluminum foil–lined rimmed baking sheet. Broil corn until well browned on 1 side, 15 to 20 minutes. Flip corn and broil until browned on opposite side, 15 to 20 minutes.

2 Meanwhile, whisk mayonnaise, queso fresco, cilantro, lime juice, garlic, chili powder, and salt in bowl until incorporated. Remove corn from oven and brush evenly on all sides with mayonnaise mixture. Season with salt and pepper to taste. Serve with lime wedges and any extra mayonnaise mixture.

Roasted Kale with Garlic, Red Pepper Flakes, and Lemon

Serves 4 | **Total Time** 30 minutes

Why This Recipe Works Make kale taste like a real treat by taking it to the oven for deliciously crisp leaves. Massaging oil and salt into the kale directly on a sheet pan seasons all the leaves and kick-starts the wilting process before cooking. By skipping any stirring, we end up with kale that has a delightful mix of textures: tender, crisp, and crunchy. Washing the kale and drying it in the salad spinner leaves it with just the right amount of surface moisture to facilitate cooking; kneading and squeezing the kale softens its texture and evenly distributes seasonings. Kale bunches can vary in the amount of usable leaves; buy 1 pound to ensure that you end up with 12 cups (10 ounces) of kale pieces. To minimize waste, look for bunches where leaves run the length of the stem. Serve the kale as a side or mix it into pastas, scrambles, or grain bowls.

- 1 pound curly kale, stemmed and torn into 1½- to 2-inch pieces (12 cups)
- 2 tablespoons vegetable oil
- 2 garlic cloves, minced
- 1 teaspoon grated lemon zest
- ½ teaspoon table salt
- ¼ teaspoon red pepper flakes

1 Adjust oven rack to upper-middle position and heat oven to 400 degrees. Working in 3 batches, wash kale and spin in salad spinner until leaves are mostly dry. Transfer to rimmed baking sheet.

2 Combine oil, garlic, lemon zest, salt, and pepper flakes in small bowl. Drizzle over kale. Gently knead and squeeze kale until leaves are evenly coated in oil mixture, have started to soften, and are slightly wilted, about 1 minute.

3 Roast kale until leaves are tender and some edges of leaves are crisp and brown, about 10 minutes. Serve immediately (leaves will soften as they stand).

VARIATIONS

Roasted Kale with Coriander, Ginger, and Coconut

Omit lemon zest. Substitute 2 teaspoons grated fresh ginger for garlic and ½ teaspoon ground coriander for pepper flakes. Sprinkle ½ cup unsweetened coconut chips over kale after roasting.

Roasted Kale with Parmesan, Shallot, and Nutmeg

Substitute ½ cup grated Parmesan for garlic, 2 tablespoons minced shallot for lemon zest, and ground nutmeg for pepper flakes.

Roasted Mushrooms with Parmesan and Pine Nuts

Serves 4 | **Total Time** 1¼ hours

Why This Recipe Works Mushrooms can be magical when they're treated with care. The unusual step of brining the mushrooms before roasting seasons the mushrooms evenly and allows them to absorb moisture through their gills and cut surfaces, which improves their texture through roasting. The shallow rimmed baking sheet allows excess moisture to evaporate during cooking, and the mushrooms become darkly browned. For a rich finish, we toss the mushrooms in butter, lemon juice, Parmesan, parsley, and pine nuts.

- 5 teaspoons table salt, for brining
- 1½ pounds cremini mushrooms, trimmed and left whole if small, halved if medium, or quartered if large
- 1 pound shiitake mushrooms, stemmed, caps larger than 3 inches halved
- 2 tablespoons extra-virgin olive oil
- 1 ounce Parmesan cheese, grated (½ cup)
- 2 tablespoons chopped fresh parsley
- 2 tablespoons pine nuts, toasted
- 2 tablespoons unsalted butter, melted
- 1 teaspoon lemon juice

Roasted Mushrooms with Parmesan and Pine Nuts

1 Adjust oven rack to lowest position and heat oven to 450 degrees. Whisk 5 teaspoons salt into 2 quarts water in large container until dissolved. Add cremini and shiitake mushrooms, cover with plate or bowl to submerge, and let sit for 10 minutes.

2 Drain mushrooms, then pat dry with paper towels. Transfer mushrooms to rimmed baking sheet and toss with oil to coat. Roast until liquid has completely evaporated, 35 to 45 minutes.

3 Carefully stir mushrooms and continue to roast until mushrooms are deeply browned, 5 to 10 minutes.

4 Transfer mushrooms to large serving bowl and toss with Parmesan, parsley, pine nuts, melted butter, and lemon juice. Season with salt and pepper to taste. Serve immediately.

VARIATIONS

Roasted Mushrooms with Harissa and Mint

Omit Parmesan and pine nuts and increase lemon juice to 2 teaspoons. Substitute 2 tablespoons mint for parsley. Add 1 minced garlic clove, 2 teaspoons harissa, ¼ teaspoon ground cumin, and ¼ teaspoon salt to mushroom mixture in step 4.

Roasted Mushrooms with Roasted Garlic and Smoked Paprika

Add 3 unpeeled garlic cloves to sheet with mushrooms in step 2. Remove garlic from sheet in step 3 when stirring mushrooms. When garlic is cool to touch, peel and mash. Omit Parmesan and pine nuts and substitute 2 teaspoons sherry vinegar for lemon juice. Add mashed garlic, ½ teaspoon smoked paprika, and ¼ teaspoon salt to mushroom mixture in step 4.

Foil-Roasted Potatoes

Serves 6 | **Total Time** 1 hour

Why This Recipe Works This potato recipe yields what everyone wants: creamy interiors, nicely browned cut sides, and tons of flavor—all with an easy method that, as a bonus, makes cleanup a breeze and serves a generous amount. Encasing the red potatoes in a foil pouch on a sheet pan allows them to steam in the oven so they become ultracreamy. Including butter and herbs inside infuses the potatoes with flavor while they cook. The butter helps create some browning but not enough, so we place the baking sheet on the bottom oven rack, close to the heat source, so the potatoes become nicely burnished, even within the packet.

- 2 pounds small red potatoes, unpeeled, halved
- 2 teaspoons chopped fresh rosemary
- 1¼ teaspoons table salt
- 1 teaspoon chopped fresh thyme
- ½ teaspoon pepper
- 4 tablespoons unsalted butter, cut into ½-inch pieces
- 3 garlic cloves, sliced thin

1 Adjust oven rack to lowest position and heat oven to 400 degrees. Toss potatoes, rosemary, salt, thyme, and pepper in large bowl until potatoes are well coated.

2 Line rimmed baking sheet with 16 by 12-inch sheet of aluminum foil. Spread potato mixture evenly over foil, leaving 1½-inch border. Flip potatoes cut sides down. Scatter butter and garlic over potatoes. Place second 16 by 12-inch sheet of foil over potatoes. Beginning at 1 corner, fold foil inward in ½-inch increments 2 to 3 times to seal edge. Continue folding around perimeter of foil to create sealed packet.

3 Transfer sheet to oven and bake until potatoes are tender, about 40 minutes. Let potatoes cool for 5 minutes. Using tongs, tear away top sheet of foil, being careful of escaping steam. Serve.

Crispy Smashed Potatoes

Serves 4 to 6 | **Total Time** 1 ½ hours

Why This Recipe Works Crispy smashed potatoes deliver mashed potato creaminess with the crackling crisp crust of roasted potatoes. How? We use one sheet pan to roast them and another to smash them.

The technique is straightforward: Skin-on spuds are parcooked in seasoned water, drained, and squashed just shy of a half-inch thick. To smash all the potatoes at once, we use a second baking sheet to press evenly and firmly on top of the pan of parcooked potatoes. Then we drizzle the potatoes with oil, season them, and spread them out on a baking sheet in the oven to render the roughened edges browned and crispy and the interiors creamy and sweet. Choose potatoes that are 1 to 2 inches in diameter. We developed this recipe with Diamond Crystal kosher salt. If using Morton kosher salt, which is denser, use only ¾ teaspoon. We like to use kosher salt here but you can use ½ teaspoon table salt if you prefer.

- 2 pounds small red potatoes
- 6 tablespoons extra-virgin olive oil, divided
- 1 teaspoon chopped fresh thyme
- 1 teaspoon kosher salt
- ¼ teaspoon pepper

1 Adjust oven racks to top and lowest positions and heat oven to 500 degrees. Spread potatoes on rimmed baking sheet, then pour ¾ cup water over top. Cover sheet with aluminum foil, crimping edges tightly (using 2 sheets and overlapping in center if necessary) and bake on lower rack until skewer or paring knife slips in and out of potatoes easily, 25 to 30 minutes (poke skewer through foil to test). Remove foil and cool for 10 minutes. If any water remains on sheet, blot dry with paper towel.

2 Drizzle 3 tablespoons oil over potatoes and roll to coat then space potatoes evenly over sheet. Place second baking sheet on top; press down uniformly on sheet to crush potatoes until roughly ⅓ to ½ inch thick. Sprinkle with thyme, salt, and pepper; drizzle evenly with remaining 3 tablespoons oil. Roast potatoes on upper rack for 15 minutes. Transfer sheet to lower rack and continue to roast until well browned, 20 to 30 minutes longer. Serve immediately.

Crispy Smashed Potatoes

Thick-Cut Oven Fries

Serves 4 to 6 | **Total Time** 55 minutes

Why This Recipe Works Can you make oven fries just as crispy as deep-fried French fries? Yes! Covering the sheet pan with foil for the first half of cooking ensures that the potatoes are tender by the time they're browned. And coating them with a cornstarch slurry provides an irresistibly crispy crust. Choose potatoes that are 4 to 6 inches in length; trimming thin slices from the ends of the potatoes in step 2 ensures that each fry has two flat surfaces for even browning.

- 3 tablespoons vegetable oil
- 2 pounds Yukon Gold potatoes, unpeeled
- ¾ cup water, plus extra as needed
- 3 tablespoons cornstarch

1 Adjust oven rack to lowest position and heat oven to 425 degrees. Generously spray rimmed baking sheet with vegetable oil spray. Pour oil into prepared sheet and tilt sheet until surface is evenly coated with oil.

2 Halve potatoes lengthwise and turn halves cut side down on cutting board. Trim thin slice from both long sides of each potato half, discarding trimmings. Slice potatoes lengthwise into ⅓- to ½-inch-thick planks.

3 Combine water and cornstarch in large bowl, making sure no lumps of cornstarch remain on bottom of bowl. Microwave, stirring every 20 seconds, until mixture begins to thicken, 1 to 3 minutes. Remove from microwave and continue to stir until mixture thickens to pudding-like consistency. (If necessary, add up to 2 tablespoons water to achieve correct consistency.)

4 Transfer potatoes to bowl with cornstarch mixture and toss until each plank is evenly coated. Arrange planks on prepared sheet, leaving small gaps between planks. (Some cornstarch mixture will remain in bowl.) Cover sheet tightly with lightly greased aluminum foil and bake for 12 minutes.

5 Remove foil and bake until bottoms are golden brown, 10 to 18 minutes. Remove sheet from oven and, using thin metal spatula, carefully flip each fry. Return sheet to oven and continue to bake until second sides are golden brown, 10 to 18 minutes. Transfer fries to paper towel–lined plate and season with kosher salt to taste. Serve.

Roasted Root Vegetables

Serves 6 | **Total Time** 1¼ hours

Why This Recipe Works Starchy root vegetables achieve enormous complexity through caramelization. We roast a combination of celery root, carrots, parsnips, and turnips to create a nice balance of deep flavors and contrasting textures. Cutting each type of vegetable into a specific shape isn't tedious; it ensures that they all cook at the same rate and brown nicely on the sheet pan. Softened shallots add flavor to the finished dish. Use turnips that are roughly 2 to 3 inches in diameter. Instead of sprinkling the roasted vegetables with chopped parsley, you can substitute tarragon or chives. We developed this recipe with Diamond Crystal kosher salt. If using Morton kosher salt, which is denser, use only ¾ teaspoon.

- 1 celery root (14 ounces), peeled
- 4 carrots, peeled and cut into 2½-inch lengths, halved or quartered lengthwise if necessary to create pieces ½ to 1 inch in diameter
- 12 ounces parsnips, peeled and sliced on bias 1 inch thick
- 10 small shallots, peeled
- 1 teaspoon kosher salt
- 12 ounces turnips, peeled, halved horizontally, and each half quartered
- 3 tablespoons vegetable oil
- 2 tablespoons chopped fresh parsley

1 Adjust oven rack to middle position, place rimmed baking sheet on rack, and heat oven to 425 degrees. Cut celery root into ¾-inch-thick rounds. Cut each round into ¾-inch-thick planks about 2½ inches in length.

2 Toss celery root, carrots, parsnips, and shallots with salt in large bowl; season with pepper to taste. Microwave, covered, until small pieces of carrot are just pliable enough to bend, 8 to 10 minutes, stirring halfway through microwaving. Drain vegetables and return them to bowl. Add turnips and oil and toss to coat.

3 Working quickly, remove sheet from oven and carefully transfer vegetables to sheet; arrange in even layer. Roast for 25 minutes.

4 Using thin metal spatula, stir vegetables and arrange in even layer. Rotate sheet and continue to roast until vegetables are golden brown and celery root is tender when pierced with tip of paring knife, 15 to 25 minutes longer. Sprinkle with parsley and serve.

Roasted Root Vegetables

Roasted Delicata Squash

Roasted Delicata Squash

Serves 4 to 6 | **Total Time** 1 hour

Why This Recipe Works Delicata is the easiest winter squash to cook because its pretty, striated skin is so thin that it can be eaten—no peeling needed. Roasting intensifies delicata's sweet and earthy flavors but can dry it out, so we cover the sheet pan with foil initially to let the squash steam before finishing it uncovered. Cooking the squash in oil and butter ensures that it roasts up golden brown. A bright herb-vinegar sauce lends a contrasting punch without overshadowing the squash. To ensure even cooking, choose squashes that are similar in size.

Herb Sauce

- ¼ cup minced fresh parsley or chives
- ¼ cup extra-virgin olive oil
- 2 tablespoons sherry vinegar
- 2 garlic cloves, minced
- 1 teaspoon smoked paprika
- ¼ teaspoon table salt

Squash

- 3 delicata squashes (12 to 16 ounces each), ends trimmed, halved lengthwise, seeded, and sliced crosswise ½ inch thick
- 4 teaspoons extra-virgin olive oil
- ½ teaspoon table salt
- 2 tablespoons unsalted butter, cut into 8 pieces

1 For the herb sauce Stir all ingredients together in bowl; set aside for serving.

2 For the squash Adjust oven rack to lowest position and heat oven to 425 degrees. Toss squash, oil, and salt in bowl to coat. Arrange squash in single layer on rimmed baking sheet. Cover tightly with aluminum foil and bake until squash is tender when pierced with tip of paring knife, 18 to 20 minutes.

3 Uncover and continue to bake until side touching baking sheet is golden brown, 8 to 11 minutes. Remove squash from oven and, using thin metal spatula, flip slices over. Scatter butter pieces over squash. Return to oven and continue to bake until side touching baking sheet is golden brown, 8 to 11 minutes. Transfer squash to serving platter and drizzle with herb sauce. Serve.

Spiralized Sweet Potatoes with Crispy Shallots, Pistachios, and Urfa

Serves 4 to 6 | **Total Time** 50 minutes

Why This Recipe Works Spiralizing sweet potatoes creates a beautiful-looking side dish but it also enables the potatoes to roast much faster than is typical. That incentivized us to dress up the potatoes further. Urfa pepper (or Urfa biber) is a Turkish chile pepper whose notes of coffee, chocolate, and molasses add lots of depth to the dish, which we expand on by incorporating crispy shallots and brighten with a lemon vinaigrette. Tossing the sweet potatoes in shallot oil from the crispy shallots before roasting stretches the ingredient and adds still more flavor to the potatoes. Finishing the sweet potatoes with tarragon and toasted pistachios contributes delicate fresh licorice flavor and sweet crunch, respectively. If you are not making the crispy shallots you can substitute 3 tablespoons extra-virgin olive oil.

- 2 pounds sweet potatoes, peeled
- ⅓ cup Crispy Shallots (page 26), plus 3 tablespoons reserved shallot oil, divided
- ¾ teaspoon table salt, divided
- 2 teaspoons Urfa pepper, divided
- 1 teaspoon grated lemon zest plus 2 tablespoons juice
- 1 teaspoon honey
- ¼ cup shelled pistachios, toasted and chopped coarse
- 2 tablespoons chopped fresh tarragon

Spiralized Sweet Potatoes with Crispy Shallots, Pistachios, and Urfa

1 Adjust oven racks to upper-middle and lower-middle positions and heat oven to 450 degrees.

2 Square off potatoes by cutting ¼-inch-thick slices from each of their 2 short sides. Using spiralizer, cut sweet potatoes into ¼-inch-thick noodles, then cut noodles into 12-inch lengths. Toss potato noodles with 2 tablespoons reserved shallot oil and ½ teaspoon salt and spread in single layer over 2 rimmed baking sheets. Roast until potatoes are just tender, 12 to 14 minutes, switching and rotating sheets halfway through baking. Transfer potatoes to serving platter.

3 Whisk 1 teaspoon Urfa, lemon zest and juice, honey, and remaining ¼ teaspoon salt together in bowl. Whisking constantly, slowly drizzle in remaining 1 tablespoon reserved shallot oil until emulsified, then drizzle vinaigrette over potatoes. Sprinkle with crispy shallots, pistachios, tarragon, and remaining 1 teaspoon Urfa. Serve.

Broiled Smashed Zucchini with Garlicky Yogurt

Serves 4 | **Total Time** 50 minutes

Why This Recipe Works Here we smash, break, and burn our way to a zucchini dish that showcases a range of textures and a surprising variety of flavors you probably didn't know the vegetable possessed. Cooked fully, zucchini turns dense and tender with a mild, nutty sweetness. We use a meat pounder to smash the squash and then break it into a couple of large pieces. After seasoning the craggy pieces, we broil them until they're charred in spots and then cut them into chunks. We serve them atop a schmear of creamy yogurt sauce garnished with crunchy nuts, spicy pepper, fresh herbs, and a drizzle of extra-virgin olive oil. We prefer zucchini that are 7 to 12 ounces each. We developed this recipe using an electric broiler. If using a gas broiler, adjust the oven rack 4 inches from the broiler element and use tongs to rearrange the zucchini pieces halfway through cooking instead of rotating the pan in step 2.

- 2 pounds zucchini
- 2 tablespoons extra-virgin olive oil, plus extra for drizzling
- 4 teaspoons lemon juice
- 2¼ teaspoons kosher salt, divided
- ½ cup plain Greek yogurt
- 2 tablespoons water
- ½ teaspoon minced garlic
- ¼ cup hazelnuts, toasted, skinned, and chopped
- Chopped fresh dill, basil, parsley, or chives
- Aleppo pepper

1 Adjust oven rack 5 inches from broiler element and heat broiler. Using meat pounder or rolling pin, firmly but gently smash zucchini until flattened and cracked lengthwise. Trim and discard ends. Break each zucchini into 2 to 4 large pieces. Transfer zucchini pieces to large bowl, including any smaller pieces that have been created during smashing and breaking. Add oil and lemon juice and toss until zucchini is evenly coated.

2 Arrange zucchini, skin side down, on aluminum foil–lined rimmed baking sheet. Sprinkle with 2 teaspoons salt, making sure to season thicker pieces more heavily than thinner pieces. Broil until zucchini are lightly charred in spots, 9 to 12 minutes, rotating pan halfway through broiling. Let cool until zucchini are warm to touch, 15 to 20 minutes.

3 Meanwhile, stir yogurt, water, garlic, and remaining ¼ teaspoon salt together in small bowl. Let sit at room temperature so flavors meld, about 10 minutes. Spread yogurt mixture on serving platter. Cut zucchini into bite-size pieces. Arrange zucchini on top of yogurt mixture. Sprinkle with hazelnuts, dill, and Aleppo pepper. Drizzle with oil and serve.

VARIATIONS

Broiled Smashed Zucchini with Herbed Sour Cream

Omit yogurt and garlic. Decrease water to 2 teaspoons and combine with ½ cup sour cream, 1 tablespoon minced fresh chives, 1 tablespoon minced fresh dill, ¼ teaspoon grated lemon zest, and remaining ¼ teaspoon salt in small bowl. Substitute ¼ cup toasted, chopped pine nuts for hazelnuts. Top with more fresh dill. Substitute coarsely ground pepper for Aleppo pepper.

Broiled Smashed Zucchini with Ricotta and Pecorino Romano

Omit yogurt and garlic. Decrease water to 2 teaspoons and combine with ½ cup whole-milk ricotta cheese, 2 tablespoons grated Pecorino Romano, and remaining ¼ teaspoon salt in small bowl. Substitute ¼ cup toasted sliced almonds for hazelnuts. Substitute parsley for dill and coarsely ground pepper for Aleppo pepper.

Broiled Smashed Zucchini with Garlicky Yogurt

Naan Tarts with Fig Jam, Blue Cheese, and Prosciutto

Garlicky Broiled Shrimp

Naan Tarts with Fig Jam, Blue Cheese, and Prosciutto

Serves 6 | **Total Time** 25 minutes

Why This Recipe Works Store-bought naan makes a great prebaked crust for a quick savory appetizer; after assembly, you simply place it on an oil-slicked sheet pan and bake it for 10 minutes. For a bold and irresistible topping, what better match is there than salty prosciutto and pungent blue cheese? A layer of fig jam, spread directly across the tarts, adds a welcome sweet and earthy element. If fig jam is not available, you can substitute caramelized onion or apricot jam. You can substitute 1 tablespoon minced fresh parsley for the scallions. You can serve the tarts warm or at room temperature. Served with a salad, they make a lovely lunch or light dinner.

- 1 tablespoon extra-virgin olive oil
- 2 naans
- ¼ cup fig jam
- 1 teaspoon water
- ⅛ teaspoon pepper
- 2 ounces blue cheese, crumbled (½ cup)
- 2 ounces thinly sliced prosciutto, cut into 1-inch strips
- ¼ teaspoon fresh thyme leaves
- 2 scallions, sliced thin

1 Adjust oven rack to lowest position and heat oven to 500 degrees. Brush baking sheet with oil and lay naans on sheet. Whisk fig jam, water, and pepper in bowl to loosen, then spread evenly over each naan, leaving ½-inch border. Sprinkle blue cheese, prosciutto, and thyme evenly over top.

2 Bake until naans are golden brown around edges, 8 to 10 minutes, rotating sheet halfway through baking. Sprinkle with scallions, cut each tart into 6 pieces, and serve.

Cheesy Nachos with Refried Beans

Serves 4 to 6 | **Total Time** 25 minutes

Why This Recipe Works There's no need to enjoy nachos only at your favorite Mexican restaurant. With a sheet pan and a handful of ingredients it's a snap to layer them up and bake them to melty perfection. The addition of refried beans ensures that these crunchy, satisfying nachos are more than just cheese and chips. And they will appeal to both meat eaters and vegetarians. To guarantee no shortage of cheese, we shred a pound and a half, using a combo of mild Jack and sharp cheddar. Add your favorite nacho toppings for serving.

- 12 ounces tortilla chips, divided
- 1 (14.5-ounce) can refried beans, divided
- 1 pound Monterey Jack cheese, shredded (4 cups), divided
- 8 ounces sharp cheddar cheese, shredded (2 cups), divided
- 2 large jalapeños, stemmed and sliced into thin rings, divided

1 Adjust oven rack to middle position and heat oven to 400 degrees. Spread half of tortilla chips in even layer in rimmed baking sheet. Dollop twelve 1 tablespoon-size spoonfuls of refried beans over chips. Sprinkle with 2 cups Monterey Jack, 1 cup cheddar, and half of jalapeños. Repeat with remaining tortilla chips, refried beans, 2 cups Monterey Jack, 1 cup cheddar, and jalapeños. Bake until cheese is melted, 7 to 10 minutes.

2 Remove nachos from oven and let cool for 2 minutes. Serve.

Garlicky Broiled Shrimp

Serves 4 as a main dish or 6 as an appetizer
Total Time 30 minutes

Why This Recipe Works We bet that you've never made a shrimp appetizer using a sheet pan. Melted butter and honey add richness and boost browning, while garlic and red pepper flakes give the shrimp an assertive flavor. We prefer untreated shrimp; if yours are treated with salt or additives such as sodium tripolyphosphate, skip the salting in step 1. This recipe was developed with Diamond Crystal kosher salt. If you're using Morton, which is denser, use a little less than ½ teaspoon.

- 1½ pounds extra-large shrimp (21 to 25 per pound), peeled and deveined, tails left on
- ½ teaspoon kosher salt
- 4 tablespoons unsalted butter
- 1 tablespoon honey
- 6 garlic cloves, minced to paste
- ½–¾ teaspoon red pepper flakes
- Lemon wedges

1 Toss shrimp and salt together in bowl; set aside and let sit for 15 to 30 minutes.

2 Combine butter and honey in small bowl. Cover and microwave until butter is melted, 30 to 60 seconds. Add garlic and pepper flakes and stir to combine. Let cool slightly, about 5 minutes. While mixture cools, adjust oven rack 4 inches from broiler element and heat broiler. Line rimmed baking sheet with aluminum foil and set wire rack in sheet.

3 Spread out shrimp on large plate or cutting board and pat dry with paper towels. Return to bowl and pour butter mixture over shrimp. Toss until shrimp are thoroughly and evenly coated, including where they are split from deveining (it's OK if butter starts to solidify). Arrange shrimp in single layer on prepared rack.

4 Broil until shrimp are opaque throughout and beginning to lightly char in spots, 3 to 5 minutes. Transfer shrimp to serving platter and serve with lemon wedges.

Soy Sauce Chicken Wings

Serves 4 to 6
Total Time 1¼ hours, plus 2 hours marinating

Why This Recipe Works These are likely the easiest chicken wings you will ever make, thanks to the sheet pan and an aromatic marinade. Spreading the marinated wings across a foil-lined baking sheet allows the hot air to circulate around them for even cooking all around. If you buy chicken wings that are already split, with the tips removed, you will need only 2½ pounds.

- ¾ cup soy sauce
- ¼ cup vegetable oil
- ¼ cup packed brown sugar
- 12 garlic cloves, smashed and peeled
- ½ teaspoon cayenne pepper
- 3 pounds chicken wings, cut at joints, wingtips discarded
- 2 scallions, sliced thin on bias

1 Combine soy sauce, oil, sugar, garlic, and cayenne in 1-gallon zipper-lock bag. Add wings to marinade, press out air, seal bag, and turn to distribute marinade. Refrigerate for at least 2 hours or up to 6 hours.

2 Adjust oven rack to middle position and heat oven to 350 degrees. Line rimmed baking sheet with aluminum foil and spray with vegetable oil spray. Remove wings from marinade and arrange in single layer, fatty side up, on prepared sheet; discard marinade. Bake until evenly well browned, about 1 hour 5 minutes. Transfer wings to platter, sprinkle with scallions, and serve.

Fire Crackers

Serves 6 to 8
Total Time 30 minutes, plus 1 hour resting

Why This Recipe Works Fire crackers are also known as Alabama fire crackers or comeback crackers—an apt name because they keep you coming back for more. That's because when you give saltines a generous coating of fat and bold flavorings, magic happens. Letting the saltines sit with oil, ranch dressing mix, and some extra flavorings (to boost the ranch profile) for at least 1 hour (but preferably 24 hours) seasons the crackers and changes their texture. Then, baking the saltines on two sheet pans turns them golden brown and gives them a flaky texture and toasty flavor. We developed this recipe using Hidden Valley Original Ranch Salad Dressing & Seasoning Mix. Two sleeves of saltines weigh about 8 ounces and contain about 72 crackers. Three teaspoons of red pepper flakes add modest heat to these crackers; feel free to increase or decrease the amount, if desired.

- ¾ cup vegetable oil
- 1 (1-ounce) package ranch dressing mix
- 2–4 teaspoons red pepper flakes
- 1 teaspoon dried dill
- 1 teaspoon garlic powder
- 8 ounces saltines

1 Add oil, ranch dressing mix, pepper flakes, dill, and garlic powder to 1-gallon zipper-lock bag. Seal bag and knead mixture with your hands until well combined. Add saltines and reseal bag. Shake and turn gently until crackers are thoroughly coated. Let sit, turning bag occasionally, for at least 1 hour or up to 24 hours.

2 Adjust oven racks to upper-middle and lower-middle positions and heat oven to 250 degrees. Spread saltines into single layer over 2 rimmed baking sheets. Bake until light golden brown and slightly puffed, 20 to 25 minutes. Let crackers cool on sheets for at least 10 minutes before serving. (Fire crackers can be stored at room temperature in airtight container for up to 1 week.)

Fire Crackers

Kale Chips

Kale Chips

Serves 4 | **Total Time** 1 hour

Why This Recipe Works For kale chips with the perfect texture, we use two sheet pans and a low oven. To ensure the air circulates above and beneath the leaves, a wire rack set inside each pan is critical. Tossed with olive oil and seasoned with crunchy kosher salt, these ultracrisp kale chips are a supersatisfying snack. We prefer to use lacinato kale in this recipe, but curly-leaf kale can be substituted; chips made with curly-leaf kale will taste a bit chewy at the edges. We prefer the larger crystal size of kosher salt here; if using table salt, reduce the amount by half.

- 12 ounces lacinato kale, stemmed and torn into 3-inch pieces
- 1 tablespoon extra-virgin olive oil
- ½ teaspoon kosher or flake sea salt

1 Adjust oven racks to upper-middle and lower-middle positions and heat oven to 200 degrees. Set wire racks in 2 rimmed baking sheets. Dry kale thoroughly between dish towels, transfer to large bowl, and toss with oil and salt.

2 Arrange kale on prepared racks, making sure leaves overlap as little as possible. Bake kale until very crisp, 45 minutes to 1 hour, switching and rotating sheets halfway through baking. Let kale chips cool completely before serving. (Chips can be stored in airtight container for up to 1 day.)

Spiced Nuts

Serves 16
Total Time 1¼ hours, plus 30 minutes cooling

Why This Recipe Works There's no shame in snacking on nuts straight from the cupboard, but these spiced nuts are an easy upgrade with a double punch of protein and flavor. We toss the nuts in a mixture of egg white, water, and salt and spread them across a sheet pan; when baked, this gives them a nice crunch and helps the spices adhere.

1 large egg white

1 tablespoon water

1 teaspoon table salt

1 pound pecans, raw cashews, walnuts, or whole unblanched almonds, or a combination

⅔ cup superfine sugar

2 teaspoons cumin

1 teaspoon cayenne pepper

1 teaspoon paprika

1 Adjust oven racks to upper-middle and lower-middle positions and heat oven to 275 degrees. Line 2 rimmed baking sheets with parchment paper. Whisk egg white, water, and salt together in medium bowl. Add nuts and toss to coat. Let nuts drain in colander for 5 minutes.

2 Mix sugar, cumin, cayenne, and paprika together in clean medium bowl. Add nuts and toss to coat. Spread nuts evenly over prepared baking sheets. Bake until nuts are dry and crisp, about 50 minutes, stirring occasionally. Let nuts cool completely on baking sheets, about 30 minutes. Break nuts apart and serve. (Spiced nuts can be stored in airtight container for up to 1 week.)

Garam Masala Peanuts

Serves 8 to 10
Total Time 45 minutes, plus 30 minutes cooling

Why This Recipe Works We wanted crunchy spiced peanuts that had a compelling array of complex seasoning and wouldn't leave our fingers greasy or sticky. Garam masala ("warm spice blend")—an incredibly aromatic, sweet, and lightly spicy blend of ingredients such as cinnamon, cardamom, black pepper, coriander, and cumin—fits the bill perfectly, complementing these sweet-salty, earthy roasted peanuts beautifully. Seasoning the nuts before and after with our spice blend ensures that they have the full spectrum of the ingredients' flavors, since some spices can be muted with long cooking. We developed this recipe using Planters Unsalted Dry Roasted Peanuts. You can substitute lightly salted dry-roasted peanuts; if you do, reduce the salt to 1 teaspoon. Do not substitute salted dry-roasted peanuts.

Garam Masala Peanuts

½ cup granulated sugar

1 large egg white

4 teaspoons garam masala, divided

1 tablespoon water

1¾ teaspoons table salt

3¼ cups (1 pound) unsalted dry-roasted peanuts

1 Adjust oven rack to middle position and heat oven to 300 degrees. Line baking sheet with parchment paper and spray with vegetable oil spray. Whisk sugar, egg white, 2 teaspoons garam masala, water, and salt together in large bowl. Add peanuts and toss until evenly coated with sugar mixture.

2 Spread peanut mixture evenly over prepared sheet and bake until peanuts are deep golden brown, dry, and crisp, about 40 minutes, rotating sheet halfway through baking.

3 Immediately sprinkle remaining 2 teaspoons garam masala evenly over hot peanuts. Transfer peanuts to bowl and stir to incorporate spices and break up any large clumps. Let cool completely, about 30 minutes. Serve. (Nuts can be stored in airtight container for up to 3 weeks.)

Nutritional Information for Our Recipes

To calculate the nutritional values of our recipes per serving, we used The Food Processor SQL by ESHA Research. When using this program, we entered all the ingredients, using weights for important ingredients such as most vegetables. We also used our preferred brands in these analyses. When the recipe called for seasoning with an unspecified amount of salt and pepper, we added ½ teaspoon of salt and ¼ teaspoon of pepper to the analysis. We did not include additional salt or pepper for food that's "seasoned to taste." If there is a range in the serving size, we used the highest number of servings to calculate the nutritional values.

	Calories	Total Fat (g)	Sat Fat (g)	Chol (mg)	Sodium (mg)	Total Carb (g)	Dietary Fiber (g)	Total Sugars (g)	Added Sugar (g)	Protein (g)
The Sheet-Pan Advantage										
Harissa (per tbsp)	110	11	1.5	0	150	2	1	0	0	1
Baharat (per tbsp)	20	1	0	0	0	5	1	0	0	1
Pesto (per ¼ cup)	460	48	7	5	170	3	1	1	0	7
Tzatziki Sauce (per 2 tbsp)	100	9	4.5	10	230	2	0	2	0	4
Lemon-Herb Sauce (per 2 tbsp)	90	10	1.5	5	90	1	0	0	0	0
Avocado Crema (per tbsp)	20	2	0	0	0	1	1	0	0	0
Lime Crema (per tbsp)	60	5	3.5	20	190	3	0	1	0	1
Creamy Apple-Mustard Sauce (per 2 tbsp)	60	1.5	0	0	630	6	0	5	4	0
Ten-Minute Tomato Salsa (per ¼ cup)	20	0	0	0	280	4	1	2	0	1
Crispy Shallots (per 2 tbsp)	260	28	2	0	0	4	1	2	0	1
Quick Sweet and Spicy Pickled Red Onion (per tbsp)	22	0	0	0	38	5	0	4	4	0
Sumac Onion (per 2 tbsp)	25	2	0	0	75	2	0	1	0	0
Chapter 1 Sandwiches, Tacos, and Pizza										
Cheddar-Crusted Grilled Cheese	480	35	19	90	790	21	1	4	0	19
with Tomato and Bacon	540	40	17	80	930	22	1	4	0	22
with Turkey and Peppadew Peppers	460	29	15	80	1010	23	1	6	2	23

	Calories	Total Fat (g)	Sat Fat (g)	Chol (mg)	Sodium (mg)	Total Carb (g)	Dietary Fiber (g)	Total Sugars (g)	Added Sugar (g)	Protein (g)
Chapter 1 Sandwiches, Tacos, and Pizza (cont.)										
Ultimate Roasted Vegetable Sandwich	530	33	9	35	1130	41	3	5	0	15
Oven-Fried Chicken Sandwiches	490	22	3.5	115	620	42	0	4	0	28
Buffalo Oven-Fried Chicken Sandwiches	550	27	7	125	1670	44	0	5	0	32
Spicy Kimchi Oven-Fried Chicken Sandwiches	500	22	4	115	690	44	0	4	0	29
Dill Pickle Mayonnaise	45	5	1	0	90	0	0	0	0	0
Chicken and Parsnip Shawarma	670	30	6	110	1090	65	5	8	0	32
Tahini-Garlic Sauce	35	2.5	0	0	75	2	0	1	0	1
Meatball Subs with Roasted Broccoli	920	44	15	210	1860	82	5	20	1	53
Pork and Broccoli Rabe Sandwiches	660	34	9	90	1050	47	5	8	0	41
Pork Gyros	610	34	9	85	1180	40	2	3	0	37
Onion Sliders	790	38	12	135	1250	67	4	13	0	53
Bacon and Onion Sliders	930	52	18	165	1250	67	4	13	0	57
Salmon Burgers with Asparagus	560	34	6	70	900	33	2	6	0	30
White Bean and Sun-Dried Tomato Patties with Lemony Spinach Salad	450	28	9	70	1020	34	8	5	0	18
Chicken Tacos with Salsa Verde	380	19	2	55	840	35	3	6	1	21
Steak Fajitas	450	19	6	75	1570	37	2	4	0	31
Salmon Tacos with Roasted Pineapple Slaw	520	21	6	60	340	61	4	18	0	24
Black Bean and Sweet Potato Tacos	380	12	1.5	0	680	63	8	19	11	7
Chipotle Mushroom and Cauliflower Tacos	310	15	3	15	830	40	3	10	4	8
Cheese Quesadillas	530	31	18	75	1140	37	0	2	0	27
Black Bean and Jalapeño Quesadillas	540	25	14	110	1100	37	0	2	0	42
Chicken and Herb Quesadillas	480	22	13	50	1460	47	3	2	0	23

	Calories	Total Fat (g)	Sat Fat (g)	Chol (mg)	Sodium (mg)	Total Carb (g)	Dietary Fiber (g)	Total Sugars (g)	Added Sugar (g)	Protein (g)
Chapter 1 Sandwiches, Tacos, and Pizza (cont.)										
Chorizo, Corn, and Tomato Tostadas	840	45	18	80	1450	79	7	9	0	29
Pepperoni Pan Pizza	700	38	14	70	2210	63	3	5	2	27
Caprese Pizza	750	44	13	50	1260	63	3	6	2	24
Pizza with 'Nduja, Ricotta, and Cherry Peppers	700	36	14	75	1540	67	4	9	2	30
Lavash Flatbreads with Romesco, Tomatoes, and Spinach	420	31	3.5	0	880	26	3	4	0	9
Chapter 2 Poultry										
Charred Broccoli Caesar Salad with Chicken	650	46	7	95	1000	24	0	4	1	34
Chicken Souvlaki	730	43	13	100	1330	45	2	7	1	42
Chicken Chilaquiles Verdes	750	42	7	95	1660	61	8	11	1	36
Chicken Packets with Fennel and Sun-Dried Tomatoes	490	24	3.5	125	600	26	3	4	0	42
with Potatoes and Carrots	460	22	3.5	125	540	22	1	3	0	41
with Sweet Potato and Radishes	430	22	3.5	125	570	17	3	4	0	40
Chicken Parmesan with Pizza-Shop Salad and Garlicky Toast	830	42	13	255	1560	46	2	5	0	64
Oven-Fried Chicken	500	24	3.5	240	1220	28	0	1	0	39
Goat Cheese–Stuffed Chicken with Roasted Carrots	510	23	7	175	910	18	4	10	3	57
Lemon-Thyme Chicken with Ratatouille	540	26	6	165	740	12	4	6	0	62
Spiced Chicken Breasts with Squash, Caramelized Shallots, and Crispy Kale	910	46	9	175	780	62	9	30	3	67
Spiced Chicken Breasts with Sweet Potato–Poblano Salad	860	40	10	180	1820	56	9	15	4	68
Singapore Noodles with Chicken and Shrimp	690	31	4.5	325	1560	64	5	6	1	39
Teriyaki Chicken Thighs with Sesame Vegetables	640	36	8	215	1920	29	3	21	9	43
Baharat Chicken with Potatoes and Herb-Date Salad	780	41	8	215	1860	56	4	19	0	44
Coriander and Aleppo Pepper-Spiced Oil	130	14	2	0	75	1	1	0	0	0

	Calories	Total Fat (g)	Sat Fat (g)	Chol (mg)	Sodium (mg)	Total Carb (g)	Dietary Fiber (g)	Total Sugars (g)	Added Sugar (g)	Protein (g)
Chapter 2 Poultry (cont.)										
Peruvian Chicken with Cauliflower and Sweet Potatoes	960	56	13	365	2570	40	9	14	3	73
Garlic-Sage Chicken Leg Quarters with Cauliflower and Shallots	810	49	12	365	1940	26	5	7	0	73
Harissa Wings with Cucumber-Tomato Salad	230	14	3	90	790	9	1	6	4	15
Chili-Rubbed Chicken with Schmaltzy Vinegar Potatoes	840	47	12	195	1130	45	1	4	3	55
Herbes de Provence Roast Chicken with Fennel	690	47	12	195	1160	15	4	7	0	50
Ras el Hanout Roast Chicken with Carrots	680	47	12	195	1150	13	6	7	0	51
Garlic Roasted Chicken with Sweet Potatoes and Green Beans	870	45	18	210	1010	57	11	14	0	59
Roasted Garlic	40	2	0	0	55	6	0	0	0	1
Roast Chicken with Warm Bread Salad	970	64	15	225	1650	34	1	6	0	62
Bulgur Bowls with Chicken Meatballs and Sumac Kale	380	26	5	65	1180	20	4	10	0	19
Mini Maple–Dijon Glazed Turkey Meatloaves with Roasted Broccoli	380	23	7	100	640	18	3	8	5	26
Green Goddess Gnocchi with Spring Vegetables and Chicken Sausage	400	22	10	105	1100	28	3	5	0	25
Chapter 3 Beef, Pork, and Lamb										
Baharat-Rubbed Steak Tips with Lemony Spinach and Pear Salad	560	34	8	115	1210	17	4	9	3	45
Hoisin and Five-Spice Beef and Vegetable Kebabs	360	15	3	80	1080	23	3	12	0	33
Coffee and Chili–Rubbed Steaks with Sweet Potato Wedges and Scallions	580	19	5	120	2110	46	9	19	7	57
Flank Steak with Roasted White Bean and Arugula Salad	510	25	5	70	1000	35	9	2	0	37
Spice-Rubbed Flank Steak with Toasted Corn and Black Bean Salad	470	25	6	105	690	24	2	5	2	37
Herbed Roast Beef with Root Vegetables	410	18	6	120	800	24	4	5	0	39

	Calories	Total Fat (g)	Sat Fat (g)	Chol (mg)	Sodium (mg)	Total Carb (g)	Dietary Fiber (g)	Total Sugars (g)	Added Sugar (g)	Protein (g)
Chapter 3 Beef, Pork, and Lamb (cont.)										
Coffee and Fennel–Rubbed Boneless Short Ribs with Celery Root Salad	560	33	9	70	1210	40	8	13	2	29
Zucchini Noodles with Pesto Meatballs	540	36	11	95	1030	21	2	8	0	32
Glazed Meatloaf with Lemon-Herb Potatoes and Brussels Sprouts	990	54	18	260	2420	61	6	13	0	62
Beef Kofte with Cucumber Salad	820	63	17	130	1200	27	7	14	0	40
Cucumber Salad	170	11	1.5	0	170	16	4	9	0	3
Yogurt-Garlic Sauce	40	3	1	5	160	3	0	2	0	2
Mustardy Apple Butter–Glazed Pork Chops with Broccoli Rabe	510	33	9	100	830	15	2	11	6	39
Parmesan-Crusted Pork Chops with Winter Squash	1090	40	13	230	1500	120	7	62	53	61
Roasted Pork Chops and Vegetables with Parsley Vinaigrette	810	36	8	190	1470	39	5	7	0	79
Lemony Roasted Radicchio, Fennel, and Root Vegetables with Sausage	480	24	6	35	1190	44	8	12	1	25
Italian Sausage with Peppers, Onions, Tomatoes, and Polenta	480	26	7	40	1350	36	2	5	0	25
Loukaniko and Lemony Potatoes with Feta-Dill Sauce	710	44	15	70	1760	46	5	6	0	38
Bratwurst Sandwiches with Potato and Kale Salad	1140	78	21	125	2620	69	3	7	0	35
Hoisin Pork Tenderloin with Green Beans, Potatoes, and Chive Butter	580	25	10	140	1080	48	7	11	0	41
Pork Tenderloins and Panzanella Salad	590	33	5	110	1040	28	3	10	3	40
Weeknight Porchetta with Lemony Broccolini	300	11	2.5	125	1450	5	3	0	0	45
Sweet Potato Vermicelli with Vegetables and Pork	320	15	4.5	45	790	30	3	14	8	16
Lamb and Bulgur–Stuffed Eggplant	430	26	7	40	1080	39	12	14	0	17
Coriander-Cumin Butterflied Leg of Lamb with Radicchio Salad and Herb-Shallot Relish	580	27	5	125	840	44	5	32	4	44
with Coriander and Fennel	580	27	5	125	840	44	5	32	4	44

	Calories	Total Fat (g)	Sat Fat (g)	Chol (mg)	Sodium (mg)	Total Carb (g)	Dietary Fiber (g)	Total Sugars (g)	Added Sugar (g)	Protein (g)
Chapter 4 Seafood										
Miso Salmon with Kabocha and Cabbage	780	44	7	95	2030	46	5	27	9	44
Lime-Glazed Salmon and Crispy Rice Salad	1000	48	7	95	1060	96	4	25	19	45
Salmon with Crispy Potatoes, Broccoli, and Mustard Sauce	670	44	8	95	1030	26	5	5	1	40
Roasted Salmon with White Beans, Fennel, and Tomatoes	750	47	17	140	1260	35	11	9	0	46
Pomegranate-Glazed Salmon with Black-Eyed Peas and Walnuts	720	43	8	95	960	39	7	13	0	44
Roasted Salmon and Broccoli Rabe with Pistachio Gremolata	510	36	7	95	580	6	4	1	0	40
Sweet Chili Salmon with Cauliflower and Lime	460	27	6	95	740	16	3	11	8	38
Curry Salmon with Sweet Potato Wedges and Asparagus	600	31	7	100	790	37	8	13	0	42
Pistachio-Crusted Cod Fillets with Broccoli Rabe	370	20	3	120	790	10	3	1	0	36
Almond-Crusted Cod Fillets	360	20	3	120	810	9	4	1	0	36
Hazelnut-Crusted Cod Fillets	370	21	3	120	790	9	3	1	0	36
Lemon-Herb Cod Fillets with Crispy Garlic Potatoes	400	15	9	110	590	32	2	1	0	34
Roasted Trout with White Bean and Tomato Salad	740	43	7	130	890	30	9	6	0	57
Lemon-Poached Halibut with Roasted Fingerling Potatoes	361	9	1	83	718	35	5	2	0	35
Old Bay Halibut with Red Potatoes, Corn, and Andouille	750	41	13	165	1740	46	5	8	0	54
Swordfish with Bulgur and Tomato-Eggplant Caponata	390	18	3	75	1000	30	7	8	4	27
Mexican Rice with Spiced Tilapia	420	15	3.5	60	930	48	2	4	0	25
Mediterranean Shrimp with Potatoes, Fennel, and Feta	320	13	4	160	1480	28	3	4	0	22
Crab Cakes with Roasted Corn and Seasoned Fries	550	27	5	135	1110	47	5	9	0	33
Chapter 5 Vegetable Mains										
Roasted Gnocchi with Blistered Cherry Tomato Sauce	280	16	6	25	1060	28	2	6	1	7
Eggplant Parmesan with Burrata and Basil	740	55	16	60	1360	43	8	19	0	26

	Calories	Total Fat (g)	Sat Fat (g)	Chol (mg)	Sodium (mg)	Total Carb (g)	Dietary Fiber (g)	Total Sugars (g)	Added Sugar (g)	Protein (g)
Chapter 5 Vegetable Mains (cont.)										
Crispy-Creamy Macaroni and Cheese	760	39	24	125	1320	74	0	11	0	31
with Asparagus and Peas	790	39	24	125	1320	79	2	13	0	34
French Onion Macaroni and Cheese	910	56	23	125	1340	71	1	14	0	33
Roasted Tomato Sauce	90	5	0.5	0	340	11	3	7	0	2
Roasted Paneer Tikka Masala	590	47	22	110	660	25	5	17	3	23
Zucchini, Leek, and Pea Soup with Crispy Prosciutto	160	9	1.5	5	940	15	3	6	0	7
Roasted Aloo Gobi	350	22	1.5	0	1100	40	6	4	0	5
Charred Cauliflower and Crispy Chickpeas with Romesco	420	32	4.5	0	1180	29	11	7	0	10
Roasted Cauliflower and Grape Salad with Chermoula	340	28	4	0	510	22	6	11	0	6
Overstuffed Sweet Potatoes with Tofu and Red Curry Vinaigrette	560	34	2.5	0	790	51	7	13	0	15
Roasted Tofu and Sweet Potato Bowls with Snap Pea Salad	560	25	3	0	2160	58	9	20	8	28
Fattoush with Butternut Squash and Apple	310	19	2.5	0	460	33	4	7	0	4
Charred Cabbage Salad with Torn Tofu and Plantain Chips	450	31	5	0	1040	37	6	20	4	14
Roasted Vegetable and Chickpea Salad	310	16	5	10	460	32	8	11	0	11
Spinach and Herb-Stuffed Mushrooms with Blistered Cherry Tomatoes and Onions	610	47	13	110	1450	26	6	9	0	23
Garlic-Roasted Mushrooms and Escarole with Couscous and Lemon Vinaigrette	490	22	3	0	980	61	13	9	0	14
Roasted Vegetables and Lentils with Feta and Herb Oil	460	28	7	25	850	41	11	13	0	14
Asparagus and Goat Cheese Tart	445	34	14	22	489	32	2	3	0	12
Fresh Tomato Galette	440	29	16	100	980	31	2	3	0	11
Eggplant and Tomato Phyllo Pie	410	28	8	20	800	28	3	4	0	10

	Calories	Total Fat (g)	Sat Fat (g)	Chol (mg)	Sodium (mg)	Total Carb (g)	Dietary Fiber (g)	Total Sugars (g)	Added Sugar (g)	Protein (g)
Chapter 5 Vegetable Mains (cont.)										
Spinach Pie for a Crowd	260	15	8	30	560	26	2	3	0	10
Potato and Parmesan Tart	390	25	13	80	500	31	1	1	0	9
with Blue Cheese and Sun-Dried Tomatoes	420	28	15	85	610	32	1	1	0	11
Chapter 6 Breakfast										
Eggs in a Hole with Tomato, Avocado, and Herb Salad	410	30	9	210	520	24	9	4	0	12
One-Pan Breakfast	680	41	15	280	1640	47	6	6	0	28
Huevos Rancheros	720	43	11	395	1870	59	12	17	3	28
Hash Browns with Smoked Salmon	640	35	10	45	1270	75	7	14	8	13
Crème Fraîche	110	11	7	40	160	1	0	1	0	1
Egg Roulade with Spinach and Gruyère	250	17	7	395	410	5	1	1	0	20
Egg Roulade with Goat Cheese and Sun-Dried Tomatoes	300	18	9	395	470	6	1	2	0	26
Sweet Potato and Poblano Frittata	390	26	10	345	740	16	3	5	0	22
Breakfast Pizza	540	31	13	240	1250	40	0	7	0	27
Smoked Salmon Breakfast Pizza	590	34	13	245	1290	40	0	6	0	32
Everyday French Toast	290	14	6	160	460	26	1	9	3	11
One Big Pancake	380	15	2.5	75	830	50	1	10	6	10
One Smaller Pancake	350	20	3.5	100	720	35	1	11	6	9
Apple Crisp Topping	210	11	4	15	150	28	3	16	6	2
Milk and Cereal Topping	320	22	14	70	140	25	0	15	4	3
S'mores Topping	260	13	8	0	35	40	3	30	23	2
Berries and Cream Topping	370	22	14	70	20	44	3	37	25	3
Almond Granola with Dried Fruit	170	8	1	0	35	22	3	11	4	3
Pecan-Orange Granola with Dried Cranberries	160	8	1	0	35	20	2	11	4	2
Spiced Walnut Granola with Dried Apple	150	8	1	0	65	17	2	6	4	3

	Calories	Total Fat (g)	Sat Fat (g)	Chol (mg)	Sodium (mg)	Total Carb (g)	Dietary Fiber (g)	Total Sugars (g)	Added Sugar (g)	Protein (g)
Chapter 6 Breakfast (cont.)										
Nutella Bread Pudding	550	30	14	170	550	57	3	19	1	14
Sausage and Cheddar Bread Pudding	520	29	15	230	780	46	2	9	3	19
Chapter 7 Sides and Snacks										
Roasted Asparagus with Mint-Orange Gremolata	80	6	1	0	190	5	3	2	0	3
with Cilantro-Lime Gremolata	80	6	1	0	190	5	3	2	0	3
with Tarragon-Lemon Gremolata	80	6	1	0	190	5	3	2	0	3
Roasted Broccoli	90	7	1	0	25	6	2	2	0	2
with Parmesan and Black Pepper Topping	120	9	1.5	5	110	6	2	2	0	4
with Sesame-Orange Topping	110	9	1	0	80	7	2	2	0	3
Broiled Broccoli Rabe	120	11	1.5	0	470	4	3	1	0	4
Roasted Brussels Sprouts with Mustard, Brown Sugar, and Pecans	180	11	1.5	0	450	19	6	8	4	6
with Chile, Mint, and Peanuts	170	11	1.5	0	490	16	6	4	0	7
with Pomegranate, Cumin, and Pistachios	170	10	1.5	0	330	18	6	7	0	6
Roasted Cabbage	110	7	0.5	0	220	9	4	5	0	2
Roasted Cabbage with Gochujang, Sesame, and Scallions	140	9	1	0	250	12	4	6	0	3
Parmesan Roasted Cauliflower	170	11	3	10	590	10	3	3	0	9
Roasted Green Beans with Goat Cheese and Hazelnuts	210	18	3.5	5	260	10	4	5	1	5
with Almonds and Mint	180	15	2	0	210	9	4	4	1	3
with Pecorino and Pine Nuts	220	19	3	5	310	9	3	4	1	5
Elote	260	21	3	10	250	19	2	5	0	5

	Calories	Total Fat (g)	Sat Fat (g)	Chol (mg)	Sodium (mg)	Total Carb (g)	Dietary Fiber (g)	Total Sugars (g)	Added Sugar (g)	Protein (g)
Chapter 7 Sides and Snacks (cont.)										
Roasted Kale with Garlic, Red Pepper Flakes and Lemon	120	8	0.5	0	330	11	4	3	0	5
with Coriander, Ginger, and Coconut	170	13	5	0	340	13	5	3	0	5
with Parmesan, Shallot, and Nutmeg	180	12	1.5	10	580	11	4	3	0	11
Roasted Mushrooms with Parmesan and Pine Nuts	250	18	6	20	290	16	4	6	0	10
with Harissa and Mint	190	13	4.5	15	330	16	4	6	0	7
with Roasted Garlic and Smoked Paprika	140	8	1	0	310	16	4	6	0	7
Foil-Roasted Potatoes	180	8	4.5	20	510	25	3	2	0	3
Crispy Smashed Potatoes	250	14	2	0	200	27	0	0	0	4
Thick-Cut Oven Fries	200	7	0.5	0	10	30	0	0	0	4
Roasted Root Vegetables	170	7	0.5	0	320	24	7	10	0	3
Roasted Delicata Squash	200	16	4	10	300	14	2	3	0	1
Spiralized Sweet Potatoes with Crispy Shallots, Pistachios, and Urfa	200	10	1.5	0	360	28	4	7	1	3
Broiled Smashed Zucchini with Garlicky Yogurt	190	15	4	5	660	10	3	6	0	6
with Herbed Sour Cream	220	19	5	20	690	11	2	6	0	5
with Ricotta and Pecorino Romano	210	16	5	20	780	9	3	5	0	10
Naan Tarts with Fig Jam, Blue Cheese, and Prosciutto	230	8	3	15	450	30	0	14	0	8
Cheesy Nachos with Refried Beans	790	52	24	245	1240	52	0	4	4	35
Garlicky Broiled Shrimp	250	13	7	245	540	8	0	4	4	24
Soy Sauce Chicken Wings	595	40	11	320	445	2	0	1	1	55
Fire Crackers	316	23	3	0	522	24	0	0	0	2
Kale Chips	60	4	0	0	160	5	2	1	0	3
Spiced Nuts	228	20	2	0	150	12	3	9	8	3
Garam Masala Peanuts	307	23	3	0	415	20	4	12	10	11

Conversions + Equivalents

Some say cooking is a science and an art. We would say that geography has a hand in it too. Flours and sugars manufactured in the United Kingdom and elsewhere will feel and taste different from those manufactured in the United States. So we cannot promise that the loaf of bread you bake in Canada or England will taste the same as a loaf baked in the States, but we can offer guidelines for converting weights and measures. We also recommend that you rely on your instincts when making our recipes. Refer to the visual cues provided.

The recipes in this book were developed using standard U.S. measures following U.S. government guidelines. The charts below offer equivalents for U.S. and metric measures. All conversions are approximate and have been rounded up or down to the nearest whole number.

EXAMPLE

1 teaspoon = 4.9292 milliliters, rounded up to 5 milliliters

1 ounce = 28.3495 grams, rounded down to 28 grams

Volume Conversions

U.S.	Metric
1 teaspoon	5 milliliters
2 teaspoons	10 milliliters
1 tablespoon	15 milliliters
2 tablespoons	30 milliliters
¼ cup	59 milliliters
⅓ cup	79 milliliters
½ cup	118 milliliters
¾ cup	177 milliliters
1 cup	237 milliliters
1¼ cups	296 milliliters
1½ cups	355 milliliters
2 cups (1 pint)	473 milliliters
2½ cups	591 milliliters
3 cups	710 milliliters
4 cups (1 quart)	0.946 liter
1.06 quarts	1 liter
4 quarts (1 gallon)	3.8 liters

Weight Conversions

Ounces	Grams
½	14
¾	21
1	28
1½	43
2	57
2½	71
3	85
3½	99
4	113
4½	128
5	142
6	170
7	198
8	227
9	255
10	283
12	340
16 (1 pound)	454

Conversions for Common Baking Ingredients

Because measuring by weight is far more accurate than measuring by volume, and thus more likely to achieve reliable results, in our recipes we provide ounce measures in addition to cup measures for many ingredients. Refer to the chart below to convert these measures into grams.

Ingredient	Ounces	Grams
Flour		
1 cup all-purpose flour*	5	142
1 cup cake flour	4	113
1 cup whole-wheat flour	5½	156
Sugar		
1 cup granulated (white) sugar	7	198
1 cup packed brown sugar (light or dark)	7	198
1 cup confectioners' sugar	4	113
Cocoa Powder		
1 cup cocoa powder	3	85
Butter †		
4 tablespoons (½ stick, or ¼ cup)	2	57
8 tablespoons (1 stick, or ½ cup)	4	113
16 tablespoons (2 sticks, or 1 cup)	8	227

* U.S. all-purpose flour, the most frequently used flour in this book, does not contain leaveners, as some European flours do. These leavened flours are called self-rising or self-raising. If you are using self-rising flour, take this into consideration before adding leavening to a recipe.

† In the United States, butter is sold both salted and unsalted. We generally recommend unsalted butter. If you are using salted butter, take this into consideration before adding salt to a recipe.

Oven Temperature

Fahrenheit	Celsius	Gas Mark
225	105	¼
250	120	½
275	135	1
300	150	2
325	165	3
350	180	4
375	190	5
400	200	6
425	220	7
450	230	8
475	245	9

Converting Temperatures from an Instant-Read Thermometer

We include doneness temperatures in many of the recipes in this book. We recommend an instant-read thermometer for the job. Refer to the table above to convert Fahrenheit degrees to Celsius. Or, for temperatures not represented in the chart, use this simple formula:

Subtract 32 degrees from the Fahrenheit reading, then divide the result by 1.8 to find the Celsius reading.

EXAMPLE

"Roast chicken until thighs register 175 degrees."

TO CONVERT

175°F − 32 = 143°
143° ÷ 1.8 = 79.44°C, rounded down to 79°C

Index

Note: Page references in *italics* indicate photographs.

H

K

L

O

P

Q

R

S

Z